WALKING ON WATER
Exploring the Arteries of England

Nick Corble

MINERVA PRESS
LONDON
MIAMI   RIO DE JANEIRO   DELHI

WALKING ON WATER: *Exploring the Arteries of England*
Copyright © Nick Corble 2000

All Rights Reserved

ISBN 0 75411 486 4

First Published 2000 by
MINERVA PRESS
315–317 Regent Street
London W1R 7YB

Printed in Great Britain for Minerva Press

WALKING ON WATER
Exploring the Arteries of England

Acknowledgements

I would like to thank Mrs Sonia Rolt for giving me permission to use extracts from the book *Narrow Boat* by LTC Rolt, published by Alan Sutton Publishing.

*For John and Brenda
and, of course, all my crew*

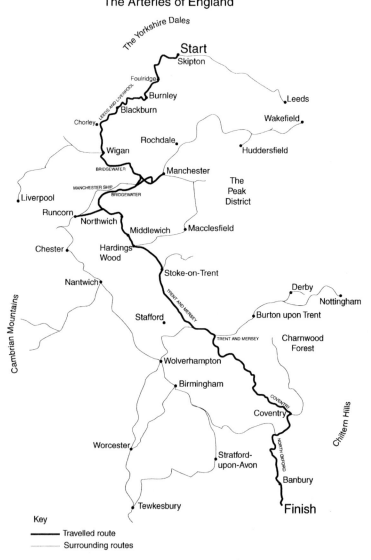

The Arteries of England

The Yorkshire Dales

Start
Skipton

Foulridge

Leeds and Liverpool

Burnley

Blackburn

Leeds

Wakefield

Chorley

Rochdale

Wigan

Huddersfield

BRIDGEWATER

Manchester

MANCHESTER SHIP

Liverpool

BRIDGEWATER

The Peak District

Runcorn

Northwich

Middlewich

Macclesfield

Chester

Hardings Wood

Nantwich

Stoke-on-Trent

Stafford

Derby

Nottingham

TRENT AND MERSEY

Burton upon Trent

TRENT AND MERSEY

Charnwood Forest

Cambrian Mountains

Wolverhampton

Birmingham

COVENTRY

Coventry

Chiltern Hills

Worcester

Stratford-upon-Avon

NORTH OXFORD

Banbury

Tewkesbury

Finish

Key
— Travelled route
— Surrounding routes

For my part I travel not to go anywhere, but to go. I travel for travel's sake. The great affair is to move.

Robert Louis Stevenson
Travels with a Donkey

Contents

Part One

Florrie

Love at First Sight (Sort of)

Her name was *Florrie*, she was twenty-three and she came from Skipton, North Yorkshire. Although recently widowed, she hid her grief well and kept herself to herself. Apparently self-sufficient, she seemed to ask nothing from anyone and expected nothing back in return. She'd recently completed her first winter alone and had survived, although she looked a little the worse for wear. Her defining aura was one of silent resignation, but coupled with dignity.

Although she was powerless to control the forces that disturbed her settled existence, she seemed somehow to know she had a voice, and was prepared to use it if necessary. Most of all she looked lonely, in need of a fresh injection of the tender loving care that had once been lavished upon her. I'd like to say that for our part it was love at first sight, but it wasn't quite like that. In those early days it would have been more accurate to say that we'd fallen for the romance of it all, rather than the realities.

It had taken my wife Annette and me a half day's hard driving to reach our rendezvous point, during which the subject of the future had been most definitely off-limits. It was only after we'd parked the car that the ins and outs of what was being proposed began finally to sink in. The responsibilities, the need for constant attention, the personal consequences of a fresh commitment, and perhaps worst of all, in the event of things going wrong, the prospect of unending maintenance. All these things hit home with the suddenness of an unexpected fall, bringing with them the same sensation of surprise, coupled with a loss of confidence in one's ability to carry out even the most simple of tasks. The whole enterprise had suddenly become quite scary.

First introductions did not go well. The image that had dragged us halfway across the country had belonged to the very best of parish magazine tradition. A grainy faxed copy of a photograph had offered splodges of black and white with the occasional defined line, through which it was just about possible to make out her basic profile. Our imaginations had filled in the gaps, and had done the job well enough to convince us the trip was worthwhile.

'Here she is,' Linda announced, with more than an ounce of pride as we walked down a newly laid towpath. Linda was *Florrie*'s guardian and advocate. We first saw her resting on a mooring post outside the boatyard's shop. Something about her, possibly her air of purpose combined with her sensible clothes and shoes, marked her out as the person we were there to meet. She looked every inch the Yorkshire farmer's wife, even though her husband had owned an engineering business.

With her introduction, our eyes rested on a graceful beauty, her bodywork an elegant shade of blue overlaid with what looked like recently applied varnish. Her tiller was decorated with a criss-cross of white, yellow and red stripes and her flanks sported elaborate designs that must have taken hours of work and patience to execute. We were impressed and checked our progress to admire the vision before us. Our imaginations hadn't done her justice.

Linda walked on.

'*Florrie*,' she announced, with more than a touch of deeply embedded pride, sweeping her arm towards the next boat but one in a way that invited – nay, demanded – that we turn our eyes towards a rather forlorn and slightly world-weary vessel ten yards further on. Our elation was pricked, and began to deflate into a dim disappointment, barely enough to keep our expectations afloat. The sheer power of Linda's very clear need for us to share her sense of pride was difficult to resist however, so we dutifully caught her up.

Even her best friends would have been hard pushed to de-scribe *Florrie* as a beauty. Her front profile emphasised her high and pointed bow, a proboscis raised just ever so slightly too high, suggesting either aristocratic or ancient Roman genes. Her roof was distinctly pitted, not with pinholes, but with whacking great big dents, where people had jumped on her from on high without regard for the damage they might cause. Her hatches were as much rust as they were paint. The sign that carried her name had been painted on wood. Although there was nothing wrong with the workmanship, the wood itself had been poorly treated and as a result had begun to rot. One more winter would be one too many.

The view from the back was hardly any more promising. No highly decorated tillerwork here, rather a simple elbow painted a deep scarlet red that merged into the muddy brown water. On her backside a dirty brown mark spilled down from the top of the diesel tank, demanding rapid action with a baby wipe, or failing that some Vim.

More with resolution than hope, we persevered, encouraged by Linda's transparent enthusiasm. It was clear that *Florrie* had known love in her lifetime, so the best tactic seemed to be concentrating on finding her inner qualities. As we focused our thoughts, it also became clear that the day's activities had suddenly become deadly serious. We'd left fantasy land behind two hundred and fifty miles away; this was the real world. The question suddenly being asked of us was whether we were suitable contenders for *Florrie*'s affection or simply time-wasters? At that particular moment none of the parties involved knew the answer. We were under the spotlight as much as the boat.

As if to accentuate our sense of having become a centre of attention, we were joined by John, a man armed with a screw-driver. Tall, with well-chiselled features, he had an air about him of quiet competence and I found his apparent dispassionate air appealing. We were not in for a hard sell. After a cursory exchange of greetings he lifted the engine hatch and began probing, seemingly at random, inside *Florrie*'s nether regions. His brief was clearly to get her started and that was what he was going to do. The bedside manner he displayed was that of a gynaecologist of the old school, more barber-surgeon than *Peak Practice*. We got the impression that he'd prod around and wait for a yelp rather than wait to be told if something hurt.

'It would take a bloody bomb to stop one of these Listers,' he announced proudly, seemingly oblivious to the fact that stopping it wasn't the problem. The only reason he was there was because the thing had so far defied efforts to make her start, with a dead battery on the towpath offering damning evidence of failure. We left him to it. As we did so, we were left with the acute feeling that

15

there were now two pairs of eyes boring into us.

After some difficulty with keys, namely working out which opened which lock, something even Linda seemed unable to fathom, we entered the cabin and our spirits lifted a little. We could just make out some splendid wood panelling lining the walls, and a beautiful cast-iron solid fuel burner dominating one of the far corners, its coal-black chimney disappearing into the roof. Linda opened the curtains and the scene which daylight revealed had a certain *Marie Celeste* quality about it. Everything was where the previous owner, Linda's husband, had left it before he'd suffered his unexpected, and unfortunately fatal, heart attack. We instantly felt uncomfortable, as if we'd broken in and were contemplating the most valuable items to steal. Linda, however, was welcoming and generous in wanting to share everything with us, inviting us to look around, explaining things as she went.

Her generosity dried up when it came to answering our carefully prepared questions. In fact, it soon became clear that when it came to information, Linda was about as much use as a bacon butty at a bar mitzvah. She shouted towards the top of John's head, all that was visible as he tinkered away in the bowels of the engine, and invited him in. Seconds later he dutifully joined us, releasing a heartfelt sign of pleasure as he came down the steps into the galley, as if reliving an ancient and cherished memory. He was either a brilliant actor or we were on to something.

'Eee, they don't do 'em like this any more,' he announced, his face full of regret as he did so, but devoid of any embarrassment from the use of such a hackneyed expression. 'It's all Formica and cushioned flooring these days – to make turnaround easier of a Friday,' he explained. What he seemed to be suggesting was that *Florrie* had character, something we found difficult to deny. Apparently standards these days were driven by the caravan trade, although comparisons with the annoying tin boxes which clogged up the motorways wasn't something calculated to warm me to boating. Everyone, Annette included, seemed surprised by my observation that I'd never set foot in a caravan, as if I'd casually commented that I'd never used an indoor toilet. It was perhaps just as well that I hadn't added my lifelong understanding that this was something that would only ever be achieved over my dead body.

Immediate questions answered, John returned to the engine, perhaps embarrassed by his outward display of emotion, and we continued our tour. Just inside the hatch was an airing cupboard, adjacent to a boiler of a type that apparently they didn't make any more, mainly because the latest European directive banned them from being installed on new boats. Not encouraging. John assured us as he once more descended into the engine compartment outside, whilst displaying a confidence only a madman would doubt, that you could still get the parts. Beyond this was the kitchen or galley, a three-ringed cooker, a preparation area, cupboards and a fridge. The last apparently took a couple of hours to cool down after being switched on and had to be left empty when you left, otherwise a particularly virulent kind of mould would invade.

Already I was approaching information overload; we seemed to be entering a parallel universe with its own rules, second nature to the cognoscenti and designed to mark out the novice for ritual humiliation. The main living area was dominated by an L-shaped seat, which folded out into a double bed, whilst forward we found a set of bunks and the bathroom, bisected by a corridor and separated from the main area by their own door. Beyond that lay what I regarded as the foredeck, with removable wooden bench-ing either side. I could just imagine our two boys, then aged six and eight, their life jackets catching the sun, sitting there and shouting warnings of oncoming shipping or low hanging branches to the feckless driver at the back.

I decided to leave the women to detailed discussions of the domestic arrangements and went to see if I could offer John some moral support at the back. Besides, my curiosity had now been rekindled and I had become keen to see *Florrie* in action. I approached with caution. John's legs had disappeared and he seemed to be bent over in a position not seen since the heyday of East European gymnasts. Although impressive, the way he was maintaining his balance seemed precarious and unsustainable, and I stood perfectly still lest one bad rocking motion relieved him of his manhood.

We struck up a conversation and it turned out that John was

no simple grease monkey. In fact, he was the boatyard owner and it was he who had had *Florrie* built in the first place. This explained his reaction a few minutes before. He'd subsequently hired her out to novices and professionals alike for the first fifteen years of her life before selling her on to the now recently departed Roy. His tone carried an undercurrent of 'even a blind idiot could drive one of these things' (and judging by some of the scratches and dents plenty had), which I wasn't sure I welcomed. Anyway, I remember thinking, this tone was a bit rich from someone who couldn't even get her to start.

Within seconds he resumed his role as provider of a torrent of information and I attempted to concentrate to take it all in. He stressed that the hull was solid and – important this – that the engine had been very well maintained. The latter fact was critical because successfully changing the inner tube on a bike was something I normally had to set aside half a day for. I wasn't what you'd call a natural when it came to anything that clicked, whirred or, in this case, chugged.

Her vital statistics were forty-four feet long and six feet eleven inches wide, narrow enough to give us the freedom of the canal network, but long enough to sleep and house four people. She needed a little attention (a little!), but John assured me this was mainly cosmetic, as he poked the screwdriver down ever deeper into the boat's workings. This was an area dominated by oil, pistons, camshafts, cylinder heads and other paraphernalia of a kind which tends to be fascinating to grandads or the kind of sad people who hang around railway restoration schemes.

Clearly I would have helped if only I'd remembered to bring some overalls with me – and if I'd known the first thing about engines. The only comfort I was drawing from his exertions was the complete lack of embarrassment he seemed to feel. He was either displaying his thespian side again or this sort of thing was perfectly normal. Suddenly even that small measure of comfort turned icy cold as I digested the implications of what constituted normal.

'There!' he announced in a raised voice coloured with just a hint of triumph, as the engine throbbed into life sending out thick clouds of pungent, oil-burning smoke. 'It was the ignition that was the problem. Soon get that fixed.'

The noise that now surrounded us was a familiar one, reminiscent of a canal boat holiday fully sixteen years before. It sounded good, solid as the Bank of England, like a narrowboat's engine should sound. All of a sudden our dream had been kick-started back into reality along with the engine, the vague notion that we had been staring a dud in the face, and therefore were going to have the decision made for us, having been snatched away.

The metal flooring was slid back into place over the engine hatch. Out of sight, out of mind, I thought, if not earshot. Standing over it I could feel its rhythmic chugging vibrate up from my feet, through my legs and into my belly. It was almost sensual. Almost, but not quite.

'Of course, the one drawback of these is the knees,' John yelled as he passed me the tiller. I nodded out of politeness and raised a thumb in acknowledgement. It was true that my knees were vibrating a little, but nothing to be too worried about. Perhaps the effect built up over time, I wondered. Maybe there was a condition known as narrowboatman's knee, a bit like housemaid's knee or tennis elbow. No, surely that couldn't be right.

'The what?' I shouted back, cupping a hand to one ear whilst keeping a firm grip on the tiller with the other.

'The boys,' he replied, pointing down into the now hidden engine compartment, as if this was some kind of term of endearment for the various bits of machinery which were now doing what they did best.

'A modern Jap job is much quieter, but I don't know, they just don't seem to sound right, and anyway, they need more work.' He sighed, grabbing the tiller from me and pushing it firmly, but with no little determination, in the direction opposite to the one I'd adopted. He managed this while at the same time wiping his nose on a disgusting, grime-encrusted rag.

The noise! That was what he'd been going on about. I was with him on that and in fact I didn't find it a problem. This was the soundtrack I'd been expecting; anything else would have been a disappointment. Besides, everything's relative and there was no one else on the water we could compare ourselves against. It would do, I concluded. If this was the price for low maintenance, I'd pay it. Without leaving any instructions, he waltzed to the front of the boat and untied her ropes. The front began to swing out as he did the same at the stern before jumping back on board. The boat rocked alarmingly with his weight. We were free from the bank and ready to motor.

The steady vibration of the engine made conversation impossible and we were left alone with our thoughts. Perhaps belatedly, the question now buzzing round in my mind was simple. Did we really want to buy a boat? Was it, well, was it sensible? For the second time in two years I was on the verge of leaving a safe, well-paid job in favour of the uncertainty of self-employment. Perhaps we should have been conserving rather than possibly squandering our limited resources. An army of niggling safe options marched to the forefront of my consciousness and charged at the veneer of confidence we'd carefully laid over our unspoken doubts.

And yet it was partly this very uncertainty that made the whole thing attractive, exciting, and even dangerous. This dream, of somewhere to escape to, a bolt hole from the nine to five, was the mirage we'd been chasing before being confronted by the sheer physicality of the boat itself and the intricacies of her unpredictable innards. In rapid succession, before we'd found out she wouldn't start, we'd been told how to get her warmed up, about the need for regular pump-outs, and the occasional requirement for blacking her bottom. Memories of nappy changes and the frustrations of trying to get baby equipment to function as it is supposed to were all too recent and raw not to offer a prescience, as well as a warning, of what we might be letting ourselves in for.

Back in the real world, John was showing me how to engage the throttle and how to find reverse. As he did so I could almost feel some gold braid forming on the peak of my baseball hat. Space here was generous, in line with the cruiser style *Florrie* had been designed to. There was enough room to set up a couple of garden chairs, with some high wooden benching-cum-safety rail curving round the stern, so there was somewhere to rest your backside on those steady slow stretches of strait. It didn't take too great a leap of the imagination to see myself leaning on the tiller, beer bottle in hand (assuming the fridge had got working in time), Annette inside, reading as usual, and the boys keeping pace alongside on the towpath on their bikes.

After a hundred yards of cruising John brought the boat in while I leapt on the shore, rope in hand, and gently pulled the bow back parallel to the path. The engine slipped into idle and then, reluctantly, for it had only just got going again after its winter lay-up, died. A couple of final putts suggested a disappointment in being cut off in its prime. Our two-minute trial period was apparently over.

'Well, what do you think?' John asked, my ears still readjusting to the sudden silence. Linda's face looked up from the hatch, her clear expectation being that negotiation was also man's work. I felt the pressure beginning to build; Annette also seemed to be looking for me to take a lead. Before I had time to frame an answer the moment passed, as John filled the embarrassment of the silence by asking if I had any more questions.

I seized the moment to inject some uncertainty. Presenting my best poker face I suggested that although we liked what we had seen, there was clearly a need for Annette and I to have a chat on the way home. Anyone thinking we were going to make an instant decision could think again.

The situation was clearly a delicate one. For Linda the boat clearly held many memories and she had yet to remove her rose-tinted spectacles. For John, we guessed there was the small matter of a selling commission, notably whether he was in for one at all, seeing as Linda had made it clear that we were to deal with her direct when it came to any discussions about actual folding stuff. For us, there was a genuine need to talk, which was actually quite unusual. That's not to suggest that we never talk, the opposite in fact, merely that whenever we'd found ourselves in similar circumstances before, when we'd bought any of our houses for example, one of us had always ended up selling the virtues of the purchase to the other. In the past we had found this to be a remarkably effective way of testing pros and cons. This decision, however, was different; neither of us was sure which way to fall, and we knew each other well enough to sense it.

The exchange of concerns and plus points started as soon as we'd managed to negotiate the confusion of Skipton's market and find the right road out. Although the childcare clock was ticking against us, we had a clear three hours, minimum, before us to swap the pluses and minuses of boat ownership, or, more specifically, taking on the guardianship of *Florrie*. Were we prepared to take on the mantle of one family's cherished past and make it part of our own family's future?

The concerns column was not long, but significant nevertheless. It centred around three sets of issues: the engine, the paintwork and the responsibility. Each was capable of being rationalised away, but taken together did they constitute enough to swing a decision?

To take them in order, the engine was clearly not the most modern available, but neither was it a museum piece. At some point it might need replacing, but on the other hand it could go on for years. Only time would tell, but at least we were aware of the risks. The paintwork was more straightforward. The previous owner had been an engineer, and clearly disapproved of fripperies such as decoration. For us, however, the opportunity of making our contribution to the picture postcard image of the canals by adding a few splashes of colour was part of the attraction. This could easily be solved, but would take time and, undoubtedly, money. The dull blood clot red and mucus green would have to go. Altogether too visceral.

The third set of issues was the most uncertain. It had been years since either of us had even owned our own car, let alone a boat, so the burdens of maintenance, of the constant nagging thoughts that there was always something we should be doing of a weekend, were habits we had both lost. Would we find ourselves repeatedly writing cheques with not enough time to get any pleasure out of the recipient of all this cash and attention? It was possible, but even this we were able to reason away. If the worst came to the worst, we argued, we could always sell her.

The plus column was less tangible, and had more to do with gut feeling. Both being optimists, we found it hard to reject the dream which had caused us to undertake a nigh on five-hundred-mile round trip in the first place. We agreed that the old girl had a certain charm, but it went deeper than that. Looking back, there was evidence that we'd both always had an attachment to the idea of owning a boat. We had even gone to numerous regattas and boat shows simply to satiate this desire, without having any intention of ever knowingly consummating it. The opportunity to take on *Florrie* had come about through a series of unusual circumstances, and perhaps, we reasoned, sometimes in life you're simply forced to take, rather than make, decisions. Fate might have been slightly too strong a word for it, but it was close.

There was of course another concern and one that had been burrowing away in the back of my mind since the opportunity had first surfaced. How the hell were we to get her down from the wilds of North Yorkshire to the sedate flatlands of Oxfordshire, where we'd need to moor her? How would she take to being dragged from her homeland, which I doubted she'd ever left, and made to live 'down south'? If she was anything like any of her fellow Yorkshire folk, I suspected her reaction would be one of initial resistance, followed by sheer bloody-mindedness about her new surroundings, constantly comparing and finding fault. Could I stand it? Annette shared my concerns about the practicalities of the journey, but was less prejudiced about the boat's origins. For her, given her northern upbringing, I suspected the Yorkshire connection was in fact a plus point.

Taking everything into consideration, we'd effectively made up our minds, in principle at least, before we reached Sheffield. We would make an offer the next day. The issue of how to bring the boat down remained unresolved, however. Given our concerns, and the backstop position of a sale if things didn't work out, the obvious answer was to engage upon a courtship prior to a full commitment. I, of course, had some time on my hands and the promise of summer was stretching out before us. One option would be for me to use that time to good effect and bring her down myself. The thought lodged in my brain and began to germinate.

I would need help, of course. Controlling forty-four feet of narrowboat as well as operating swing bridges and locks, not to mention the dreaded pump-out stations, on my own was not an attractive prospect. In fact it was bloody stupid according to John, to whom I'd floated the idea. More attractive was meeting these challenges accompanied by a combination of family and friends acting as crew, people whose company was usually sampled only at set piece events or hurried weekends, and performing the journey in a series of short to middling bursts over a couple of months.

Once we had resolved the practicalities, the final pieces of the jigsaw, less easy to explain but important nevertheless, began to slot into place. These had been buzzing round my mind for a while, a series of unconnected thoughts that predated the opportunity to buy *Florrie*. Put together they seemed to offer a set of questions which I thought it was probably worthwhile trying to answer. I was reminded of the first of these as we cruised along the motorway, the milometer silently sanding down the distance between us and home. The predictable flowing movement of the three-lane highway heading south offered an inviting prospect of progress, albeit at the price of boredom. Three dead hours stretched before us and the comforts of home.

As the car accelerated effortlessly, doing what it was designed to do, it occurred to me, not for the first time, that this was what travel in Britain had become. Centres of population had become important less for their intrinsic value and the differences they offered than as staging posts between a starting point and a destination.

Motorway service stations had taken on the aura of watering holes, offering exactly the same range of adequate amenities and fast foods, and visited by many more people than the towns some were named after. Indeed, many had assumed a notoriety greater than their namesakes such as Keele (home of a fine university), Newport Pagnell (more or less subsumed by Milton Keynes) and, of course, the infamous Watford Gap, named for the Northamptonshire Watford rather than its more famous cousin (home to a fine football team), which for many marked the border between north and south. The motorways had become the new railways, minus the charm and companionship. Simple conduits for busy isolated people who no longer travelled in the true sense of the word, but moved.

Indeed, the meaning of travel had changed, becoming

synonymous with necessary movement; its benchmark of success being how quickly it could be got over with. It was something you did because you had to, rather than for its own sake, its purpose the destination rather than the journey. Gone were the days of the Sunday drive; the idea of a gentle roll out had become a thought entertained only by the masochist or the terminally insane. Whilst I agreed with the view that travel is primarily a state of mind, an emotional as much as a physical experience this nirvana had become a luxury open only to the privileged few. Could *Florrie* be our passport to join that elite?

The modern view of travel, with its predetermination and single-mindedness, had allowed fresh phenomena to emerge, none of them pretty. These included road rage, the breakdown of lane discipline on motorways (unknown when I'd learnt to drive twenty years before) and a general disregard for, and disinterest in, fellow travellers, which at times seemed to border upon contempt. Far from being the exception, each of these phenomena seemed to have become the norm, almost *de rigueur*.

Not that I was without fault, in fact I was as guilty as the next man, and this had been one of the thoughts troubling me. Even as these contemplations absorbed some of the attention I should have been applying to the road I was becoming exasperated by yet another set of roadworks and the prospect of having to slow to a mere fifty miles per hour. This was going to add a full five minutes to my journey time – nothing less than a disaster! The canals, with their maximum speed of four miles an hour, seemed to offer an antidote to all this rushing around. But was this enough? After all, there was the surely more serious business of earning a living to be got on with, with no idea as to how this was going to be achieved. Luckily, before doubt had a chance to begin to set, other thoughts rushed in to shore up my shaky defences.

I returned to the theme of different towns and places, what made them what they were and what made them different from each other. It had become fashionable to suggest that trends in retailing, work and social activities had had a general homogenising effect upon us. If you were dropped blindfolded into any community in England, it might take some time to work out where you were. Schools operated to the same curriculum and young boys and girls supported football teams hundreds of miles from their home, teams which they would never see play. High streets sported the same fascias and the pubs all looked the same and served the same beers.

Local cheeses, breads and even accents had been massaged out of the system. According to this theory, regionalism had fallen foul of greater mobility of labour, instant communications technology, the need to establish national markets and the greater insularity of people's lives. Only exceptionally did communities come together any more. It didn't seem that long ago that the Queen's silver jubilee had spawned a series of spontaneous street parties and a general feeling of self-worth as a nation. It was difficult to see this happening for her golden jubilee three years hence. Although no royalist I regretted this as much for what it said about us as a people, and about the environments we had allowed to develop around us as a kind of self-protecting, inward-looking cocoon. Rather than street parties I saw barbecues in back gardens and people using the inevitable bank holiday flicking through a multiplicity of equally poor TV channels or catching up on the DIY, anything it seemed to avoid interaction with their fellow human beings.

Once again, I was no paragon of virtue and was equally guilty of being seduced by the ephemeral comfort, materialism and, ultimately, the shallowness of it all. And yet here we were being presented with a chance to pause, to look around and see if there was any hope. Bringing *Florrie* through the canal system offered this opportunity, and I wanted us to take it.

Even as these thoughts began to crystallise, I was aware of the likely reactions I could expect from those who knew me. Some would point to my having recently turned forty and shake their head ruefully, worrying about the impact such a break might have on my pension arrangements. The words 'midlife crisis' echoed inside my head. Others would mutter 'lucky sod', point at the healthy redundancy cheque coming to me after less than a year in a new job and might say something about a classic case of being in the right place at the right time. But to be perfectly honest, and perhaps this was a symptom of the wider problem I was diagnosing, I didn't much care what other people thought.

The clincher was the canals themselves and what they represented. I had long harboured a dream of walking from John
o'Groat's to Land's End, but the idea had been filed away under
'retirement projects' and never seriously investigated. The
attraction of this had been to get under the skin of what made our
nation what it was, to connect with some of the ingredients which
made up different regions and answer some of the questions that
were now rising to the surface through these ruminations.

The problem was, walking was such bloody hard work, and a
project of that scale was pretty daunting, even for someone of my
relatively tender years. Travelling from the northernmost tip of
the main body of the English canal system, close to its southern-
most point, offered the same potential rewards with considerably
less effort. What was more, it was available now, when we were
young and (relatively) fit, not that either of us had any illusions
about the scale of the task ahead and how exhausting it might be.
Given the speeds involved it would be like walking – but on
water.

The canals had been the industrial arteries of England. Over
two thousand miles of navigable waterways remained from the
marvel of British ingenuity that had made the migration from the
land into the towns possible. From their beginning, the narrowboats had brought the food to feed the burgeoning urban
population, and then, in time, they had carried the raw materials
to sustain the glowing fire of the industrial revolution. The canals
had, in many ways, watered the roots of what made modern-day
Britain. Even the briefest of study of a map of them suggested an
intricate web gripping the edges of our island at its key points,
London, Liverpool, Bristol and Hull, supplying the tension which
pulled the nation together.

By using the canals as my guide I could drift stealthily (well, as
stealthily as the Lister engine would allow) into the backyards of
different communities and peep over the fence to see what was
going on. Was the life force still flowing down these channels, or
were we, as a country, spiritually and physically wasting away? I
didn't know, and part of the point of this exercise would be to
gather some evidence.

A list of the canals I would need to use alone hinted at the potential: the Leeds and Liverpool, the Bridgewater, the Trent and Mersey, the Coventry and the Oxford. Equally, a list of the places I would go through suggested either greatness and vibrancy or faded grandeur and depression, depending upon your point of view and prejudices. Places like Blackburn, Wigan, Manchester, Stoke-on-Trent, Birmingham and Coventry. To not only go to these places, places I would otherwise have needed a reason to visit, but also to stop and stare, to wander and gather information and finally to make up my own mind: these were my reasons for the journey.

That my subject was England was relevant too. During the week we first saw *Florrie* the Scots and Welsh had voted in their new parliaments and campaigning had begun (albeit with a whimper rather than a bang) for elections to the European Assembly. What did it mean to be English any more? Were the external forces acting upon us having the effect of accentuating or denying our differentness? Did enough defining characteristics survive, and if so were they thriving? I knew my sample would be selective, my analysis personal and entirely qualitative. But as the industrial age gave way to the information age, it seemed a reasonable quest to tap into the country's psyche and see how it was coping. Anyway, the trip was not intended to be a scientific experiment, more of a prolonged bout of personal nosiness.

This then was my thesis, the justification for spending the best part of the summer accompanied by the steady chug of a diesel engine, a sound that I was already beginning to feel nostalgic for. We were both able to recognise it as just that, a justification, for if we were being totally honest the decision had been made some time before, we just hadn't known it.

We both wanted to slow down, do something different, find a way of earning a living and raising a family which didn't simply 'go with the flow'. The redundancy cheque gave us the opportunity; we'd have been mad to ignore it. These were the ideas we'd fallen in love with and had nurtured the days before trekking to Skipton. *Florrie* was simply the vehicle, quite literally, by which we hoped to achieve them.

Most of all, we were in the market for some fun. The previous few months had been a tiresome battle against the body corporate and I was exhausted. Like *Florrie* after her winter lay-up I needed to recharge my batteries, both intellectual and physical. This final rationalisation was probably the most selfish, but also the most important of the lot. Naturally, therefore, it was the last to be chalked up on the list.

All these thoughts can be put down on paper now, but at the time we slept on it and spoke briefly the next day about next steps before I dashed out to help run a fun day for the local Beaver Scouts with my youngest son. The realities of herding a group of fifteen eager six- and seven-year-old boys through a programme of sports and set events had focused my mind wonderfully. When I got home therefore, tired and ready for a reviving G&T, I was a little bit fazed by Annette's nervous expression and announcement that 'the deed has been done'.

We were the proud owners of forty-four feet of narrowboat. All that needed to be done now was to arrange the licence, fix the insurance, negotiate some permanent moorings, organise the finance, buy extra cutlery, bedding…

Nine-Tenths of the Pleasure

Predictably, a kind of stalemate followed, characterised by mounting frustration and an almost dreamlike scepticism – had we really committed ourselves to this abstract notion of a summer, perhaps endless summers, spent on a boat? As a kind of reinforcement therapy we consumed all the information we could get our hands on and even attended a narrowboat rally on the Grand Union Canal, but none of this was a substitute for the real thing. She was idling two hundred and fifty miles away blissfully unaware of the plans being laid for her, swaying on the water like a child on a dying swing.

Back at work, I was like a student who had finished his exams while everyone else was still swotting. I had run out of things to do and was waiting for my own personal term to come to an end with enthusiasm for the task ahead. This lack of activity provided a contrast with what was to come, heightening the air of anticipation, which, the old adage insisted, was nine-tenths of the pleasure. By rights, we should have been rubbing our hands and getting excited. Instead, the overwhelming sensation was one of frustration.

In the meantime we tried to use the days constructively, doing some research, sorting out the administrative details and, not least, hustling up some crew members for what had now been termed the Grand Trek South. Reactions to our proposed adventure were pretty much as had been predicted, but on the whole favourable. No one seemed to think we were mad, well, not completely mad anyway, with the main problem being friends and family struggling to see how they might find the time to join us between holiday commitments made to fit in with restrictive rules on annual leave. I was already beginning to enjoy my coming freedom from such nonsenses.

Both of these reactions in their own way seemed to vindicate what we were planning, suggesting as they did that we were still sane, and that the whole adventure would provide a refreshing antidote to the often artificial demands of modern life. Perhaps the most reassuring comment was from a colleague of Annette's, someone who himself had put down the corporate millstone some years before, but seemed to be doing well enough on it. On hearing of our plans his response was simple, straightforward and reaffirming. 'You want to be careful,' he suggested, 'you're in danger of getting yourself a life.'

It was during this research phase that I first came across the man many regard as the saviour of the British canal system, LTC Rolt (never, I learnt, simply L Rolt, he was in fact known as Tom). Rolt's seminal work, the imaginatively titled *Narrow Boat*, was published just after the war and described his travels with his wife around the system on board his boat *Cressy*. His book placed a particular emphasis on comparing the values he found on the canals with those of a Britain finally completing the process of urbanisation.

It is from Rolt that many of the idyllic images now associated with the canal system have sprung, and many have credited him with reversing the tide of opinion which had, at the time he was writing, all but written off that system. It was about then, for example, that it had became fashionable to call for the draining of canals on the grounds that they were a danger to young children, with drownings always highly publicised. Canals had gained a reputation of being ugly and uneconomic, populated by people who were effectively water-borne gypsies. Partly as a result of this, they were for years the victims of a process of almost wilful neglect by those ostensibly responsible for them.

The villains were first the railway companies, which from the middle 1800s onwards had steadily bought up the canals as a way of eradicating competition. When they, in turn, were superseded by the roads and nationalised, the canals came as part of the package. Unfortunately, no one knew quite what to do with them; they were, in effect, an embarrassment to their new owners, the state. This was despite the evidence from elsewhere in Europe that a well-maintained inland waterway system could be a national asset, offering particular advantages over roads for bulk transport.

Perhaps a healthy disregard for the opinions of foreigners is a timeless part of the English psyche? It was during this phase that the circular argument that no one used the canals because they were silting up, but they weren't worth dredging because no one used them, took hold.

The publication of *Narrow Boat*, at first on rough war economy standard paper, followed by his leadership in helping to establish the Inland Waterways Association, meant that LTC Rolt played a large part in reversing these opinions. It is interesting to note, however, that in a particularly English way they were saved less to act as a commercial resource but as a leisure amenity, demonstrating perhaps where we, as a nation, like to place our priorities.

As King Canute ably demonstrated, tide turning is something not to be taken lightly – indeed, contrary to popular myth he failed miserably, albeit deliberately. It was only relatively recently, certainly in my memory, that the future of the canal system was secured, and indeed parts of the system which had become derelict have now been restored, in some cases beyond their former glory. In fact, at the time of writing, more miles of canal are being restored each year than were opened in the heyday of canal building in the 1790s. Despite this, some local authorities, still operating a few decades adrift from the available evidence, occasionally come up with schemes that are little short of heritage vandalism. Fortunately, thanks to the likes of Rolt and his followers, these can be guaranteed to spark a regatta or two to shame the decision-makers into a volte-face.

In the vacant state into which I descended during this time between decision and action, Rolt's book began to take on a strangely mesmeric quality, sending out sharp shoves of encouragement in the form of coincidences. To what extent these were simply the desperate graspings of a frustrated mind it's difficult to judge; it's easier to make something out of nothing when nothing's all you've got to play with.

For a start, his journey, and his book, started at Banbury in Oxfordshire, significant not only for being close to where we were thinking of finally berthing our boat, but also for being familiar, as we had lived many of the first years of our married life around there. Secondly, and more obtusely (and I readily acknowledge a certain clutching at straws here), early on in the book, Rolt describes in detail his fascination of the work carried out on a boat called *Florence*, work not dissimilar to the beautification we intended for *Florrie*. My reading was beginning to take on a certain spooky quality.

Perhaps more significantly, I hadn't got much beyond the Introduction before comparisons between the rationalised justifications I had come up with for undertaking the Grand Trek South and Rolt's own ruminations became painfully apparent. In the process some of the smugness I'd begun to wallow in began to deflate. Reading Rolt showed that that there is no such thing as a new idea, simply a variation on someone else's thoughts.

In reading his book it became clear that many of my still ill-formed concerns had been already been succinctly summed up fifty years before, even though the context then had been the demise of the agrarian economy in favour, if Rolt would approve of that word, of industrialisation. Like me, Rolt had a rather irritating tendency to rail perhaps rather too loudly against his own particular prejudices, not least the despoliation of the countryside. The essence of his message continued to ring true, however. Before I'd consumed too many pages it had become clear that certain passages could even be lifted seamlessly into this book, so perfectly did they echo my own painfully unoriginal meanderings.

It is without shame therefore that I reproduce some quotes here. Take this one, for example: 'It [canal travel] seemed to me to fulfil in the fullest sense the meaning of travel as opposed to mere blind hurrying from place to place, and I felt certain that there could be no better way of approaching what is left to us of that older England of tradition which is fast disappearing.'

Uncanny, eh? Try this one in the next paragraph: 'The rush of traffic on the road above' – remember this was 1939 he was talking about – 'seems to become the purposeless scurrying of an overturned anthill beside the unruffled calm of the water, which even the slow passage of the boats does not disturb.'

It struck me that there was one significant difference between us. One of Rolt's biggest concerns was the coming world of industrialisation and the stripping away of the ancient craftsmanship and skills of artisan England, which he regarded as somehow honest and worthy. My concerns were similar, only over fifty years on and within a different context. What troubled me were the issues of a post-industrial age, of affluence rather than hardship, and how we, as a society, were shaping up in the face of the next, electronic, age.

The contexts of our times were clearly very different in another way too. Despite Rolt's eulogising, life on the canals during his day was undoubtedly punishingly hard. Many of those who made their living, and indeed lived, on the canals were unable to read or write and were beholden to the canal companies for their daily crust. By way of contrast, life for all but the small minority in late twentieth-century Britain is, equally undeniably, comfortable; if not downright cushy – certainly by comparison.

All this theorising was clearly in danger of disappearing up its own backside. I was sliding towards the need to justify myself again. Why not simply take the journey at face value and enjoy it? Rolt's simple if at times frustrating book therefore became part of the process of waiting, and later provided a useful comparator with parts of my own journey.

There is of course an alternative explanation to how I latched on to this work. Like me, Rolt was at a critical juncture in his life when he was writing (he was about to get married when he started to plan the journey). Also like me, he clearly did not have an immediate need to earn a living, although my respite was only temporary. Perhaps we were just two privileged dreamers looking for solutions to problems which didn't really exist and over which we had no control. Perhaps we should have just kept our thoughts to ourselves and got on with life.

Containing our anticipation while we were waiting for the paperwork to come through became a major challenge. Fortunately two separate diversions managed to alleviate the waiting. The first of these was planned; the second was more serendipitous. As is often the way, once you become alert to signs they start to pop up everywhere, like spots on a teenager's face; for where had we chosen to go to celebrate Annette's fortieth birthday but Venice? Venice, home to twenty-eight miles of canal system and a top speed of five miles an hour – on one of our own canals this was enough to get you a ticket.

It's easy to be cynical about Venice, and as I write this the temptation to slip into sneering clichés in order to build some kind of modern sophisticate credentials is almost overwhelming. Almost, but not quite, for our experience was that there is a sheer gentility and joy about Venice, which is both charming and, well, so Italian. There is about Venice something that tells you that it shouldn't really exist, and yet despite this you're glad that it does; like an orchid blossoming above the treeline, it clings tenaciously and proclaims its virtues, inviting you to look and admire, and then move on.

But for us one of its main virtues was its intimate relationship with water. By the time we had settled in we found ourselves immediately searching out someone capable of delivering the inevitable gondola ride. After a brief bout of bargaining we found ourselves sliding into the highly polished craft, lined with ecclesiastical purple silk, and succumbing to the experience. Once settled in, the gentle movement and natural symmetry of the gondolier's action eased us instantly into a semi-catatonic state of relaxation. Like someone making a Christmas pudding, our new friend stirred the oar acrobatically in the uniquely Venetian forcola, a curiously carved block of wood acting as an rowlock, keeping up a steady almost hypnotic commentary. Occasionally he placed his plimsolled foot against the base of one of the high walls surrounding us to give extra momentum or to execute a turn, but it was done effortlessly and without show.

It was then, in what became a seminal moment, that any residual concerns that we might have made a terrible mistake over *Florrie* finally dissolved. As we shut our eyes and gave ourselves up to the rhythm of the gentle sloshing of the waves against the boat's sides, we both imagined ourselves moored up somewhere in the middle of nowhere without a care in the world. The feeling was unique, and yet it was replicable. The next time we experienced it our location was unlikely to share the romance of Venice, but its essence would remain the same, a realisation which was strangely satisfying.

The second diversion emerged when I was lucky to secure a place on the Royal Yachting Association's one-day Inland Helmsmanship Course at less than twenty-four hours' notice. Although pure luck, the way things were going I took this as no mere coincidence, but rather yet a further sign that the summer's plans were simply meant to be.

I was halfway up the motorway to Coventry before I remembered I had forgotten my waterproofs, something I was sure would immediately mark me out as a novice, as the forecast was for thunderstorms and all in all some pretty ugly weather. In the event the clouds parted to allow a glorious early June day to emerge, which, rather than demanding anoraks and cagoules, called out for sun hats and glasses.

Our rendezvous was Hawkesbury Junction, at the meeting of the Coventry and Oxford Canals, although true canalites know it as Sutton Stop, after the name of the original family of lock-keepers who'd taken the tolls and kept the lock for generations. Unbeknown to me this was one of the most historically significant landmarks of the inland waterways system, but at the time it was just another canal.

On first sight the lock itself is insignificant, with a negligible drop of around six inches, but I reasoned that if you added that up over the length of a canal you'd probably get a lake's worth. Reading the local noticeboards, I learnt that Sutton Stop was important for its strategic location, the two canals effectively running in parallel until they touched at a hair-raising 180-degree bend. This location used to be a favoured congregation point for working boats, but these days, to the uninitiated, it is simply a pretty spot by the canal crowned by a spectacular arched iron bridge.

Eventually the two companies controlling the canals merged and this lock was the result. A further differentiation between them had been that the towpaths were on opposite sides from each other, which had led to the construction of an S-shaped turnover bridge, designed so that a horse could cross from one side to the other without getting the tow rope knotted up. This was a marvellous brick construction, as solid as the much wider spanned iron bridge which crossed at the technical point of the junction itself. This in turn was quite defiantly black and white, a kind of industrial age attempt at half-timbering. It had been cast in Derby and still bore the name of The Britannia Foundry, Derby on its side, along with the date of its construction, 1837.

There was one other trainee on the course, a woman who had considerably more experience than me of the water, having had a number of canal boat holidays. Her husband, however, had never let her take control of the steering, except on the straight bits. As a result over the years her confidence had been shot to pieces and she'd been relegated to permanent lock setting and tea-making duties. Hats off to her, we all agreed at introductions time; all being well after the course she'd be the one with the certificate, not her bossy husband.

Our trainer was Keith, accompanied by his wife Kath and two other crew, Tony and Bob. Keith came across as what is popularly known as a 'strong silent type'. He emitted an air of serenity that seemed almost too good to be true. Although he was happy to talk, he only did so when he needed to, for example to impart information or to answer a question; he had little time for small talk. He seemed to be a man in control of himself, but that maintaining that control was something he worked at, as if he didn't trust himself to freewheel. His walk and general bearing hinted at a military past, erect and disciplined, as if waiting for permission to stand at ease.

His boat was called *Narroway*, and she was moored at the head of a line of boats on the private, non-towpath side of the canal. It was only later that I noticed the subtitle to the boat's nameplate – Matt 7:5, 13–14 – and the first thing that caught my eye once inside, other than the fact that the wood panelling was so similar to *Florrie*'s, was the computer-generated dedication of the boat to God's glory. It turned out that *Narroway* was owned by the Centre-Light Trust. This was a Christian charity Keith had set up in the early 1990s to provide a focus and purpose for those who needed it most, mainly young adolescents and the very old, although presumably not at the same time. This went some way to explain my first impressions of the charity's founder.

There was also a suspicion that the trust also offered a purpose for Keith, and possibly Kath too, although it turned out she had a landlocked Noah's ark of animals back at home to keep her busy, one of whom, her Labrador, was also part of the boat's crew. When I later questioned him gently about what had led him to set up the charity he replied simply, and with just a hint of embarrassment, that he'd 'got the call of God,' which is one of those answers which can be filed under 'conversation stoppers'.

Running courses was an income earner for the charity, and I was happy to add to its coffers. Keith was excellent at his job, imparting a combination of both basic theory and solid practical advice at the helm, all delivered with the sort of patience which probably comes as part of the package once you've taken a call from upstairs. Only once did I see him stressed, and this was when his mobile phone went off to the tune of Beethoven's Ninth for the third time, and he was unable to resolve the query as everything he needed was back at the office. His exasperation at this point hinted at a more stressful past, so inadequate was his response. I saw a little of myself in all that.

Although originally a whim, the course turned out to give an invaluable insight into the demands and responsibilities of owning and operating a narrowboat. There seemed to be so much to learn. When Keith informed us that the average boat hirer only gets around twenty minutes' tuition we looked at him in shock. My shock was perhaps the deeper, as I was the one planning to spend the summer apparently surrounded by near novices. Despite being no Boy Scout, and therefore knowing nothing about knots, even before we broke for elevenses I was doing a round turn and two half hitches as well as a locking hitch with the best of them.

Keith also introduced us to his engine, which for me was the equivalent to taking the back off a computer and trying to make out what bit did what. The exercise was valuable, however, if for no other reason than it highlighted the critical importance of the stern prop shaft gland. This is the point where the boat's propeller meets the water and it needs to be kept regularly greased, ideally every night after cruising, if water is not to creep into the boat and slowly sink it. Fortunately this basic yet vital task is achieved through the simple turn of a tap, which on the *Narroway* was near the throttle, but on *Florrie* I knew was deep in the innards of the engine compartment.

Inevitably, perhaps, once on the water we trainees tended to make comparisons with car travel and our driving test, although for both of us the latter was too long ago to be a clear memory. As it turned out, both of these analogies were misplaced, as the differences between driving a car and steering a boat outnumber the similarities. For a start, tarmacadam is a solid, visible platform, whilst water is a moving, transient master out to play tricks on you. Once understood and accepted, a happy medium can be achieved under which these quirks can be turned to the helmsman's advantage. The secret, we learnt, was to work with, and not fight against, the elements.

Even the basic act of steering is 180 degrees different. In a car, if you pull to the right you quite reasonably swing your vehicle to the right. At the tiller it's the other way round, requiring you to relearn your instincts, something which only experience can deliver. The comparison with a driving test was more reasonable, although given that most people on the water have had no formal tuition, this basic skills course was probably more analogous with the advanced motorist's test. This observation made us feel quite good about ourselves, even if it did little to improve my second attempt at bringing the boat in for mooring.

Although the thump which resulted from my efforts was felt all down the left-hand side of the boat, I took some comfort in the fact that it wasn't followed by the sound of breaking crockery. We also successfully learnt the act of using a winding hole (the canal equivalent of a three-point turn), the emergency stop (holding the boat stationary without moving up or downstream or drifting from side to side) and even reversing, the trickiest manoeuvre of the lot.

The winding hole was particular fun, involving as it did deliberately slamming the bow of the boat into a muddy dip taken out of the side of the canal and pivoting the boat round. Apparently in the days before engines this was achieved using the natural forces of the wind to push the boat round, hence the term. Signalling was more fun than in a car, involving dramatic mimes to fellow skippers and, if all else failed, a hand cupped to mouth, from the bottom of the belly, yell.

It felt tremendous to feel the imbalance of water again, even if the *Narroway*'s engine was disappointingly smooth, clean and quiet, and no doubt considerably more efficient than my Lister. Over lunch we had the chance to swap biographies and dig a bit deeper. I asked Keith what was the worst thing that had ever happened to him on a canal, and without hesitation he told how the canal he was on had once run out of water. This can apparently be achieved as simply as pulling the plug out of the bath if you fetch up a certain type of idiot and give him a windlass or lock key. Open enough locks up and it doesn't take long to drain a canal. Although this sounded pretty horrendous, on deeper examination it hardly rated a ten on the trauma scale, as it turned out it had only taken about three hours' waiting to get afloat again.

Things livened up when I asked whether there was such a thing as canal rage, a waterbound equivalent to road rage. It was at this point that I learnt of the three distinct classes of canal user: the professional, who knows what he is doing; the holidaymaker, who doesn't, but doesn't really care, and the owner. The owner, a rank I was about to join, apparently often doesn't know what he's doing either, but thinks he does. As Keith so succinctly put it, they think they own the water as well as the boat. I hid my discomfort with the thought that he was talking about other people, not me. I'd have an Inland Helmsman's Certificate to differentiate me from the herd. At least I hoped I would; when he was telling us all this we hadn't had our results yet.

His greatest vitriol, delivered with what seemed like an un-christian relish, was reserved for British Waterways, a friction I'd read about elsewhere and wanted to delve into. To date this organisation had been more than accommodating with me. Part of the animosity between this official body and the regular canal user was, I learned, driven by the rate of increase in the cost of licences without, seemingly, a commensurate increase in investment in the canals themselves. As Keith put it, the order in which money was spent seemed to be towpath first, overhanging trees second and canal dredging third, when to Keith's mind the priorities should be the other way round.

Another component was the perceived lack of respect for canal heritage, with important landmarks left to rot or facilities still used by working canal boats being shut down. Finally, I put some of it down to good old-fashioned conflict between those in authority and those who paid their wages, for what was the licence at the end of the day but a form of taxation? British Waterways probably also carried some of the stigma from previous incarnations of authority which had done so much to destroy the system. Like the Irishman, the canalite has a deep sense of history and can use it to continue to carry a sense of grievance seemingly for centuries.

For the moment, I was prepared to suspend judgement. However, later on that same day I was disturbed to see a development of new luxury flats, loudly boasting canalside frontage and each with their own pristine white metal balconies, complete with view. Standing alongside them was a derelict listed building, once a key feature of the wharfside and no doubt soon to be shut in with ugly barbed wire and strident notices warning people to stay away due to dangers from its unsound structure until it all fell down. This was the sort of thing that kept the feud between authority and user alive.

As the course drew to a close, so the clouds began to congregate above us and we began a series of protracted goodbyes. The prospect of the motorway seemed alien now, and in the end I took the A-roads for as long as it made sense. We picked up our course notes, a sort of inland waterways' Highway Code, complete with explanations of canalside signs on the back, and exchanged one last handshake.

As he took my hand, Keith leant forward to impart a final reminder. 'Always remember,' he insisted, his eyes staring deep into mine, 'to grease your stern prop shaft gland at night.' Somehow I was able to resist the temptation to add a comment of the 'oo-er, missus' variety.

As we loitered on the bank, finding it difficult to leave, a couple approached us, not exactly elderly, but old enough for their children to have fled the nest. They were unhappy. Were the British Waterways toilets always locked, they asked, and how were you supposed to use them? Even I knew the answer to this one, and I watched to see how Keith would handle it. Once again demonstrating the benefits of a divinely inspired sense of patience, he enquired whether they had a key.

They didn't think so. Could he look at their key ring? There it was, a Yale key with BWB printed on the side of it, representing the old British Waterways Board. He explained what it did and they were suitably grateful, although indignant that this hadn't been explained to them beforehand. While she had our attention, and being on the subject of keys, the wife wondered if we could tell her what a particular small square-shaped one on her key ring was for. That, it turned out, was for the ignition.

Although ink was not yet dry on my Inland Helmsman's Certificate, the inscription ceremony having been performed by Bob, an ex-draftsman, who'd brought along his calligraphy pens specially, I now felt that I at least had an inkling of what I was supposed to be doing, even if I lacked the experience in actually doing it. In short, I was ready. The time for waiting was coming to a close, soon I would be a proper boater.

One thing did bother me. Did I really want to be associated with people who, on the evidence we'd just seen, spent a reasonable proportion of their time standing cross-legged at their tiller trying to work out how the hell you got an engine to start?

Part Two
Denis

Skipton – Gateway to the Dales

The boxes were packed, the shopping done, the maps consulted and the relevant bookings had been made. There was nothing left to do, and I was managing to keep a reasonable balance between excited anticipation and trepidation. It was in this state of mind that I decided to have a celebratory haircut. Big mistake.

The trend around our way is for the traditional gentlemen's barber, the type which offers both a razor on the neck and 'A little something for the weekend, sir?' to have been replaced by much shinier, but not necessarily that much more hygienic, and certainly more expensive, establishments. These are run either by young, slim, often heavily made-up magazine models or by older and considerably more, shall we say, cuddlier women. There is no middle ground. My knowledge of hairdressing skills, like my need of them given my glistening pate, is at best limited, so I feel unqualified to comment on the abilities of these women. However, I have never left one of them without having gained the impression that these are not practitioners operating at the height of their profession. More likely they are 'filling in' prior to getting a proper job, in hairdressing or elsewhere, possibly as topiarists.

Like most men, my perspective on haircuts is that they are simply something that has to be done, a chore rather than a pleasure. They do not represent a social opportunity, neither are they really that important in the great scheme of things. In short, I do not really go to the barber for a conversation, preferring to spend my time in the chair to reorder my day's 'to do' list or generally to meditate. There seems to be an unwritten rule however, possibly one instituted by the Hairdressers' Guild or something, that at least an attempt at conversation has to be made. Typically, in my case, this involves an opening line such as 'Not working today, then?'

This time was different. The short, not unattractive but, let's face it, gabby girl circulating round my head came out from nowhere with the question 'How far do you think it is to Hampshire, then?' On the face of it this was a reasonable question, although made slightly less reasonable by the fact that it was asked at a time when the clippers were buzzing in my ear. A moment's thought, however, threw up a volley of sub-questions, such as which mode of transport was going to be employed, where exactly in Hampshire were we talking about here, what time of day would the journey be taking place and where did we expect to start from?

She continued to flutter about my person with the imprecision of a demented butterfly and none of the grace, occasionally peering intently at my tonsure as if trying to find a hair she could cut. With something of a sense of dread, I asked why she wanted to know. In the end the explanation was distressingly simple; it turned out she was selling her aged VW Beetle and the prospective purchasers were coming from, you've guessed it, somewhere in Hampshire. Her second greatest concern, after when they were likely to turn up, was whether the car would make it back. It turned out she'd only ever used it for local journeys and it had never been required to motor for more than half an hour before. Would it make it the journey?

The analogy with *Florrie* hit me along with the bright sunlight that broke through the clouds as I made my way back to the car park. For years *Florrie* too had been confined essentially to day trips only, and it had been ten years since she'd been kept going for more than a week. Would she make it through the trial we'd selfishly set for her? It wasn't something we'd considered in any depth. Suddenly the equilibrium of my mood slid twenty points down the pessimism scale, a shift arrested from further decline only by a fresh consultation of maps of our planned route once back home, something I'd found increasingly able to provide comfort at times of doubt. The nagging thought stayed with me that night, however, tapping me on the shoulder every time my brain contemplated shifting into a deep sleep.

I woke the household up at six and we packed. We had a long way to go and I was fed up with waiting. And so it was, with an indigestion of hope and fear fermenting in my stomach, that we headed up the M6 for the third time in a month. At roughly the same time, coming from points east, was my first crew member, Denis, my father-in-law (who for the sake of convenience I shall refer to henceforth as the F-in-L).

We had arranged to meet fifty miles down the canal from Skipton, just outside Chorley at a place called Adlington, which was to be our target destination for this first tranche of the journey. The route had been planned carefully, not only to include a variety of canal obstacles in order to build up experience levels, but also some potentially interesting places to visit. Adlington had also been chosen as it lay just north of the precipitous Wigan flight of twenty plus locks, which I felt it was probably unfair to subject the F-in-L to. At the time this was a reasonable calculation, although on reflection I doubt it would have been a problem. During the planning stage, however, we were erring on the side of caution. For all of us this quest was heavy with unanswered questions.

I was glad that the F-in-L had won the ballot to be my first crew, as this would be the first occasion in the ten plus years we had known each other when we would be able to pass what the childcare manuals call some extended 'quality time' together. He was a retired geography schoolmaster, and as my knowledge of escarpments, weather patterns, moraines (terminal or otherwise) and oxbow lakes was peripheral at best I was looking to him to inject some feature detail into our journey. Most especially I was looking forward to the opportunity to discover finally what a drumlin was, a phenomenon which I had singularly failed to understand at school despite its unnerving ability to turn up in exam questions.

Besides, he was approaching seventy and, without wishing to be a Jeremiah, we might not have that many more similar opportunities. Although when first approached he'd appeared reticent to take part, a reaction I put down in large measure to the fact that he had yet to gauge what 'Grandma's' view might be, as time passed he seemed to become more keen. On the eve of our adventure, therefore, there was a kind of schoolboyish anticipation for both of us over events to come.

As a travelling companion though, the F-in-L suffered from two significant drawbacks. The first was that he didn't swim, and if anything had a bit of a fear of water. This hadn't stopped him going on a number of cruise holidays of course, but there would be a world of difference between taking tea with the captain of a multi-thousand ton floating hotel and the realities of canal life. I was particularly concerned about his possible willingness to leap from the bow of the boat, rope in hand, when the time came for mooring. This would be a critical manoeuvre, and one that would need to be repeated on a number of occasions, so he would have to be comfortable with it. The solution, I'd concluded, would be to conduct a few rehearsals, and to try to pass on a little at least of my extensive knowledge as a bona fide qualified Inland Helmsman (complete with certificate to prove it).

The second drawback was potentially more worrying. The F-in-L was a renowned snorer. His snores, it was said, could shake the apples off the trees. Up until now, my only experience of this phenomenon had been through solid walls, and even then it had been pretty frightening, putting a whole new perspective on being asked whether the earth moved for you. More recently the power of his snores had been confirmed by our children, who had shared a room with their grandparents while we'd been in Venice. Their limited experience of life had ill equipped them with sufficient descriptive power to articulate the effect; suffice it to say that words like 'awesome', 'wicked' and 'mega' were used, none of which I took as promising.

Alone, this habit would have been sufficient cause for concern. The reality, however, was that I too was currently a champion in this field. In the run-up to the first leg we'd enjoyed a mini-heatwave (two days, which qualifies in English terms) and I had become a martyr to my hay fever. Two bunged up nostrils and periods of sleeplessness interspersed with bouts of deep coma had made me a menace to society. When I asked Annette if she'd miss me, her reply was unnecessarily cruel but, I concluded, heartfelt. She responded that she was looking forward to a decent night of uninterrupted sleep on her own – for all the wrong reasons.

The thought of us both vibrating away on the water, where sound travels further, was a cause for concern. Not so much personally – after all, we would both be asleep – but what if our snoring became synchronised and built up a resonance that, in time, could spark a chain reaction, like a nuclear device? The consequences could be horrifying, and certainly wouldn't be covered under the insurance.

We managed to meet at the White Bear Marina in Adlington, our pre-arranged location, without difficulty, and attempted to go through our checklist of tasks without unnecessary delay. We were still a long hour away from Skipton and *Florrie*. Key amongst the duties to be carried out here were confirming arrangements for mooring up in a few days' time, which the boatyard seemed pretty relaxed about, and buying some life jackets, both for the boys and, quite naturally, for their grandad. I also had a nagging concern that some more ropes might be useful, being sure that I'd read somewhere, either in a note the previous owner had written to himself or in one of the survey reports, that fresh ropes would be a good idea. In the event, I decided to put this off until I'd had a chance to carry out a status report *in situ*. If we were to make lunch in Skipton we needed to get our skates on.

The six of us crammed into a car designed for a maximum of five with some difficulty, the resulting discomfort being another reason for making haste. The weather was glorious: a perfect early summer's afternoon with warm sunshine reflecting off deep green pastures not yet turned brown. We hoped it was a portent of things to come. The motorways and A-roads parted for us like the Red Sea until finally a dun-coloured sign, of the type only a committee could regard as inspirational, came into view proclaiming SKIPTON – GATEWAY TO THE DALES. Seeing this sign prompted a question on why smaller pseudo-tourist towns always have to be the gateway to somewhere else – wasn't there enough inherent within the town itself to justify a visit? My mind was too focused on other things, however, to spare any thinking capacity, so I let the thought wither and die unformed.

In Skipton's case, simply to pass through on the way to somewhere else would be a shame. It is indeed worth visiting, if for nothing else than the intriguing unbalanced symmetry of the town, its dark yet attractive buildings of solid Pennine stone, and the Bizzie Lizzy fish and chip shop. The meals served here are of the quality, and indeed quantity, I had learnt over the years to associate with the area. Whenever we were tempted to make a visit, however, I couldn't help but recall Linda's observation the day she'd shown us *Florrie* for the first time, that it had probably been too many visits to this particular restaurant, and others like it, which had contributed to her husband's heart attack. Still, I reasoned, his bad luck had turned out to be our good fortune, or so we hoped. In the event, we settled for healthy sandwiches.

Taken at face value, Skipton does indeed have a self-effacing air about it, functional without being showy, in a solid Yorkshire kind of a way. The place is a combination of the day-to-day practical, which you expect from a market town, and the peripheral, those features which are more common in towns which have come to depend upon the income from tourists and day trippers. Examples of these included specialist shops, amazingly extensive menus in wine bars and elaborate signposts, each of which were predicated on a high number of strangers trampling through the town on a regular basis.

Skipton is what the F-in-L later referred to as a honeypot location, a gloriously descriptive term which just about summed it up. People were drawn to it without really knowing why, and it was good when you got there. Like honey, it was good to sample, but it wasn't something you'd necessarily want to have as your staple diet. In other words, nice place to visit, wouldn't want to live there.

A glance at the map shows the town standing at the intersection of the roads linking Harrogate, Yorkshire, in the east and Blackburn, Lancashire, in the west, and as such could have suffered from a white and red rose schizophrenia. Fortunately, certainly from a local perspective, the road south takes you into the very definite territory of Bradford and Leeds, in the heart of West Yorkshire. The town's county credentials are finally sealed by its position on the very tip of the Yorkshire Dales National Park, a location which confers its 'gateway' status.

The town itself isn't quite at the most northerly point of the Leeds and Liverpool Canal, and therefore of the main English canal system, but it is near enough to make no difference; anyway, a few hours' chugging to the west takes you to that point. Neither is it the summit of the canal, its highest point in terms of altitude, although this too was on our itinerary. No, the town has a more important claim to fame which, I felt, made it a fitting place to begin our odyssey. It was in Skipton, in July 1766, where the meeting had been held at which the idea of forging a canal link across the Pennines was first seriously considered.

At the time, this was an eighteenth-century version of big thinking, creating as it would, via connections with the Aire and Calder Navigation, a through route from the east coast of the country at Hull to the Irish Sea. In effect, the new canal would cut the country in two, in a higgledy-piggledy kind of way, through what was destined to emerge as its industrial heartland.

Comparisons with the Channel Tunnel in our own time are not altogether fanciful, not least in the time it actually took to fulfil the dream and the political, financial and engineering problems that were encountered along the way. It took fully fifty years to complete the project, during which time the original route of 108 miles expanded to 127, largely to accommodate various objections from towns along the way. Amazingly, however, only seven years passed between that first meeting and the opening of the first section, appropriately that which linked Skipton to Bingley, albeit heading east deeper into Yorkshire, rather than the route west and south into the heart of Lancashire which circumstances dictated we would follow.

Perhaps some of the political objections were predictable, as the canal brought together the two proud county titans of northern England, with each determined that the other would not gain an unfair advantage from the enterprise. At the same time each was jockeying to ensure that they emerged triumphant from the inevitable compromise over the route. In less than two years this rivalry was formalised by the creation of two separate committees, each protecting the very definite and discrete interests held either side of the Pennines. When, in 1768, there was sufficient agreement to seek an Act of Parliament to build the canal, its designated name was, perhaps predictably, the Yorkshire and Lancashire Canal. One can only suppose that either an arm-wrestling or a black pudding whanging competition had decided the ordering of counties in the name.

Substitute the UK and France for Yorkshire and Lancashire

and comparisons with the Channel Tunnel continue to resonate. Although the engineering feats behind both are now largely taken for granted by the people who enjoy them, it is interesting to speculate on whether the current link will still be in use two hundred years hence. By the way, it took eighty years for the company to finally pay off all outstanding debts incurred in building the canal, a period Eurotunnel might eventually look upon with envy.

Dog shit lay in the grass verges of the newly laid gravel path leading us to *Florrie*, a symbol we were to learn to make synonymous with the towpath over the coming weeks. It had been a while since we'd seen her, but during this time we'd had photographs to remind us of what she looked like, so there were no surprises when we finally approached her, keys in hand. She looked serene, floating gently on the water, as if nothing at all had happened in the three weeks since we'd last visited, which for her at least was largely true.

Plenty had, of course, not least our preparations. As we staggered up the pathway, it wasn't the burden of expectation that dragged us down so much, but rather an improbable number of Tesco bags full of food and any number of cardboard boxes. These were laden with odds and sods that during the time we'd been waiting we'd thought 'might come in useful on the boat'.

Sliding the keys into the padlocks gave us an immense satisfaction. At last we were actually getting somewhere. Beneath our feet the boat rocked gently as it absorbed the weight of others joining me at the stern. The lock sprang open and I removed it. With not much of a shove the hatchway to the galley slid open to reveal the inside. The stern doors followed and I descended into the dark below. As I did so *Florrie* gave me her version of a Glaswegian handshake as I bumped my forehead ever so gently, but no less meaningfully, on the edge of the hatch. Fortunately there was no blood, just wounded pride.

As the various supplies were being brought on board, I wandered over to the boatyard and reacquainted myself with John the boatyard owner, who generously volunteered a few minutes of his time on a busy Saturday turnaround day to show us where everything was. His checklist covered all those things it would probably have taken us days, if not years, to work out for ourselves otherwise. As he did so, however, it was clear that even he was struggling to remember some of the boat's features, this particular style of boat having passed out of his hands some ten years before, a period which represented two or three generations in hire boat terms. Much of it was common sense; you just had to know where the appropriate knob or button was and what sort of thing you might be looking for, something which I've always found comes as a distinct advantage in these matters. Naturally, there were a number of things we forgot to ask simply by dint of the fact that we didn't know they existed. It was these which were to require the application of a combination of cunning and luck over the coming days.

Eventually the moment of truth arrived. Actually starting the engine and edging our way out of town could be put off no longer. Unfortunately the bow was pointing in a direction opposite to one we wanted to go. The option of chugging downstream and turning round, away from the glaring attention of the audience gathering on the bridge above, was denied to us by virtue of the fact that we were on a short spur that terminated in a dead end, without so much as a winding hole en route. There was nothing for it but to reverse out.

If my short Inland Helmsman's course had taught me any-thing, it was that reversing is possibly the most difficult manoeuvre to execute with a canal boat. The flow of water is all against you and the steerage offered by the tiller is practically non-existent. To coin a phrase however, at that moment there was no alternative.

My tactics were clear: to get her straightened up and to chug very slowly but ever so surely backwards, through the narrow channel created by the privately owned boats moored behind us on one side, and the hire boats tied up double on the other. A perfectly sound strategy, on paper anyway. Mercifully she started first time, John and his crew having done the necessary repairs, and I grasped the tiller with determination.

We began to move forwards, but our cruising speed was

agonisingly slow. As I pushed the throttle forward the engine note deepened and the machinery below audibly announced that it was trying – it wasn't its fault – but still nothing seemed to happen. A model on a boating lake would have offered more control. While all this was happening, the momentum created by our push-off was carrying us rapidly towards the underside of the bridge ahead, where the crowd had now multiplied, attracted like rubber neckers to an accident. The master plan, it was becoming clear, was unravelling with alarming speed, with no time to devise a plan B.

With a mixture of relief and alarm, I realised where I was going wrong – I hadn't engaged the propeller and the engine was revving in neutral, a schoolboy error. Pulling the throttle back to the twelve o'clock position, I pushed the clutch in with my thumb and the engine responded with a roar, as if its energies had been caged and finally set free. Grabbing the tiller, I tried to rescue the situation and we only managed to avoid careering into the bridge with a helping hand, well, two actually, from the F-in-L up front. I shot *Florrie* into reverse and arrested our forward movement. On a canal boat reverse is your only brake, and it takes a while to come into effect. It comes at a cost, and that cost is a complete loss of control over the direction your backside chooses to take and we were now lying at an oblique thirty-five-degree angle to the shore. Still we were floating free at last. I selected neutral to buy some time to think.

Through a combination of the effect of a side wind and the F-in-L's shove we began to right ourselves into a line parallel to the shore and I decided the time had come to begin to take her backwards. Inside, Annette, her mother and the boys had all gone mysteriously quiet, invisible even to those on the towpath as they sensibly kept their heads so low they must have been lying on the floor. I was on my own at the back, in every sense of the phrase.

As I've already described, *Florrie*'s backside in those days was not a pretty sight, the ugly brown stain spilling out from her diesel suggesting a bad case of the trots. To have it coming towards you, at whatever speed, would on any occasion be enough to ignite concern, if not disgust. If you took any level of pride in the appearance of your boat, this would soon escalate to real fear.

It came as no surprise to find therefore that the first boat we had to get past was, of course, immaculate. A sixty-footer with what looked like a fresh paint job, she positively shimmered in the early summer sunshine, sending out a message of serenity and pride. She was the object of envy from all around, a position she clearly revelled in. Indeed, I had the impression that she was moored where she was simply to be admired rather than to be used. A bit like keeping a Rolls-Royce in your garage and inviting visitors to take a sit in her.

Inside, the owners appeared to have guests, and I had time to notice that afternoon tea was being laid out, complete with china cups. Very brave. I also noticed that on the shore they'd placed large cages complete with exotic birds and dwarf rabbits, adding to the air of circus.

We hit her for the first time with a gentle bump and proceeded to bounce off her side, a predictable encounter which caused little real damage, inside or out. What was less foreseeable was the pall of thick black smoke, the burning residue of diesel which had lain untroubled for months, which filled the air as I decided to go for maximum revs in reverse. My timing couldn't have been more perfect if I'd tried, as the instant cloud that resulted was sucked into their galley, leaving small black smuts on the window.

It was at this point that their patience ran out. The male partner, a pretend captain if ever I saw one, emerged with a boathook, which he proceeded to brandish in such a way that it was difficult to interpret his intentions. His subsequent efforts to keep us from smashing into him again were valiant, but in vain. You can't compete with a Lister in these matters.

This time we were serious, as if we were daring him to join in our game of dodgems. The resulting thump echoed loudly inside our cabin, so goodness knows what it was like inside theirs. The lady of the boat finally emerged, shrieking a heartfelt 'Well really!' in her best Margaret Thatcher voice.

The momentum that resulted from the subsequent deflection made steering even more difficult to my inexperienced arm. Juggling the benefits (greater control) and disbenefits (more speed) of higher revs was proving to be a difficult art to master. The following three minutes lasted a lifetime. Through a combination of artful dodging, judicious use of the throttle and shoves from all those we surrounded (it had now become impossible for anyone within a fifty-yard radius to ignore our passage), we eventually made it out into the clear water of the junction between the branch line and the main canal.

Unfortunately, in a wish to get it all over and done with, this had required a final burst of revs in reverse and these had sent us careering towards the far shore. This would not have been so bad if it hadn't been for a small cruiser, a stupid interloper in my view, moored exactly at the top of the T of the junction. This in turn was occupied by two twenty-somethings in swimming gear, sunning themselves and flirting, their world at that moment confined to the few disappearing inches that kept them apart. They seemed to have little comprehension of how appropriate their bathing garb might soon be as we headed at a reasonable rate of knots towards their altogether less sturdy plywood craft.

This time a burst of forward revs was required, although accompanied by a swing of the tiller if we were not to ram our old friend once again. Another collision would seem like malice, as, to the captain's mind, the danger we represented had clearly passed and he had descended back down below, no doubt muttering as he went. More by luck than judgement, I pulled the right way and we entered a perfect parabola to send us down the Lancastrian arm of the canal. A signpost pointed our way declaring LIVERPOOL 92 MILES. At that moment we would have been happy to complete just one of them and leave behind for ever the appreciative crowd for whom the afternoon's entertainment was now over.

Going forward at last, I corrected our trajectory just in time to avoid the giant pleasure boat now heading our way. Three or four times our size, this had the virtue of being impossible to miss, visually, if not physically. I remembered to head for starboard, keeping port side to port side as taught by the venerable Keith, allowing us to sneak past the first swing bridge which had been opened for her convenience.

It was at this point that Annette emerged, suggesting that she really had best be on her way. The original plan of motoring for half an hour and turning round had somehow lost some of its attraction. I agreed without too much argument and instructed the

F-in-L to head for the front and take up a mooring rope. This was to be his first practice, a moment of truth.

He coped admirably, which was encouraging, and we moored without too much difficulty. The chance to take stock as well as breath was grasped greedily by all involved. Our goodbyes were brief but poignant, with neither Annette's nor Grandma's face showing any of the concern they were both surely feeling at that moment. It was past four, although we'd all probably aged a lot more than the span covered by the hands on any clock. Time enough remained to get away from the crowds and find a good pub.

Between us and that oasis stood a few more hurdles. The first of these was our first real casting off, completed successfully once the wife was out of view, and the next swing bridge, a hundred yards down the path, which turned out to be a bit trickier. Once again, the F-in-L demonstrated an agility I didn't know he had in him by jumping onto the towpath without a need for me to stop, and sprinting to the business end of the bridge. While I tried to keep *Florrie* stationary, again as taught, he crouched down and fiddled with the chain at the base of the bridge.

Before long, he stood up and gestured incomprehensibly. There was nothing for it but to wave him back to the boat and moor up. The sheer noise of the engine made any kind of verbal communication impossible. Fortunately, he understood my intent as I edged *Florrie*'s bow bankside and he leapt on board (who was this gazelle?) and grabbed a rope. Without too much difficulty we effected a temporary mooring and the F-in-L explained that the BWB key didn't seem to be the right one, and the lock that seemed to be keeping it fast belonged to a padlock.

As we were not short of bunches of keys, I armed him with a couple of jailer's rings' worth and sent him back. Within a couple of minutes he returned. Being a trusting soul, I went and checked for myself, only to find, to my annoyance, that he was right; none of the fifty or so keys we had seemed to fit. This was crazy. Roy, the previous owner, must have come this way hundreds of times; the key must be on board somewhere.

'Having trouble?'

The enquiry came from a short bearded man, apparently

boatless, but clearly knowledgeable in the ways of swing bridges. He seemed overly pleased to be able to tell us that what we needed was known as a handcuff key, the lock of which neither of us had noticed. We had been fixated on the padlock which, our Mr Fixit informed us, was simply for the convenience of the farmer on the other side of the bridge.

Handcuff key, handcuff key, there had to be one somewhere, but no. It was T-shaped apparently, about three inches long. Wistfully I glanced back to the boatyard, still within view. There was nothing for it but to jog back and buy one.

I decided to take the back route, reasoning that with any luck no one would recognise me, or, even better, the people who were still milling about as if they had nothing better to do (they hadn't) might have had some other even more absorbing distraction since our reversing incident. As I passed, I noticed the small cruiser had gone, either the flirting had reached a stage where it needed to be consummated or they had realised how vulnerable they were at the apex of the canal. I entered the boatyard shop nonchalantly.

'Handcuff key,' I demanded with what I hoped was an air of authority which suggested that sarcastic comments would not be appropriate at that particular moment in time.

'Three pounds forty-eight,' came the equally efficient reply, my mood having clearly being picked up on.

The shiny silver key I'd come for was wrapped in a paper bag with all the efficiency of a female pharmacist bagging a large box of novelty condoms before I could get a good chance to look at it. I gave a silent prayer of thanks that handcuff keys didn't come in different sizes, thus preventing the opportunity to look a complete novice, which of course I wasn't. I had ten minutes' experience.

Back at the boat, the F-in-L was getting his first taste of what we came to recognise over the following few days as a general phenomenon amongst canal folk, namely their high propensity towards chat. This process is largely one-way and difficult to disengage from. We both put it down to the relative lack of human contact once you're actually on the water and the need for compensatory behaviour when you actually meet a fellow human being.

It turned out that our new friend had known *Florrie*'s previous owner and was keen to know how and why we'd acquired her. Once imparted, I got the impression that this intelligence would pass its way down the canal via bush telegraph faster than we would. This previous relationship at first warmed us to our new friend, but our estimation of him took a retrograde step when he rubbished John and the local boatyard. Our experiences had been nothing but good, so we took the next piece of advice he offered with a pinch of salt.

This regarded the Lister engine, which he suggested we should treat like we treated our wives. That was to say his advice was to give them a thoroughly good thrashing every now and then when no one was looking. It was at this point that I decided that this man reminded me of a pixie, small and bearded, he seemed to have an underlying quality of evil about him. The more he hung around and continued to talk, the more this quality seemed to rise to the surface.

I decided I didn't want to share his company any longer – it was only a matter of time before he'd materialise a shovel, sling it over his shoulder and begin to sing 'heigh-ho' – so we made noises about getting on and the F-in-L once more meandered up to the bridge. This time he was successful, a broad grin spreading across his face like butter melting in a frying pan. As I wandered through the boat having pulled up the back mooring pin, I noticed that the bread bin was open. Inside were yet more keys, including, quite naturally, two handcuff keys. The bread bin, of course. Obvious when you think about it.

There was one comment which stuck in my mind from the conversation we'd just had with the pixie, and that was the nickname originally given to *Florrie*'s class of boat. This was Randall's Rammers, after the man who made them, a term of endearment derived from the high and slight upward curve of the bow of the boat. I hoped we wouldn't do too much ramming over the coming weeks to justify this tag.

With the F-in-L back on board we did the narrowboat equivalent of sitting back and enjoying ourselves. In our case this meant me manning the tiller while the F-in-L either stood beside me awaiting instructions or leant forward on the hatch taking in the view. This was perfect, with the sun low in the sky, sending out long shadows and occasionally getting in our eyes, and the steady throb of the engine vibrating the skin on the backs of our shins like jelly. The khaki of the canal complemented the rich deep greens of the pastures beautifully, the whole scene framed by the overhanging branches of the trees, providing a tunnel-like effect.

We soon left the environs of the town and were rapidly surrounded by a typically rural scene of the sort which normally exists only on the top of jigsaw boxes. Cows chewed the cud and sheep gambolled innocently. It was easy to imagine a milkmaid coming round the corner complete with two wooden pails full of thick creamy milk, a foaming froth on their tops.

On the canal's surface, a variety of waterfowl watched us pass by disinterestedly, looking up only to see if we might be in the mood to throw them some bread, a tendency they'd noticed amongst these strange stick-like creatures who passed by on their noisy machines. Noticeable was the high proportion of young – ducklings, cygnets and even some goslings, with the ducklings the most adventurous, some even trying to race us for a while. Frankly, given the speed we were travelling it was an evens bet.

And the engine was indeed noisy, but in a rhythmic, satisfying way, living fully up to the expectations I'd vested in it during the long waiting time before this moment. It also sent a warm current of air up from one of the cracks down the side of the engine hatch, a phenomenon we were to welcome in the colder days ahead. The sound was strangely localised however, and seemed much less intrusive and almost normal when sitting at the front.

Our course twisted and turned on itself as the canal stuck faithfully to the contours, a legacy from the original designers who were happy to add extra distance if it meant avoiding the expense and delay of an additional lock. Eventually a climb in height was required, and our first encounter with those instruments of both excitement (for they represent a break from routine) and fear (born both from the inherent danger they represent and, for the novice, the potential for doing things in the wrong order): the lock.

By this time we had started to consult our Nicholson guide, the canal users' bible, which shows the passage of the canal through snippets of Ordnance Survey maps. As such, we were ready for it in good time. Holme Bridge Lock was mercifully rural, allowing us to put into practice the theory we had by now absorbed *ad nauseam* without an audience. It was a double width lock, in keeping with the tradition on the Leeds and Liverpool, giving an ample aperture to aim for, even if it was going to mean some negotiating as to which side to take once we were in.

Becoming quite practised in the art, I glided slowly alongside the towpath and allowed the F-in-L to jump off. He had volunteered to be on lock duty, not yet having had much experience of steering, an arrangement which suited us both down to the ground. Using hand gestures, he indicated the need to empty the lock before I could enter it. I returned my understanding with a thumbs-up and idled patiently at the side of the canal, pleased with my ability to keep the boat steady for periods at a time. This had been earmarked on my training day as something that would only come with time and here I was managing it on our first day. Keith would have been proud of me.

Eventually the F-in-L leant into the lock gates and opened them, one at a time. They seemed to be yawning, but it was a welcoming yawn. I waited until they were both open and pushed the throttle forward. For the second time that day nothing happened. I checked the clutch. No, that was fine. Almost immediately the awful truth dawned: we were stuck on the mud. The humiliation of it all had barely had a chance to sink in, which was more than you could say for *Florrie*, before a hire boat rounded the corner and offered a tug. I accepted with all the grace I could muster and gestured him into the lock first as a thanks.

Both this lock and its successor were negotiated successfully, allowing us to start building up a reservoir of confidence. For the third and final lock of the day the F-in-L took the tiller and I wandered up ahead. The lock was set for us and I went through the routine I had up until then only watched from the back of the boat, and then at some distance. This time, however, there was an audience in the form of an incomprehensible local, who offered advice as freely as a radio show host from his vantage point leaning on the far lock gate. From what I could understand, his advice seemed to involve mainly where the best water points were, when I should, and most definitely should not, begin to operate the gate paddles and where the next winding hole was.

The most annoying thing about this chap was not so much the unremitting way he was right about everything he said, but the self-righteous way in which he said it. I took some solace though in his pronunciation of winding as in winding hole. Even through the churning of vowels and consonants which made up his accent I was able to detect that he rhymed wind with find, rather than wind as in a gust of. The latter was how Keith had pronounced it, and with reason, as he'd shown us; anyway, Keith was my guru on these sorts of things. I thanked the local kindly and moved on, feeling the scores between us were equal.

Once through we moored up for the final time that day and paused to take in our achievements. We had reached Gargrave, felt by some to be the most beautiful spot on the Leeds and Liverpool Canal, and in the early evening sunlight we weren't about to argue. It had taken us exactly three and a quarter hours, as suggested on the planning map we had used, and we had covered four and three quarter miles. Most important of all, we were now at the most northerly point of the whole system. In many ways the next day would represent the true start of our journey south. It was the perfect symbolic place to stop.

The run had, in many ways, been a perfect 'breaking-in' session. We had encountered both problems of our own, as well as more natural obstacles, and had negotiated them all successfully. As important, we were now well away from the crowds and the family. The enterprise, which even that morning had been merely an abstract notion, was now a reality. Significantly we had moved out of the concept stage. Equally, we now had some idea of the sheer scale of what lay before us, or more accurately me and *Florrie*, for only we two would complete the entire journey. This was not an unhappy thought, although it was no less daunting for that.

After due reflection, we got changed and headed into Gargrave for that long promised pint. The village itself seemed on the surface fairly sleepy, although it didn't take much of a scratch to reveal signs of life. This was true especially in the village hall whose car park was full and whose doors were open for air. Inside, too many couples to count were engaged in a mélange of sequence dancing to a slightly over-amplified record player, unaware that their perambulations were public property.

Houses round about seemed well kept and, all in all, the place seemed to have some of the characteristics of a honeypot location, with its bed and breakfast signs and free visitors' car parks. The village was in fact unduly blessed, having not only the canal but also the River Aire flowing through it, the latter bisecting it to the west, with a bridge over the river forming what most regarded as the village's centre.

At night however, it seemed that the visitors went and the villagers reclaimed their streets. They did not seem to congregate in the local. The Old Swan when we got there was curiously empty of either locals or out-of-towners, with the single exception of ourselves. We didn't mind though; our weariness had taken us beyond the point where the tonic of a vibrant atmosphere would help. We simply wanted to sit down, compare notes and eat a good meal, and the pub and its attentive staff allowed us to fulfil these three requirements admirably.

Before too long we were wandering back to the boat, accompanied still by a soundtrack of sequence dancing music which only faded totally when we reached the towpath. We unlocked the various padlocks and I banged my head once more on the hatch, this time significantly harder than before, the beer having clearly deadened both my attention and, mercifully, the pain. As we stepped on board the boat swayed gently from side to side, enhancing the effect of three pints of Tetley's to a point where it was impossible to distinguish causation. Outside, it was overwhelmingly quiet and sleep came without any further prompting as our forty-four-foot cradle rocked us into the arms of Morpheus.

We were under way. We'd travelled a whole quarter of an inch on the map. Only another twenty inches to go.

Mad Cows and Englishmen

An untroubled sleep was broken only by a desperate need to empty my bladder. That and the sound of birds chirping away in unison, as if in rehearsal for the warbler's equivalent of the last night of the proms. I had also woken at four stricken by the thought that we had done the unforgivable and forgotten to grease the stern prop shaft gland. As it seemed inadvisable to do this in my pyjamas, and my imagination was allowing me to sense a slight list at the back of the boat, there was nothing for it but to get up and get dressed.

Going through the well-rehearsed rituals of rising, I was struck by the realisation that neither of us had snored during the night. The clear air was clearly doing wonders for my sinuses and it seemed that all the bad press the F-in-L had received had been poorly deserved. To my mind it also added credence to a theory that I've long held that the whole snoring thing is a power device exerted by women to make men feel guilty. Either that or the effect is in fact a symptom of an allergic reaction to women and children. Take them out of the equation and all is sweetness and light. An interesting theory, I concluded, worthy of being worked up later, possibly during an idle moment at the helm.

Once outside it took a nanosecond to realise that the weather had changed, and as it could hardly have got better from the previous day this was discernible through a marked deterioration in conditions. Even as we breakfasted the slight drizzle I'd experienced when trying to lift the engine hatch with one hand, whilst turning the greasing tap with the other, had turned to a steady and seemingly settled pitter-patter on the steel roof of the boat. Unlike Handel sheltering under his anvil, we were inspired less to compose music than to dig out our waterproofs and consult the Nicholson to see what lay in front of us.

It was at this point that I first encountered one of the F-in-L's less endearing features. Whilst he may have been great on the big practical things like getting the radiators to work, he was less useful when it came to details – like remembering to bring the Nicholson back from the pub. So it was, by dint of the fact that I was already dressed and we were keen to get going, that I returned to Gargrave and the Old Swan pub. Luckily the cleaners were in and although it was difficult to make myself heard above their vacuum cleaners, the cleaners' equivalent to a Lister it seemed, I managed to recover the guide, without which further progress now seemed inconceivable. At this stage in our apprenticeship, knowing what lay immediately ahead was half the battle, the old adage that forewarned is forearmed being certainly true in our case.

Whilst in Gargrave I also bought an umbrella. The overcast skies above us were distinctly smoky, in places as black as our exhaust when in reverse, and the geographer on the crew claimed that the lack of wind suggested that the rain would settle in and stay for a while. The glossy patina applied by the moisture to the grey Pennine stone gave the village a distinctly different look from the previous evening. No less pleasant to look at and admire, just different. Walking less purposefully than the previous night – going we'd been desperate for a pint, coming back we'd been looking forward to our pit – allowed me to gain a fresh perspective on the village.

It was Sunday and raining, so the chances of anyone on the street being a local rose proportionately. Greetings were exchanged more liberally, possibly because I'd probably been spotted emerging from the pub at nine thirty in the morning, and an air of normality had descended. I noticed that an estate of new housing, probably council built, had been added in the heart of the village, but it had been done so sympathetically, with stone that blended with the much older houses surrounding it. People were out buying papers and walking dogs. I felt like an observer, albeit an unobtrusive one on a scene of determined normality.

Back at the boat I jumped the last two steps into the galley, remembering to duck my head as I did so. The F-in-L was up, so we cast off and made for the imminent Bank Newtown flight of locks. This collection of six locks raises the canal up from the Upper Airedale a total of fifty-six feet and is situated in open moorland. The Nicholson offered the prospect of excellent views, but these were unlikely to be available for us. Besides, we reasoned, this was to be our first real sustained test. There was going to be a chance to practise, with three relatively evenly spaced locks acting as an overture to the main event.

With no one in sight we turned the corner out of Gargrave and immediately reached the first of these, Anchor Lock. This and the two which followed presented little in the way of problems. Approaching the flight itself, we had to wait, the first in the series being set against us. Waiting for it to empty, the telltale sign of a fellow canal user, windlass or lock key in hand, suggested we had company. Although no boat could be seen, they were fortunately going the same way as us and, as courtesy demands on these occasions, we waited for them to catch up.

The utilitarian level of decoration on the *Caraway* suggested it was a hire boat. The name confirmed this, as I had spotted a number from the same company also named after herbs and spices. She was green and red like us, although the boatyard had sensibly applied a high gloss to her, which contrasted favourably with *Florrie*'s dull matt finish. As soon as she hove into view I pushed the throttle forward gently and eased our boat into the lock. With the engine idling nicely and mooring ropes looped loosely round the posts up top, I went down below to fetch my camera. From this point on there was little for me to do except make sure we missed the cill, the concrete step at the front of the lock which is traditionally the cause of most sinkings when boats get caught on it.

It was as I emerged through the doorway that the *Caraway* hit us firmly and squarely on the stern. Instinctively I stood up to see what had happened and inevitably banged my head on the hatch. I was beginning to feel like Pavlov's dog. Our assailant, an embarrassed father of two pre-school children, smiled his apologies as he strained to get his boat under control, but they were forced smiles, a type I knew too well.

I fended him off and in so doing began to generate a tiny sense of guilt towards the owners of the boat we'd rammed so comprehensively at Skipton. Some but, to be perfectly honest, not that much. Collisions in a canal boat are all part of the experience; the hardened steel of most boats takes some denting. I took the view that it was foolish to invest in these boats the sort of pride that most people place in their cars, as both scratches and disappointment will be inevitable.

Once in the lock the two boats rose up slowly, as if in an ancient lift, and exited without further incident. Standing next to each other we took the opportunity to swap 'ow dos and details of what we were both up to. They were on a week's hire and expected to meet up with some friends somewhere along the flight, and at that moment they were awaiting a call on the mobile. I hoped it didn't come when he was heading towards me, but didn't tell him that. He anticipated that they'd moor up at that point, something I suspected he was quite looking forward to.

Truth be told, however, going through the lock with another boat was extraordinarily helpful, as, although it is perfectly possible to go through a lock single-handed, one crew member is the highly advisable minimum, with two preferable. Even more hands were therefore welcome and eased both our passages considerably. Besides, it was a bit of company.

Halfway through the flight, the helmsman of the *Caraway* asked if he could go in first 'for a change'. I agreed, not least because his lack of aim was beginning to become a little embarrassing. In theory, aiming for a narrower berth is easier, as if done gently enough the boat should slide into the available space, like a peg into a well-greased hole. Inevitably, however, I made a complete dog's breakfast of my first approach and was able to give some cold comfort to the *Caraway*'s skipper who from that moment on was able to feel slightly less inadequate.

By the time I looked up I noticed that the F-in-L was apparently giving a lecture to a group of around twenty fully kitted-up walkers, showing them what he was doing and why. This breed has its own name on the canal, being known as gongoozlers, although the origin of this name is unknown. Its Tolkienesque phrasing suggests gypsy roots. We'd already noticed that the canals seemed to have this effect on people, making them drop their guard and relearn the joy of simple human contact. On the water or by it we are stripped of the markings that classify us, our suits or the types of car we drive, breaking down barriers and making it easier to break the conversational ice.

Pleasant change though this was, we had a job to do and I could tell by his body language that the F-in-L was being polite rather than enthusiastic. Once a teacher, always a teacher I reasoned, as I watched him extricate himself expertly from the situation and put the theory he'd been busily explaining into practice. The gongoozlers went on their way, seemingly satisfied, filing off two by two like children in a crocodile to class. They seemed oblivious to the rain as stalactite-like droplets formed round the hoods of their waterproofs, eventually falling on their fronts and shoulders with a sharp 'plick'.

The remaining locks were accomplished without further incident. The *Caraway*'s guests duly arrived and rather than stopping for coffee they elected to provide yet more assistance. As we went through the flight, the sheer undiluted pleasure that the F-in-L seemed to be extracting from the proceedings became ever more apparent. His tongue hung out the side of his mouth when he put his back into opening the gates and his general state of alertness, checking and rechecking the lock paddles, winching only slowly at first and watching carefully so he could judge the best moment to speed up the flow of water, all betrayed a growing absorption in the whole process. Watching him, I gave him a new nickname, christening him the Lockmeister.

Going through the Bank Newtown flight got me wondering. Perhaps it was simply the wanderings of a mind in neutral, or more a symptom of being away from home for a couple of nights, but the whole process of negotiating a lock brought to mind other activities. First there was the process of assessing the state of play, then the preparation followed by a parting of the gates and eventual entry. This, of course, was followed by the gentle movement of the water, rising and falling, with a gushing towards the end and the inevitable climax, withdrawal and the satisfaction of a pleasure successfully completed to each party's mutual satisfaction. There were differences, of course, not least a frequency of occurrence that would qualify any water-borne Don Juan for serious tabloid coverage. On this day alone we managed twelve locks, and later in the journey the count was likely to get as high as thirty. The very thought made my eyes water.

After Bank Newtown the canal calmed down, which was more than could be said for the weather. If anything the rain had stepped up and my inadequate wet weather gear was beginning to show the strain. Unfortunately there'd been some confusion when it came to packing and I had but one pair of long trousers with me. In order to preserve these for the evenings, until we could get to some civilisation to buy some more, I had taken to wearing my shorts. This was no intense hardship, as although it was wet it was still warm, and the improvisation worked.

We were both surprised by how little we were affected by the rain, almost revelling in it and accepting it as simply part of the surroundings when normally I for one would have expected to curse it. We were both clearly beginning to enter that altered state of mind we'd hoped for, appreciating the journey for what it was rather than for the distance we were travelling. When the rain combined with a strong wind, however, things began to get beyond a joke. Not only did the gusts blow the rain into our faces, sometimes unexpectedly when we turned a corner, but it also made steering difficult, forty-four feet of boat proving an effective sail.

As a result, we were forced to learn yet another new skill, that of crabbing, steering the bow of the boat at an angle to make it assume some sense of straightness. When doing this, I was reminded of the old David Niven story about the crab who had to learn to walk straight to impress his lobster girlfriend's parents. When he unexpectedly succeeded his girlfriend turned to him and asked him how he did it. The reply was blunt and not a little desperate. 'Shudup!' he said. 'I'm drunk.'

All the time we were crabbing, the canal continued to follow the contours of the surrounding hills wherever possible, and it was difficult to keep track of which direction we were actually heading in. The net effect of all these factors was a need to maintain absolute concentration, and it was good to have someone to share the steering with during this spell, not simply to provide a break, but also to give the opportunity for an occasional towelling down.

During this period we stepped on the gas a bit, partly simply to get through it, and partly because of the greater manoeuvrability this provided, not in order to follow the advice of the gnome in Skipton. Needless to say, traffic levels were light, with the only boats on the water those like ours, where there was a mad need to keep going come what may. Although we opened the throttle, we took care to ensure that the boat was not breaking wash on the sides of the canal. Even in these enlightened times breaking wash remains something one simply doesn't do in public, don't you know?

It was during this time that I almost began to feel nostalgic for a lock, and as I hadn't consulted the Guide for a while it came as some surprise when one duly appeared. The Lockmeister's eyes positively lit up and he was at the front of the boat before I'd even had a chance to ask how he wanted to play it. I'd been fully prepared to do it myself, both for the experience and because, to be perfectly honest, I'd begun to have concerns for his health.

All went smoothly and once we were through the skies thinned out and the rain slowed down to a fine spray and eventually stopped, all within minutes. Far on the horizon I could even make out some blue sky and for a moment the light visibly brightened. Slight ripples in the water gave an oil painting artificiality to the reflection on the water, as if they were trying to deconstruct the image.

Any joy at the expectation of sunshine was short-lived. Pulling into the pound after the lock, I approached too fast, and in attempting to lasso a mooring bollard in order to wrench the last half a mile an hour out of our momentum, the rope snapped with a dull crack, as if someone had stepped on a dry stick. Suddenly, from pulling in, *Florrie* was shooting out into the centre of the canal, her speed unchecked, a pathetic yard or so of rope dangling behind like the docked tail of a pedigree dog. I cursed both my luck and my failure to follow my instincts the day before, when something had warned me that the ropes required attention.

Having recovered the Lockmeister, I slipped *Florrie* into idle and consulted the book, as we had taken to calling the Nicholson. As luck would have it there was a boatyard two miles downstream and what was more there was some spare rope in the hold. Although not thick enough to act permanently as mooring rope, this was good enough to hold us for a single stay. I chugged the required distance contritely, conscious that I had done something stupid, but reassured that there had been no permanent harm done. When we got there, the stop was a great success. Not only did we manage to buy more rope, but I was also able to get some proper wet weather gear, all nicely green and smelling solidly of rubber, almost good enough to see me through five days' cod fishing off Iceland.

Best of all, however, there was the opportunity to gain the silent victory that always flowed from having a crap in someone else's toilet, thus delaying the inevitable toilet pump-out just a little while longer. The system on our boat was of the kind which had a chemical holding tank, which to my mind was preferable to the alternative style of the Elsan, the so called 'bucket and chucket' system, even if you were always aware that you were sitting on nothing more than a floating cesspit. At least this way the emptying process was something that was conducted remotely. Later reading revealed that for earlier generations disposal had involved a spade and furtive nocturnal visits to adjacent fields, an even less alluring prospect.

As we entered the fringes of the village of Barnoldswick we began to pass through a semi-built-up area for the first time on our journey. Put it this way, we were peering into people's backyards rather than up cows' backsides. This was my first chance to meet some of the objectives I'd set myself way back when first trying to rationalise the writing of a book on the journey, that is, having a peek over the back fences of England and reporting back on what I saw.

The results from this stretch were, sad to report, inconclusive. The gardens could have belonged anywhere in the country, although in a fit of xenophobia I doubted I'd have viewed some of the attempts at humour offered by some of the house owners along this stretch in Germany, say, or Scandinavia. When I say attempts, the word has been chosen deliberately, for the net effect of these was less to produce an open chortle than to register an understanding somewhere deep in the brain that what we were seeing was not supposed to be taken seriously and might, should the fancy have taken us, titillate. The difference was a bit like comparing the forced humour of a sketch show on TV, which sets out to be funny, and the subtler effect of a well-written light entertainment programme whose purpose is to amuse lightly. Take the fishing gnome placed against a NO FISHING sign. Anarchic or what? Or the DOWNING STREET sign to which an old-fashioned toilet chain has been attached. Satire already! This far north!

Overall, the most lasting impression I was left with was of junk, both floating in the canal, as if the water was seen by some as a convenient municipal dump, as well as in people's gardens. The former was exemplified by smaller items such as lager cans, rising up through milk crates and traffic cones, to positive hazards to shipping, which would have been marked as such on any ordinary navigational chart. Perhaps the most extreme example of the last of these was the guard rail from a small cruiser sticking up near a bridge, which caused us to swing violently to avoid it. On closer inspection we could see that it wasn't just the guard rail but the whole boat, which had clearly sunk and been left there.

Junk in people's gardens never fails to fascinate. How is it possible to open your curtains every day and gaze out on a sepia rusted caravan at the bottom of your garden? How it got there in the first place was part of the fascination as there was no discernible side passage to the house in question. Either it had been there before the houses had been built (a builder's, perhaps), brought through in pieces (some kind of initiation ceremony) or perhaps British Waterways has a barge with a crane which glides along silently at night and places such items in the back gardens of people who've misbehaved. This could even be their ultimate sanction against lager can throwers and those who think it's amusing to remove traffic cones, balance them on the head and then tip them into the canal. Beware, litter louts, there may be secret cameras about and, like one poor house I saw, you may one day find twenty dead satellite TV aerials at the bottom of your garden. Don't try to kick them into the water, however, because they've been booby-trapped.

The one thing nearly all the gardens had in common was some kind of play equipment for children, whether slides, climbing frames or swings. Despite the turn in the weather (it was becoming positively warm, which was probably inevitable as by then I'd climbed into my new wet weather gear) there was no sign of any little darlings using them. I guessed they were safely inside, probably watching TV or playing computer games.

This stretch represented the start of the summit of the Leeds and Liverpool. From here on in, as they say, it was downhill all the way to beyond Wigan. My reading had told me that given the heights transversed by the canal, its technical summit, at only six miles in length, has always been inadequate to feed sufficient water into the system. One indicator of the heights involved is the ninety-one locks on either side of the canal needed to bring it up to this point. The summit of a canal is effectively the reservoir which tops it up, and the relative shortness of this one has always meant a constant battle to keep it flowing, a battle which in its heyday was lost in times of drought. Each time a lock either side of the summit was opened it sent out another fifty thousand gallons of water on a journey to either the Irish or the North Sea.

The canal seemed intent only to experiment with non-rural views, however, as none of them lasted for long, and we were soon welcoming back the familiar fields of cows which had been our staple diet for some time now. With the grass still carrying a dew-like wetness it was possible to understand why everything was so green around this part of the world, something the cattle certainly seemed to appreciate. As we took this in, we were surprised to see a huge, double width pleasure boat dominating the canal. As the serious obstacle of Foulridge Tunnel, all 1,640 yards of it, was rapidly approaching, we reconciled ourselves to a steady chug in behind them.

This was hardly a daunting prospect as the afternoon was drawing in and we were still on schedule despite some desperate weather during the day. However, from a distance it had been difficult to gauge just how slowly the vessel was going and almost despite ourselves we crept up on it in no time. Pulling the throttle back to just above idle, we aimed for their slipstream, perfectly happy to drift along behind like an obedient offspring, the banks of the canal having narrowed perceptibly over the preceding few hundred yards.

Suddenly, to our surprise the skipper pulled over – almost a yard – and invited us to try our luck on the outside, waving us on with a barely discernible flick of his left wrist. This was about as amazing as being invited to overtake by a tractor driver on an A-road, and, like a tractor, the boat's skipper had the advantage of a good view, standing as he was on a platform. This gesture meant that not to try would not only be an act of outrageous cowardice, but also effectively a vote of no confidence in the skipper's judgement.

We therefore pulled out and moved slowly past the imposing bulk of what can best be described as a floating bar, albeit a bloody miserable one on a wet Sunday afternoon. Largely devoid of any embellishments inside or out, the boat was surprisingly full of day trippers, many of whom leant out of the windows with their cameras and camcorders to record our progress for prosperity. This was our first experience of being on the receiving end of attention, *Florrie*'s utilitarian paintwork rarely marking her out as the belle of the ball. Whilst this attention was flattering, the temptation to do a Gazza, to pull a face or belch loudly, was almost irresistible. Almost, but not quite; I'm glad to report that our superior years and maturity held us back. Incredibly, I smelt their driver's aftershave as we passed, so close was our trajectory. Within a couple of minutes however, the floating bar was a memory.

As we came into Foulridge, I began to get an inkling for the first time of why British Waterways is viewed so ambiguously by serious canal users. Despite a series of signs indicating the availability of moorings it was nigh on impossible to tell whether these were permanent or of the visitors' variety. With the canal running out on us we decided to chance it and eased a path into a narrow slot about three hundred yards away from the tunnel's entrance. This was no easy task and required an almost car-like series of manoeuvres.

It turned out that the canal was precipitously shallow by the towpath, further undermining this spot's status as suitable mooring, and we were determined not to get stuck again. The more we tried different variations of approach, the more we came to realise that if we were to moor at that particular spot the price would be an abandonment of decorousness in favour of practical-ity. It was during this phase of our thinking, of course, that the floating bar hove into view again, and once more the cameras and camcorders appeared at the windows. Luckily we were unable to hear any of the no doubt helpful suggestions that were also offered as their boat glided majestically by.

Our eventual position was one in which our rear end stuck out about five feet into the canal, which was wide enough at this point for it not to matter, with the front end delicately kissing the bank. All in all a five point eight for technical ability, but a disastrous three for artistic interpretation.

As we cut the engine and its various parts ground to a metallic halt, silence once again washed over us like an incoming wave. After a pause to complete the ship's log we slipped into a rhythm of domesticity, in particular the cooking of the evening meal. We felt content and secure inside our little home from home, insulated from the world outside. Now and again the feet of representatives from this world would pass by on the towpath, our view of them distorted by our low vantage point in the water.

Although we knew we were sitting in space we were only borrowing, we felt a sense of territoriality and belonging surrounded by objects which by now, perforce, had become familiar. If anyone wanted to speak to us they would have to knock or otherwise ask permission. We were masters of our own domain and were enjoying it. Although we were both on holiday, this was a technicality. Simple chores like washing-up or wiping down the draining board meant that being on *Florrie* was more an extension of being at home. More accurately we were simply living our lives, redefining the space between home and holiday. We were travelling, but on our own terms, not the travel of swimming pools in exotic locations, but the travel of freedom and adventure, the taste of which we were beginning to savour.

Some photographers spend their entire life seeking the perfect sunset. The blending together of the various hues of pink, red, purple and orange in a constantly moving sky represents a unique challenge. The main skill of this art is gauging the moment when the scene is at its apogee, like knowing when to strike on a trout. Squeezing the shutter and watching the colours fade into one immediately afterwards through the viewfinder must be a moment of supreme satisfaction. As we began to approach the hinterland of industrial Lancashire I found myself gripped by a similar passion. I wanted to capture the perfect *Coronation Street* roofscape, and our brief experience of Foulridge so far suggested that it might offer some promising material. First of all there were the dull grey slates of the roofs. Secondly, the houses were arranged in neat terraced rows; thirdly, and most importantly from the photographer's point of view, it was on a slight hill, which provided a natural vantage point from which to capture a number of rooftops in line.

As we disembarked, I decided to take my camera with me. This seemed to worry the Lockmeister, who, with an irony I'm sure he didn't intend, kept on reminding me not to leave it behind anywhere. Our first stop in Foulridge, and don't ask me how the place got its name, it isn't worth speculating upon, was the Hole in the Wall pub. It was here that the story of Buttercup the cow was told, a tale that has passed into canal lore on this stretch and it can only be a matter of time before she is commemorated on a tea towel, if she isn't already.

Buttercup's moment of glory occurred on 24 September 1912, back in the days when cows were still given names and didn't carry an EU subsidy. No one knows how, still having become something of an expert on the vacant expressions of cows over the preceding few days it was easy to imagine the circumstances, but Buttercup had the misfortune to fall into the canal at the head of the tunnel. Rather than make for the side, the cow, possibly by now on a bid for freedom, unwisely decided to swim the length of the tunnel.

What was even more remarkable was that she was successful, and on reaching the other end was revived with, according to which version you choose to accept, a drop of the hard stuff or a pint of the best. A picture of Buttercup, looking suitably bemused, along with an engraved rendition of the tale, hangs in the bar of the Hole in the Wall, and in this version her reviver is in fact whisky. Perhaps out of respect for Buttercup, the Hole in the Wall's management did not have beef stewed in beer on the menu.

After we had read the tale of Buttercup, there was little left to do in the Hole in the Wall, an opinion which seemed to be shared by the locals, who were once again notable mostly for their absence. Those who were there were quite clearly pure-bred Lancastrians, their accents giving them away as clearly as a red rose in their buttonhole. A particular example was the stress placed at the end of words ending in '–ing', talking, bringing, asking, and the way they said 'thur' rather than 'their', or Tony Blur rather than Blair, a pronunciation which might have been deliberate. The person who seemed to be enjoying herself most was the barmaid, whose stereo at home had clearly broken down, as she was taking the opportunity to utilise the tape system to play and dance along to all her favourite songs. Fair enough, we thought, she lives here, we don't, so we left in search of a telephone box.

As we pounded the cobbled streets of Foulridge, it became clear that we had emerged from the land of honeypots and entered a more prosaic, workaday environment with factory units and washing left out to dry, something which presumably took weeks in this part of the world. Neither did it offer my *Coronation Street* vista; the angles were all wrong and the inclines made it more Hovis ad than Weatherfield, and the Hole in the Wall was certainly no Rovers Return. It's difficult to swap gossip with yourself. By the time we'd realised this and checked in with home, we also recognised that we'd come to the end of a long day, and we made our way back to *Florrie*, who was shamelessly showing her rear end to all passers-by like some bitch on heat.

A mist had begun to rise off the surface of the canal, giving the whole scene an eerie feel, and I half expected a damask covered arm to emerge holding a sword, until I remembered we were in Lancashire and things like that 'don't 'appen round here like'. Still, it augured well for better weather the next day.

I awoke the next day at two thirty in the morning to the sound of rain clattering on the roof. Not the simple pitter-patter of light summer rain, but the dull insistent thumping of heavy drops, as if someone was aiming a jet wash at us. It started at the back and came through in waves, regular as clockwork in a metronomic pattern which actually lulled me back to sleep. The same thing happened at four, and then again at five fifteen, each sudden awakening interrupting a deep sleep, so deep in fact that being roused from it brought about a strong sense of grievance.

When I woke for the last time at seven it was not so much the sound of the rain that did it but rather the lack of it, as if something deep in my brain had said something was missing. It was either that or the sound of the ducks outside, who were making a terrible squawking noise. Whilst it was clearly the proverbially nice weather for them, it was difficult to see why they had to be so triumphant about it. Their celebrations could only be described as flamboyant, with whole families standing up on the surface of the water whilst simultaneously flapping their wings and quacking discordantly. After a while it became impossible to ignore, almost infectious, and I pulled back the curtains to take in their rituals.

Meanwhile one of the Lockmeister's pyjama-clad legs had appeared from the top bunk, signalling life, so I lit the gas and put a kettle on. As it happened, an early start suited us as there was only a ten-minute window every hour when the green lights indicated we could go down the tunnel from our direction. The problem was that we didn't know at what point on the hour the ten minutes started, so we planned to camp out at the entrance to catch it.

Fortunately, with our rear end and therefore the propeller in the deeper water, extracting ourselves from our mooring presented none of the problems it might have done. Equally fortunately there was no one else around to get in our way or observe, which probably accounts for the fact that our manoeuvre was textbook in its execution. Getting to the mouth of the tunnel would not even have required second gear, if we'd had one. By then the rain had returned with a vengeance and we moored loosely to the permanent bollards made available for the purpose.

Behind us sat a beautifully painted sixty-footer, its skipper decked out in what looked like a professional golfer's wet weather gear. He looked the perfect stoic Englishman, oblivious to the weather and focused on the task in hand. Stiff upper lip and all that. When I turned *Florrie*'s engine off it was possible to detect in the ensuing silence that his boat was idling, and further examination revealed that he was preparing to cast off. We said hello and learnt from him that the lights were due to turn green on the hour and at that moment it was two minutes to.

Panic ensued, as the F-in-L and I had failed to have a sensible conversation about tunnel protocol, so I sent him off to the front so he could at least turn the headlamp on, while I prepared the ropes and got the engine going again. At that moment the lights changed with the abruptness of a grand prix start, but without quite as much urgency. I bought a few seconds by waving our companion through and followed dutifully in his wake. If nothing else, I reasoned, I could follow him.

We were a matter of yards from the tunnel's mouth when the F-in-L cupped his mouth and yelled down the length of the boat that the light wasn't working. There was nothing I could do; it had been fine last time I checked. There had to be a simple explanation. I yelled back to him to fetch a torch and he ducked into the boat, trying every electrical switch he could find in a frantic effort to get the headlamp working. Eventually, when we were about ten yards in (1,630 left to go), much to my relief he emerged with our most powerful torch and shined it into the murkiness ahead.

The tunnel's exit was barely visible, but straight ahead, giving a tiny aperture to aim for. What was worse was that the boat in front had clearly decided to adopt a policy of 'get it over with as soon as possible' and was already several lengths in front. I decided not to attempt to keep up and we soon adopted a simple but effective stratagem whereby the F-in-L aimed his torch at the side of the wall I was about to hit next. This he usually did in plenty of time to allow me to avoid this happening, despite the fact that my slow speed made steerage more of an art than a science, relying on good anticipation as much as accurate turns of the tiller.

This routine proved extremely effective and we fell into a kind of catatonic state in which concentration was absolute, there being no margin for error within the narrow confines of the tunnel walls. A predictable eerie silence fell on us as we focused on our respective responsibilities, a silence which was, of course, underscored by the amplified chug of the engine in the narrow confines. Luckily, the ghost that is supposed to haunt all canal tunnels, known by various names, but the most common is Kit

Crewbucket, failed to materialise and slowly the glimmer that was the exit grew bigger. As it did so we began to appreciate the true impact of the phrase 'seeing the light at the end of the tunnel'.

Our growing complacency was shattered temporarily by a sudden downpour of water down a ventilation shaft. I had seen this coming, and to a degree had anticipated it, but there was only so far I could swing away without affecting the delicate balance on the tiller. As a result, I only felt part of the effect, which was more than could be said for the F-in-L, who was so wrapped up in his torch-shining duties that he copped for the lot. I reasoned that it was all part of a learning experience; he was too far away for me to offer sympathy.

Another curiosity of tunnel steerage was the need to crab slightly due to the forces generated by the water hitting the sides of the tunnel walls. Whilst I didn't quite understand the hydrodynamics of this, the practical reality of it was all too real, although I found that the compensatory actions I was taking were more intuitive than calculated. This was something I didn't realise until afterwards, when we were talking through the experience. It was something I took considerable comfort from, it meant I was beginning to become a more natural helmsman, operating by instinct rather than rote. The effect was not dissimilar to learning a foreign language and realising for the first time that you are reading in the strange tongue rather than translating.

Although unorthodox, our Heath Robinson arrangements eventually saw us through the tunnel, a journey of twenty minutes. As we emerged, the light, although still dull, hit us with a flash, making negotiation of the bend that greeted us an immediate challenge. Reaching the open air also made me realise the sheer level of focus and concentration the preceding minutes had required. The overall effect had provided a kind of adrenaline rush, and I realised that coming through had put me on a kind of high of exhilaration it took a few minutes to come down from as the chemicals in my brain re-established their equilibrium.

It was only later that the sheer scale of our achievement stuck me fully. Although not by any means the longest tunnel in the system – there is disagreement on which has that distinction, with the favourite being the Harecastle near Stoke – it was certainly in the top ten in terms of length. We were due to encounter the Harecastle later on in our journey, which at over 2,900 yards was getting on for twice as long as the one we'd just been down. In this sense Foulridge was a good example to lose our innocence on. What was more, it had the added virtue of being straight, which not all tunnels are, with some including dog-legs, thus removing the solace of a distant light to aim at for at least part of the passage.

Although certainly an experience, our passage had been relatively straightforward, and put into perspective the achievements both of Buttercup and of the original builders of the tunnel. Considering the technology of the time (the tunnel was opened in 1796, over two hundred years ago), tunnel boring must have been a long, arduous, not to say dangerous occupation. It's easy to see why engineers preferred to follow the contours and dug tunnels only when there was no alternative.

In fact, the canal builders of the time were faced with two major predicaments, not only actually creating a giant hole through a hillside, but also making sure it was level, for obvious reasons. Most digging was purely manual, carried out by a crude combination of pickaxes and shovels, and conducted by candlelight. Geological surveys were practically non-existent at that time, so those actually doing the digging had no knowledge of the ground they had to shift or when it would change. One minute they might be dynamiting solid rock, the next shifting wet sand. What was more, during the building ventilation shafts had to be dug from above (fancy trying to get that right), and the excavated sections of tunnel lined. Against this background, our twenty minutes had been a picnic.

Even when a tunnel was opened it often created as many problems as it solved. Some collapsed and many were significant financial burdens to the independent canal companies. Some were wide enough for two boats to overtake each other, but it was more normal for a one-way system to operate, as at Foulridge. Very few of the longer tunnels had towpaths, which meant that the horses that normally provided the motive power got a rest. Instead, getting through a tunnel required genuine manpower, accessed through the process known as 'legging' in which a plank is strapped to the boat's roof and two men lie either side, literally walking the boat down the inside of the tunnel walls. This practice is now banned on the UK system, thankfully removing any temptation to try.

For us, going through the tunnel had been like a real life computer simulation, if such a description isn't too contradictory. In this case, however, the punishment for getting things wrong was not simply a discordant noise and warning message, but a loud thump, complete with a real-life reverberation through the length of the boat and probably the loss of a little more paint from the side.

Twenty minutes was enough, and once it was over my excitement was tempered by a calming dose of relief. If we'd had some sun and a yardarm, and if they'd been in the correct alignment to each other, we'd have given ourselves a tot of something warming to celebrate.

Of Cills and Mills

The excitement of the Foulridge Tunnel was only to be the start of it. By the time we had emerged it was still only half past eight in the morning and before us lay the prospect of Barrowford Locks. This flight of seven marks the end of the summit and from here on the order of the locks would be reversed. I already knew that the Lockmeister was relishing this challenge, mainly because he'd told me half a dozen times, taking great pains to describe the differences.

As far as I could see these were mainly vested in the fact that we'd be going down not up and that when we entered the lock it would be full not empty. I also knew that I should be paying more attention to the back of the boat and the potential disaster of the cill. From now on this would be visible, whereas previously it had existed more as an abstract notion, marked by a white line on the lock wall. Finally, the threat of oncoming water was about to be replaced by the equal and opposite threat of water from behind.

In theory, from Barrowford it would be possible to view the actual reservoirs that top up the canal, but in reality the driving rain made seeing more than twenty or thirty yards ahead an impossibility. Instead we had to take comfort in the fact that at least they were being refilled, removing any prospect at all of us being grounded. Anyway, we reasoned, this was not a day for admiring the view but rather one to get on with the job in hand. As we approached the first lock we spotted the sixty-footer we'd seen the other side of Foulridge, last seen merging into the optical illusion of the tunnel's exit. Its skipper was clearly not happy. His round face was puce, his whole demeanour one of aggravation as he clenched and unclenched his fists. We drew alongside, not knowing what to expect.

'Some idiot's emptied all the pounds,' he fumed. 'The lock-keeper's seeing what he can do,' he added, seemingly as an afterthought.

We didn't quite know the significance of this intelligence, but knew that the prospect of sitting on the top of the canal all day in the pouring rain was not an enticing one. I'll admit that the idea of having to keep the Lockmeister on his leash so near his quarry for any length of time was also a worry.

Fortunately it soon became apparent that the panic was over-stated as the gates, which previously had been so damningly barred to us, swung open to reveal a full lock.

'Do you want to tie up?'

This query is an odd one at the best of times, but in the circumstances it took me a couple of seconds to understand the true meaning of the offer being made. Our new friend, now returned to what was presumably his normal state, was offering to tie the boats together and go down the flight in tandem. This was something we hadn't experienced before and, in theory at least, was going to make our lives a lot easier. Besides, Mr Previously Angry had that air shared by so many on the canals of absolute certainty in his abilities, which, given our position at the reverse of this spectrum, was comforting. At the very least we'd learn something.

The sixty-footer was called *Orion Dawn* and was skippered by Alan, who, it turned out, spent eight months a year cruising the canal system with his wife. She, the boat, that is, was immaculate, although his wife seemed to be thriving too, and, as we were later to find out, was as impressive inside as she was out.

The act of tying up was as simple as its name suggested and required the use of a sturdy rope to clamp two boats together so that they became as one, powered by a single engine. Thankfully, this wasn't to be ours, as Alan's engine had already become an object of envy. Whilst ours was functional, even in the short period we'd been motoring some of its deficiencies had already become apparent, the most significant of which was the relative lack of responsiveness. Up until meeting Alan I'd regarded this as normal, but watching him move his boat backwards and forwards with barely any effort at all, as if powered by the wind and just as quietly, had provoked a degree of genuine envy in me. He literally had fingertip control. What was more, his manoeuvring was achieved with barely an audible chug, the engine purring contentedly like a sleeping cat.

I was rendered virtually unemployed as we worked our way steadily down the locks. I tried to look busy, fending off with a rather intricate rope fender I'd found in the hold, and occasionally tightening up one of the ropes that bound us together. I suspected that the rope fender was meant to be ornamental rather than practical but under the circumstances thought this was okay because so too, it seemed, was my role in proceedings. The Lockmeister and Alan's wife seemed to have struck up a routine of signals and their own little language and everything was going smoothly. Having little to occupy my mind, I returned to my locks-as-sex metaphor and concluded that two was definitely more satisfactory than one.

Halfway down the flight, a soot-black cloud approached us overhead at a rate of knots I could only envy and threatened to engulf our contented scene. It was at this point that the workers went on strike and we were invited to have a coffee aboard the *Orion Dawn*. As I got off and walked round to the back I could see our two boats floating together as if in conspiratorial conversation in the as yet unemptied lock, their two bows touching at a slight angle as if one was leaning into the other's ear. We were working on the assumption that no one would be mad enough to be coming up the flight on a day like this. An assumption that proved to be absolutely correct.

Bending my head as I entered, I eased off my waterproofs in the cramped confines of the back of Alan's boat, revealing the by now rather tired shorts and T-shirt underneath. The warmth was especially welcome, as was the coffee. Inside, the *Orion Dawn* was beautiful, with wood panelling and personalised features installed by Alan himself. With just pride, they pointed some of these out, including some commissioned stained glass and an ingenious cupboard which pulled out rather than swinging on hinges, taking up hardly any space but acting as a more than adequate pantry. This sort of detail was new to me, being completely unacquainted with the boating and caravanning scene, and was filed away for the day when we might have the will, or indeed the funds, to refit *Florrie*.

This couple were typical of many we met on the canals, true

enthusiasts who had negotiated most of the system and spent months at a time on it. They were, as they put it, spending their kids' inheritance. They were also following a dream, having commissioned the hull and designed the boat themselves to their own specifications. They were typical too in the division of labour they employed between steering and lock work. Not once during this leg of the journey did we see the wife of one of these couples steer into a lock leaving the husband to work it, despite the latter being by far more physically demanding. It seemed to be the natural order of things for this generation and probably said as much about their marriage as it did their respective abilities, a theory backed up by the experience of my fellow trainee on the Inland Helmsman's course. On further reflection, however, I wondered how things would work out when the boat was manned by me and Annette, as was scheduled for the leg after next.

Such people were invariably a mine of information, although like all opinions the intelligence received did not always tally. Alan was particularly damning of Blackburn and Manchester, both of which were on our itinerary, with the former looming up fast. He had tales of vandalism and of children throwing rocks at him from the bridges. His adamant advice was to limit motoring in these places to school hours, as if the sort of children who threw rocks at boats for fun dutifully went to school. As for mooring up in either of these cities, this would, in his opinion, provide sufficient grounds for committal to a mental asylum.

We talked about ourselves too, and about our plans to make the South Oxford Canal our home. This met with approval all round, the South Oxford being both picturesque and, what was more, safe. This phase of the conversation also allowed us to explain why we had gone through Foulridge by torchlight, something Alan admitted had surprised him but he'd clearly been too polite to enquire about up until then. This honesty allowed us to avoid any embarrassment and it was a pleasure to spend a few minutes with these people before the rain eased up and we began to robe up again for the rain.

Before going, I couldn't resist asking Alan about his engine. This it turned out was also a Lister, but with four cylinders, against our two, and water cooled rather than air. I expressed my admiration and filed that information away also, as I was beginning to adopt the view that a fresh supply of motive power might not be such a bad thing after all, reassuring chug or not.

One thing we found it hard to agree with Alan and his wife on was their opinion of the Leeds and Liverpool Canal, or L & L. In their view this was one of their least favoured parts of the system, and they'd even turned round just past Skipton and retraced their steps rather than complete the loop via Leeds. Although our experience was by force limited, we'd both enjoyed the canal so far and were happy to defend it. If this was the worst the system could offer, then we had some delights in store.

True, the L & L does not quite fit the picture book, romantic view of canals, being often really quite wide and almost river-like, and this may have been part of the problem. The locks too are wide and functional rather than fitting tightly round your boat. These made travelling through the canal a very demanding exercise, and although my seventy-year-old Lockmeister seemed to be thriving on them, I could see that they could begin to become quite daunting if you were female and not quite so invigorated by the challenge as he was. Surely though, I concluded, this was a comment less on the canal than on how you chose to tackle it.

These characteristics of the L & L largely reflect its origins as a conduit for heavy loads, carried by wider but shorter vessels – only boats of sixty or less feet can navigate this canal, against the longer seventy feet of the traditional narrowboat. We had already come across some of these monsters, sometimes referred to as barges, and had more to come. This did not make it unique on the system however, as many of the other canals are similarly wide. The L & L also had the additional feature of over fifty-swing bridges which, although sometimes a pain to get past, were part of what made it different.

Back outside, it immediately became clear that the Lockmeister and his able (and vastly more experienced) lieutenant had lost their rhythm. In their first lock after coffee they were busy opening the front paddles to release the water back into the canal when a panicked cry screamed out from the rear of *Orion Dawn*. At that point I was at the front, going through my fendering exercises, but even I could hear what he was saying.

'Close the paddles, close the paddles,' he screamed, clearly in dire straits, 'I'm getting soaked, quick, quick!' The tone of his calls was becoming more and more extreme. Message received and understood, the workers lockside quickly reversed their direction of winding in a desperate effort to shut the front paddles.

'Get a bloody move on! Shut the paddles,' yelled Alan.

'We're going as fast as we can, stop getting at me,' his wife hollered back at him, as if this degree of crisis was a perfectly normal occurrence. From my vantage point I could see the danger and appreciated Alan's growing desperation. Water was pouring out from the gate behind him in a parabola of foam, most of it landing on his short platform, filling it faster than it could drain. It was a matter of time before it started to seep into their boat itself and I was reminded of the line from the film *Titanic* when the ship's fate is sealed. Asked if sinking is inevitable, the ship's designer says something like 'It's a mathematical certainty.' At the same time, the turbulence created by the water was dragging his backside onto the cill. One way or the other, the stern of his boat was in danger of either going down or staying up.

Visions of the back of his boat tilting, taking *Florrie* with it, began to take shape and I wondered what to do for the best. One thing was for certain, adding more weight to the back of the combined boat at that moment probably wasn't a good idea. Besides, I didn't want to get wetter than I had to. Both the crew working the locks were still winding like fury, and I could see that they were nearly there, and yet Alan's insistent cries had, if anything, got worse. 'I'm in trouble here,' he shouted, 'for God's sake get a move on.'

The problem was that the Lockmeister, Alan's wife and I had all misunderstood what the problem was. The priority was not so much to close the front paddles but to plug the gap caused by an inadequate shutting of the one at the back. We had all interpreted his instructions as a need to close the front paddles first, as a precaution, not to meet the more real and immediate danger from behind. Luckily the F-in-L realised this as soon as the front paddles were shut, and it was the work of moments to close down the source of the danger.

Relief flowed all round as the moment passed. I couldn't guess how close we'd been to real disaster, but knew enough to know that the danger had existed real enough. Nothing more was said, although lessons could be drawn from the incident, not least the need for clear communication in a crisis. I was only grateful there had been the four of us, as I very much doubted if the result would have been the same if the pair of them had been on their own. Equally, maybe the problem wouldn't have occurred in those circumstances, Alan's wife following her routine by instinct. Then again...

Two more locks followed and then there came that point that occurs in most friendships when it becomes natural to part, in our case quite literally. It was with a mixture of gratitude and a feeling of looking forward to motoring under our own steam again that we undid the ropes keeping us together and went our separate ways. The canal can do that to you, at times encouraging an almost Garboesque desire for solitude.

We motored on ahead and put a respectable stretch of water between us before slowing down. We'd travelled the grand total of two miles since breakfast, but a lot had happened. The stretch which followed was briefly rural before some initial signs of encroaching urbanisation merged together to form the outskirts of some civilisation. Unlike our previous experience of built-up areas, this was a proper bona fide town, Nelson in fact. Nelson, it turned out, was a convenient label for a series of small villages which came together during the industrial heyday of the nineteenth century to form a town, and this impression is reinforced in the approach to it by canal.

You could tell it was a proper town by the quality of the rubbish in the canal and by the colour of the canal water itself, which was distinctly greyer with a hint of chemicals. Particularly noticeable was the number of dead fish, and whether this was a by-product of pollution or simply clumsy fishermen we could only speculate. Perhaps the most surreal and unpleasant sight was a dead chicken, bloated to twice its natural size so that at first it was unrecognisable.

The most distinguishing characteristic was the sheer number of derelict mills lining the canal's banks, providing an echo of hustle and bustle now long since gone. Loading bays were bricked up and cranes which still extended out into the canal were rusted up, surely for ever. The few that remained open, albeit partially, were operating as mill shops, a telling reminder of the economy's shift away from manufacturing to retail. Those that had died had clearly done so suddenly, with only makeshift attempts to seal them or tidy them up. One day busy, the next dead, as if they'd suffered a sudden and unforeseen heart attack. Industrial debris littered the scene, and it was hardly surprising that over the years much of it had found its way into the canal. One even sported a recent sign saying WARNING – GUARD DOGS, but guarding what? It was almost a sick joke. An arsonist might be doing these buildings a favour, architectural heritage or not.

As we motored through this scene, through necessity quite slowly in case we came up against something we'd rather not ram, the sides of the canal became noticeably more overgrown, as if this stretch of the water had been abandoned to its own devices. For the first time we were forced to choose our channel to avoid being brushed by overhanging branches. The towpath side of the canal had been reinforced with steel plating, which whilst no doubt utilitarian was ugly and rusting in places. Treatment of the canal in this way, as a problem to be contained rather than an asset to be cherished and even exploited, said much about how these whole areas had been given up for lost, the mills rotting, the cost of knocking them down before they fell down no doubt uneconomic.

During the period of my life when I used to work for a living, my job had taken me around most parts of the country. Part of the pleasure of this travel was the opportunity it provided to taste different subcultures and to observe how different communities both viewed each other and what they typically regarded as the amorphous south, which was usually lumped together simply as London. More often than not, these towns exhibited a fierce pride in their existence. Sometimes this could be put down to a reliance on a single industry or interest which had the effect of acting as a binding agent creating a common cause. Other times it was less understandable, and altogether less laudable, being more of a defensive reaction in the face of long-term decline.

As an aside, I'd often also noted a dislike, sometimes bordering on loathing, of a particular neighbouring community, if you like a mini-example of the sort of rivalry discussed earlier between Lancashire and Yorkshire, although worse – if that is plausible. This competitive edge was usually self-defeating, with both communities, in their refusal to work co-operatively out of sheer bloody-mindedness, or out of fear that one party would get the upper hand, ending up losing out in the competition for the public resources they both craved.

Let's dwell on the positive side of this pride, however, this community spirit. Testing whether this still existed was one of my many objectives in carrying out this journey. I also wanted to check whether my original thesis was correct, whether this sense of local exclusion existed at all; after all, it had been formed on the basis of often extremely light contact, with an unrepresentative sample of the local population. Approaching a town by canal and lingering for a couple of hours seemed hardly any more of a scientific approach; it was, however, an alternative which could be used to confirm, deny or otherwise test my theories.

The lucky winner in the draw to be the first subject in this exercise was Burnley, which was rapidly emerging from the morass that was Nelson. Where the one ended and the other began was unclear, but like a good pub you knew it when you got there. It was chosen not only because it was the first major town we had encountered, but also because the need to boost my wardrobe had by then become pressing.

Burnley is approached circumspectly, with the canal looping round the town so that it is difficult to know where best to stop and moor to reach the centre. The town itself is hidden in a hollow and the approach from the north is via the attractive Thompson Park, which even seemed to have a bandstand, although it was difficult to be sure through the trees. It certainly had a boating lake.

Then comes the surprise. The so-called Burnley Mile, al-though it is in fact only three-quarters of a mile long: one of the supposed seven wonders of the UK canal system. Opened at the turn of the century, the nineteenth century that is, this is an embankment sixty feet high which stretches out in a straight line, part of which is an aqueduct over the main road. Building it had practically bankrupted the canal company, with building interrupted so that more money could be raised to finish it.

We were glad they had managed to finish it though, and we slowed down, the better to enjoy the privileged view afforded by floating past other people's rooftops. Then, suddenly, a thought hit me and I passed the tiller to the F-in-L and ran through the interior of the boat, picking up my camera as I went.

This was it, a unique opportunity: the perfect, absolutely bloody perfect, *Coronation Street* skyline. I stood on the roof of the boat and began snapping away. The rain had stopped for a moment and the slates of the roofs had a watery sheen on them. All that was needed was a sleepy cat and the scene would have been a hundred per cent. More pictures followed, I couldn't help myself, until I ran out of film. Five minutes of undiluted opportunity, and I'd taken it. I couldn't wait to get the film developed.

Whilst standing on the roof I had seen a domed building which experience suggested could only be a town hall, signifying a spot close to the centre of the town, so I rushed back to the stern and prepared the F-in-L for a landing. This was achieved without too much difficulty alongside Bridge 130. More by luck than judgement, this location turned out to be entirely appropriate as it was here that a small visitors' centre called the Weavers' Triangle was based in an old wharfmaster's house and canal toll office. It also included a stretch of wharf, but this was the other side of the bridge and had been invisible to us as we'd moored.

In its heyday, Burnley was the world's centre for cotton weaving, a role celebrated in this centre, which we were fortunate to find able to accommodate us as it was only open two hours a day. It seemed the climate in this area, which is damp and cool (as we could testify), was ideally suited to the working of cotton. Although the climate had remained constant, world economic forces had changed, making cotton now part of Burnley's history.

The custodians of the visitors' centre were delighted to see us, as they'd been watching us as we'd moored up and were always disappointed when canal users failed to call in, a phenomenon they simply couldn't understand. In fact, delighted was an understatement, it was as if they'd been waiting all their lives to meet us. My house is your house, they seemed to be saying, come in, rest your weary feet, make love to my wife and eat what meagre food we have left in the fridge. Until our arrival it had been a visitors' centre singularly uncontaminated by visitors. This was despite the fact that admission was free, although donations were encouraged. We duly obliged and were given a couple of tickets, as they liked to keep a headcount of custom, something I guessed could have been achieved just as easily through the use of fingers.

We were instantly allotted our own personal guide, in fact guides, with both the custodians following us as we wandered from room to room, seeking approval for the exhibits and providing a running commentary. This, more often than not, was abstract, taking as its starting point one of the features of the exhibition and plaiting it into an aspect of their own lives. Perhaps this was why it was called the Weavers' Triangle? The appearance of an old chair, for example, segued neatly into a discussion of how the woman of the pair had helped her daughter move into her new flat the day before. A model fairground led into a discussion of her holidays that year, and so on.

One of the F-in-L's most endearing qualities is his ability to maintain a feigned interest with people of this type, a quality I don't share, so I moved on and sought out a Gents, it being that time of day. I do recommend the Weavers' Triangle though, should you ever find yourself in Burnley. The exhibits are compact, well labelled and interesting. I picked up a number of titbits of knowledge that are bound to come in handy one day when playing Trivial Pursuit. Here's an example: did you know that the tradition of having set weeks off in certain industries, called Wakes Weeks, was so called because the lack of soot and eerie calm in the deserted town was felt to resemble a wake? Well, I didn't, and probably never would have if it hadn't been for the Weavers' Triangle visitors' centre.

Out of a sense of obligation we also inspected the canal toll office, which meant going outside. This too was impressive and included a list of tolls laid out on an old clerk's desk which read as follows:

CLAY, BRICK AND STONE – ½D PER TON PER MILE.
COAL – 1D PER TON PER MILE.
TIMBER AND MERCHANDISE – 1½D PER TON PER MILE.

I don't know about you, but this actually seemed rather a lot to me, given the weights it is possible to carry by water, although I suppose it rather depends upon your definition of merchandise. A subsidiary sign underneath again solicited donations, although they joked that they did not charge by weight. This, I thought, was a shame, as they would surely clean up on any Americans or Germans who might, by any chance, be visiting.

Going back in, we were encouraged by another member of staff to take two more tickets, and although it was tempting to oblige in order to boost their numbers, we declined. On leaving I decided that perhaps the most depressing exhibit in the centre was the last loom to produce cotton in the triangle. I supposed it had to be somewhere, but seeing it seemed so, well, final.

Having decided we'd had enough of viewing the past, we stepped into the present, climbing the two hundred yards or so uphill which took us to a pleasant and open town centre, clearly the recent recipient of major investment. This route took us past both the town hall we'd seen from the roof of our boat and what was the local Mechanics Institute, which the F-in-L was able to inform me was a kind of charity which existed for the betterment of the working man. It was this sort of insight that I'd brought him along for. These days the institute in Burnley is a theatre, which doesn't seem a bad use for it. It would have been good to step inside as one sensed it would be ornate and spectacular, in an arrogant Victorian kind of way, but the shops beckoned. We needed fresh food for the evening meal and there was the small matter of some trousers.

As luck would have it, Burnley has a particularly strong tradition of markets, having first been granted a charter in 1294. Although the modern-day market is now covered, we were able to get not only the vegetables our bodies were beginning to crave (much longer and we'd have been at risk of scurvy) but also some extremely reasonably priced trainers.

Prices in general were excellent, this being a definite difference between the north and south of the country. We baulked, however, at paying threepence for a carrier bag at the greengrocer's and as a result of our principles had to wander around the rest of our time in the town with courgettes, spring onions and sweet peppers stuffed into every available pocket. I thought it was only a matter of time before someone came up to me and asked 'Is that a courgette in your pocket or are you just pleased to see me?' but these things simply don't happen in real life.

Despite looking hard, I was unable to detect any sign of a specifically regional food in the market, only Lancashire cheese and that hardly counts (I doubted it was even made in Lancashire, although on the evidence of our own eyes there was certainly no shortage of dairy cattle). The only candidate was a form of compressed meat, which was laid out on a slab in an unnatural rectangle with bits of tan-coloured jelly clinging to the outside. This, the F-in-L, now becoming a regular mine of information, told me was brawn, a polite term for mangled-up calf's muscle. I decided this naming was a bit like the practice of some fishmongers of calling dogfish rock salmon. I nearly threw up on the spot. The only conceivable use I could see for something of that consistency was as putty. Eat it? No way!

The rest of the shopping was distressing familiar, the place having inevitably fallen victim to the levelling down of the high street which has afflicted every major, and indeed minor, town in the UK. This though is an old and well-worn gripe and not worth going through again here. In its favour, it was clean and the people friendly when we were trying to find places, virtues which can never be taken for granted and worth remarking on when found. Overall, we were left with a highly favourable impression of Burnley, which seemed to have made a successful effort to create a fresh identity for itself. At the same time, it had not forgotten the legacy offered by its past, but neither did it dwell on it to the point of desperation, as is often the case.

We cast off and headed out for Hapton, which, according to the helpful booklet *Welcome to Burnley* that we'd picked up in the visitors' centre, saw pioneering work on electrical power and is believed to be the first place to have had electrical street lighting. Deeming a brew to be a good idea, the F-in-L went down below to put a kettle on and came back with the distressing news that we'd run out of water. The poignancy of this announcement was heightened by the fact that there seemed to be no shortage of it falling on my head at that particular moment.

That did it. Another tunnel, the Gannow (a mere 559 yards long), was our next scheduled piece of excitement in what was turning out to be an incident-filled day. As we still hadn't diagnosed why the headlamp wasn't working, this news convinced us that a stop for some routine maintenance was in order. In what was rapidly becoming a day of firsts we managed to locate a British Waterways water point and tied up. Our hose fitted the tap, something we'd somehow thought wouldn't happen, although there was no logical justification for such pessimism, and we waited for the tank to fill.

And waited, and waited. When we consulted the original instruction sheets that used to accompany *Florrie* when she was a hire boat, we saw that the tank held six hundred gallons. I lifted the hose. The dribble that was coming out of it barely formed a continuous stream. It immediately became clear that filling the tank was not going to be a quick operation. I stuffed the hose deep into the tank and opened a couple of taps so we'd know when the water was on again. Although it occurred to us that the taps should work with only a minimal amount of water in the tank, we rationalised away the lack of flow by the belief that a head of pressure needed to build up, thus demonstrating a lack of grasp of even elementary level physics. It was a wonder we'd got this far.

It was time to turn our attention to the headlamp. It was the work of seconds to find the switch on the side of the lamp that the F-in-L had, in his haste, failed to locate. I flicked it a couple of times on and off in the confident expectation that it would work, and that if it didn't then it would be the result of faulty wiring. It didn't. What was more, the wiring was fine, so far as I could make out anyway. Straight incompetence on the part of the F-in-L, up until then my favoured theory, was out. I went back to basics and sought out another switch. These were all located down at the back of the boat near the rear exit, and on approaching them I flicked one of them on at random.

A whirring noise started up behind me and the galley tap

spluttered into life. In an instant the horrible truth hit me. The whirring had been caused by the pump that drew water up from the tank. The F-in-L had only gone and turned the whole electricity supply to the boat off, hadn't he! It must have happened in the flurry of activity before we'd entered Foulridge Tunnel. Incompetence was back on the agenda, leavened with a generous helping of frustration, and finally spiced with a certain satisfaction that we were back on track.

I closed the tap and called out for the F-in-L to join me. Only one problem was troubling me. Should I insert the hose down the back of his shirt or the front of his trousers?

Devil Worship, Isolation and Celebration

Rising to the novelty of sunshine and a sense of renewal, I decided to embark upon a programme of cleanliness. First on the list was personal hygiene and I checked out the on-board shower, which turned out to be pretty effective. If there's anything I can't stand it's a shower which just dribbles all over you like a leaking tap. Once in my groove, I started to fill buckets with detergent and gave *Florrie* a good old scrubbing down, using brushes acquired only the day before for this very purpose from Burnley Market. Some good old-fashioned elbow grease was required to scrape off the encrusted bird shit and grass cuttings which had clung to her side since we left Skipton. From now on, I reflected, any muck we collected would be our muck, not inherited.

Aware of how long it took to refill our water tank, I started off by rinsing the suds off with canal water, but as I went on I decided this was slightly defeating the object, especially having seen how some people seemed to regard the canal as a convenient open drain. In the middle of filling a bucket with fresh water from the tap a scream came up from the bathroom as, deprived of cold water, the F-in-L's own nice warm shower became instantly scalding. Back to Plan A, but I felt my lack of foresight made up for his own failings with water the day before.

Hapton, the nearest place to our overnight mooring, had failed to live up to its advance billing in the *Welcome to Burnley* booklet. There was nothing wrong with it, it was an ordinary village with ordinary houses and seemingly ordinary people, but it would have been hard to justify a day trip. We'd managed to find a pub the previous evening, but had only stayed for a half as the TV was blaring away and it was hard to make yourself think. Somehow the TV had become discordant with the tone of our days.

While we were drinking the reporter had been investigating the price differentiation between houses in the north and south, with the example of a house in London being used, the value of which would have bought an entire street in Manchester. I tend to find this kind of stuff almost entirely depressing and pointless and didn't want to listen to it. As it was unavoidable, however, the alternative was striking up a discussion with a fellow drinker. At least it would have been if there'd been anyone else there. Not even a barmaid was visible, and if I'd had a mind to it would have been easy to have made off with the empty gallon of whisky bottle full of coppers without anyone noticing. Another weekend pub we concluded, an impression partly confirmed by the pretty serious karaoke and disco equipment stacked up against a far wall.

Our mooring, about half a mile out of the village, had been pleasantly rural, however, and we'd taken all the sleep our bodies demanded, uninterrupted by the artificial demands of an alarm, and this was quite a lot after the exertions of the previous day. Although our surroundings were unexceptional, we felt a glow of exclusiveness about the little bit of rural England we'd requisitioned for the night. We were alone, in charge and happy. Once recharged, we set off when we were ready.

Upon leaving Hapton we notched up a few more swing bridges. Some of these turned out to be difficult to manoeuvre, requiring three hands to operate them, which can be a bit tricky when the normal complement is two. I gained the impression that the Lockmeister was less enamoured of these obstacles than he was of locks, not that that stopped him volunteering, which was to his credit. It was just possible he was still feeling a twinge of guilt over the previous day's shenanigans.

We were compensated after the second such bridge by passing a boatload of teenage girls still in their nightdresses drinking coffee. Their boat was clearly not a normal hire boat, being highly decorated and decked out with enough of the traditional clubs, hearts and spades to suggest it had once been a floating casino. It was the full sixty feet and, as was often the way with older craft, had a side hatch about a third of the way down, which regrettably on this occasion was shut. These girls were clearly even later starters than we were and completely unabashed by their state of dishabille, facts we were able to be grateful to the Fates for. Something told me we were in for a good day.

With the sunshine placing everything into sharper focus the

scenery along this stretch was inspirational, almost Constable-like in its depiction of rural harmony. The bright greens of the pasture underscored occasional flecks of yellow dandelions. Trees in full leaf drooped their branches down to tickle the water and tease out ripples as the wind gently swayed them from side to side. These scenes drifted by in slow motion, giving us ample time to take them in before the next bend demanded our attention.

If it was more rural to look at it, it was certainly a good deal more rural to the nose, something we put down not so much to the cows themselves but to the variety of breeds represented. This, we surmised, in one of our many idle moments at the tiller, when the brain casts off and starts to probe new areas, was probably created by some kind of reaction yet to be investigated by chemists.

Although the fields included the standard Friesians, there were also brown strains, which certainly weren't Jerseys, as well as greys and whites, and all manner of variations in between. The calves seemed oblivious to the differences, with brown ones suckling from grey mothers and so on. Either there was a terrible skin problem with the cows around here, we thought, or the local farmer was into eugenics as a hobby. This cultivation of the lost art of idle speculation had became an unexpected by-product of our journey and one which we both welcomed. How many times, in the course of an ordinary day, do you get the chance to let your thoughts wander down previously completely unexplored avenues?

Whatever the cause of their differences, these cows seemed to share the same sorts of attitudes to our boat as their brethren elsewhere, being almost contemptuous of us, looking up only briefly with a look of utter disdain before turning away and returning to the important business of getting their cud thoroughly chewed. We were barely an interruption in their day. I welcomed this variety, which I was happy to put down as a regional difference, the very fact that it was noticeable meant that it was different from what I was used to.

The canal on this stretch at times drew uncomfortably close to the motorway, without ever actually coming into contact with it. The fact that both the planners from over two hundred years ago and their more recent colleagues had chosen the same route seemed at the time noteworthy. On reflection, however, it was hardly surprising, given the fact that we were effectively going through a valley, with significant hills rising either side of us. As with earlier on the journey, these were swathed in a verdant lushness which seemed almost luxuriant.

Indeed, such was the magnificence of the scene that it moved the Lockmeister to slip into geographer mode. He pointed out the feature of the treeline which described an almost straight line over the range of hills, above which all was bare, although not barren. Peppered amongst the grass on the horizon were spots of white (sheep) and black (silage bags) as well as strings of telegraph poles. Nearer to the canal, the sun had brought the buttercups out, providing a reminder of the mad cow at Foulridge (why hadn't she simply turned round?). At points these carpeted the fields, giving a local version of the fields of rape I was more accustomed to seeing at this time of year in the south, although clearly much more attractive.

One of the hills, we think we worked out which one, was the famous, or infamous, Pendle Hill. Conspicuous by being slightly higher than those surrounding it (it is in fact only 1,831 feet high), it also conveyed a certain magisterial air, as if it knew it was the stuff of legends and therefore more important than the others around it. These legends centred on witchcraft, and Lancashire's own and earlier version of a Salem-style story of fear, accusation, superstition and ultimately the pitching of families both against others and against themselves.

Although there's probably some element of a kind of pre-industrial equivalent of an urban (rural?) myth in all this, the story goes that in 1612 a hornets' nest of devilry was uncovered in Pendle, quite by chance. At the time the climate was very definitely anti-witch, something which was largely reflected in the then king's beliefs, James I not being hot on witches, whom he decried as evil. Fair enough. In an age of simple beliefs, however, it took but a single episode between two people to spark what ended up becoming a cause célèbre, involving whole families and ultimately the complete community.

At the centre of the story was one Alizon Device who refused to buy some pins off a beggar. All perfectly reasonable, you might think, but following this refusal the beggar promptly collapsed and died, probably of a stroke, which naturally put a bit of a kibosh on things. Things were not to get better for Alizon though, as she was immediately accused by the dead man's son of putting a curse on him, which in turn led to her being investigated as a witch. That's the way it goes sometimes, you go out for a stroll and end up finding yourself banged up as a witch.

Then came the twist though. Under interrogation, Alizon confessed to cursing the beggar and for good measure said that her grandmother had often asked her to allow a familiar demon to come to her. No doubt intrigued, the magistrate leading the investigation pressed her and asked for more accounts of witch-craft, which she duly supplied, her young imagination running on all four cylinders. Alizon turned up allegations of turning milk sour, of bewitching a child by making a clay image of him and of murder by spells, all involving various members of local families.

After this things naturally started to get really interesting, in-deed they soon spiralled out of control. Human teeth were unearthed, as well as clay images. Most damning of all, news came through of a witches' coven on the Good Friday, where it was alleged that twenty witches had gathered to plot to blow up Lancaster Castle, where the first wave of accused were being held, and to kill the governor. This was serious stuff, and the magistrate was obliged to try those involved, a process which took all of three days from trial to actual suspension by the neck until dead. No hanging about then. Sorry.

As with the Salem trials in New England, it's possible to put a lot of this down to mass hysteria and ignorance. Just as important, however, was the undercurrent of inter- and intra-family rivalry, which suggests that certain strains of human behaviour remain constant, although they may not manifest quite so violently these days. On the other hand, a day spent in a modern magistrate's court might make you revise this view. Ultimately, it's all probably just a different version of the general suspicion of outsiders that I've already remarked upon. In the early seven-teenth century the neighbouring farm was probably as much a foreign country as the next town is now.

Closer inspection shows that the Devices had a long-standing feud going at the time with the Chattox family, who, it was alleged, had at some point broken into Alizon's grandmother's home and stolen some items they were later seen with. As a result they were obliged to pay a yearly tribute, a commitment which soon petered out. These two families were the chief protagonists in the dispute. All these antagonisms were no doubt known to the magistrate involved, but positively inundated with confessions and accusations, as well as an air of possible treason, his options were in truth fairly limited. He probably had a game of the seventeenth-century equivalent of golf lined up for the weekend (possibly something involving wenches) and didn't want to drag things out too long. What made the whole episode more alarming was that it was by no means exceptional, witch harassment being a popular sport at the time, fuelled to a great extent by the king's zeal on the subject. So much for the benefits of strong leadership.

After all this rural black magic, it was almost a relief to see fields give way once again to fences, walls and eventually buildings, alongside a very well-maintained towpath. I'd begun to lose confidence that something nasty might not be lurking behind the next cowshed. Particularly reassuring was the prospect of calm represented by a series of anglers' pitches, which were numbered from the high one hundreds and counted down, agonisingly slowly. We agreed that this must be quite a sight when full and wondered about the qualities which might make one pitch more desirable than another, a debate that in turn led to a discussion about how fish choose the best places to hang out. Less pleasing to the eye as we approached Blackburn, for this is what the buildings were about to become, was the series of mini-towns being put up by builders with what seemed to be a complete dearth of imagination.

Presumably part of the reason a canalside location had been chosen for these developments was their proximity to the water. Whilst a cynic might say this is simply cheap land, it seems a shame to waste the opportunity to share in the tranquillity of the canal. Why was it then, we wondered, that they chose to create huge banks of spoil up to thirty feet high, effectively hiding the water from view? A much more appropriate action would be to hide the houses from the canal user, for these were, almost without exception, ugly, Lego-like constructions mapped out by computer and erected by disempowered craftsmen.

These builders seemed to be engaged not in creating communities but simply huge aggregations of houses. There were no focal points where people could congregate and share experiences, no greens, churches, cornershops or even sports clubs, simply row upon row of 'executive-style' boxes with tiny gardens where it would be impossible to host a party for even two or three families with children. It didn't seem to be exaggerating things too much to suggest that we hadn't learnt anything from Pendle, with these estates offering tremendous potential for intrigue and envy of the more modern style. More likely, however, people simply wouldn't care, possibly engaging initially in a hands-off relationship with their immediate neighbours, but after that very much keeping themselves to themselves.

Perhaps the most distressing aspect of these developments was their popularity. It seemed that barely was the mortar dry than the drives were occupied by people carriers and off the road vehicles. The new owners' next move seemed to be a kind of token personalisation of their property, as if they were marking their territory with urine. These could be something relatively unobtrusive from the local garden centre, like a lattice feature on the fencing, or something altogether more ambitious like a charming Doric column by the front door. This duty fulfilled, the owners seemed to retreat behind their front doors never to be seen again. Although aspirations were being met, I wondered if they were being fulfilled.

This whole business with the housing estates we passed cracked upon a wider meditation on other aspects of what were *de facto* essentials of modern life, like TV or the media, or indeed food. There is an interesting debate to be had some time on the extent to which people accept what they are offered simply because they have been conditioned to think it's what they want, and whether, if asked, they might actually want something completely different.

Consider how opinions are gathered or ideas tested, through methods such as opinion polls or the fashionable focus groups.

These each ask people to react to a given, whether it be a state-ment or a product, more often than not an evolution of something that already exists, rather than going back to basics and trying to find out what is driving demand in the first place: what people want a political party, car or new shopping centre to provide and where it fits into their life. Instead, our lives seem to be increas-ingly made to fit into what is made available to us. Result: more of the same and, not surprisingly, more ironing out of any kind of variation or alternative viewpoint until we all do, think and see the same things. There was another rationale. These changes might be what people really do want, a prospect altogether too frightening to contemplate.

In a final stretch of open country before Blackburn we approached a family of swans – mother, father and a group of half a dozen cygnets. A children's book scene, and one that remained static, almost defiant, the closer we got to it, with the swans, not unreasonably perhaps, daring us to get out of their way rather than the other way round. At the last minute they kicked their feet and moved the necessary yard or so required to maintain clear water. All, that is, except for the father, who mysteriously disappeared, causing me to fear that we'd hit him. But no, he had taken the blind side and reappeared on our flank behind us like a sneaky dogfighter.

This analogy was not altogether inaccurate as he pulled what was clearly his angry face, ruffled up his feathers, bent back his long delicate neck into an S shape and proceeded to charge us. His legs paddled like fury to keep up with us, something he achieved admirably and went on achieving for what seemed like an age, well, at least three or four minutes, after which his family had fallen out of sight. During this time he was never less than a couple of yards away and if I'd turned off the engine I'm sure I would have heard him hissing his anger. Turning off the engine, however, was not a risk I was prepared to take. All in all it was an extraordinary performance in both its futility and its persistence. We wondered if it was normal behaviour for swans, who, let's face it, have a bit of a reputation in the aggression department, but later experience suggested otherwise. He'd either got out the wrong side of the nest that morning or he was an evil bastard. I favoured the latter.

By its own admission (check out the municipal web site), Blackburn is most famous for its football team, the Rovers, who rose from obscurity to win the Premier League in 1995. Subsequently their history has been less magnificent and at the time of our journey they were still licking their wounds after being relegated to the next division down. If you're looking for analogies, there's no need to look any further.

It also had a brief moment of fame in the late 1960s when the Beatles mentioned it in their opus 'A Day in the Life' on the Sgt Pepper album with its reference to four thousand holes in Blackburn, Lancashire. This has, perhaps inevitably, been picked up by the local football fans who have called their fanzine 4,000 Holes. Although, as always, theories abound as to the meaning of this apparent nonsense, my favourite is that John Lennon had read a newspaper report that four thousand holes had been located in the roads within Blackburn and the idea that someone had been given the task of counting them simply tickled his fertile imagination.

First, however, some facts. Blackburn is a medium-sized town of around 140,000 souls ten miles to the east of Preston, the county's capital, and thirty miles from Manchester, in whose more extensive shadow it often gets lost, much to its football supporters' chagrin. The town grew rapidly through the need to accommodate workers for the new cotton mills, most of whom were housed in the sort of terraced housing we'd had such a good view of from the Burnley Mile. Smoke from that era has given the Pennine stone of the buildings a permanent darkness, which means the area will probably never shake off the signs of its industrial past, even though it has moved on economically.

Textiles play a role locally, with some of the country's finest carpet manufacturers located in the vicinity, although other major employers include a number of paint-makers. By this token, the good burghers of Blackburn should have immaculate taste in interior design, something we were unable to test but were happy to take on trust. As is often the case in these towns, the biggest employer is local government.

Whilst the town might not be described as thriving as such, it is doing rather well, with lower than average unemployment rates and a disproportionately high number of young people, and a similarly low proportion of the older and retired. Whether these can be taken as indicators of prosperity or of inertia and poor health conditions for the elderly is always open to interpretation.

Lessons over, we decided it was time to take the temperature of the town for ourselves. The Lockmeister had been particularly impressed by the way we had been able to glide into the centre of Burnley without any of the aggravation usually associated with big towns of finding a parking space and paying, and once again so it proved with Blackburn. Choosing our spot, we simply moored up alongside Eanam Wharf, an illustration of sensitive restoration of an example of our industrial heritage. The wharf had a spectacular red roof which more than covered a large loading bay, giving shelter to the men and goods involved. The rest of the development was a business centre, bar and, perhaps inevitably, a visitors' centre. Although we were sure this was excellent, we didn't feel up to another of these so soon after the Weavers' Triangle experience; anyway, we had different fish to fry.

The Nicholson had hinted that the cathedral was worth a look at, and as one of the first things we saw was a sign directing us towards it, this is where we let our feet take us. Before then came the answer to the question that had been troubling us since our first approach to the town: exactly which brewery was it whose products were tempting our nostrils? The answer was Daniel Thwaites, a local concern which has been brewing since 1807. It was then that it struck me that at last I had found an icon of regionalism, an activity which distinguished different regions from each other. Beer was one of the few examples of something that had been threatened by the levelling-down process back in the sixties and seventies, but exceptionally had been rescued by the efforts of the good folk of CAMRA.

Alas, when I put this to the Lockmeister he had bad news. A Sunderland resident, he reported that their local brewery, Vaux, of roughly the same vintage as Thwaites, was about to close down, the victim it appeared of the financial markets rather than any problems in demand for, or the profitability of, their product. This was due to have a devastating effect on the town, taking six hundred jobs with it and leaving a massive physical gap in the heart of the city. The comparison with some of the mills we'd seen was obvious, I'd seen the Vaux Brewery site many times and its presence in the middle of the city was imposing.

Funnily enough, a couple of weeks later I heard an interview on the radio with a member of the family which had for five generations run the Vaux Brewery, by some coincidence also called Nicholson. He was distraught and clearly at a loss to understand why this thing had happened to his beloved business. He had spent the weekend before writing personally to each of what were about to become his former employees.

One thing he said stuck with me. The decision to close had been the shareholders', whose priority was to maximise return on the company's capital, and other parts of the business, principally hotels, were at that time being more successful. Although under existing rules this decision was legitimate, he suggested that if a wider perspective had been taken of accessing the interests of all stakeholders, rather than simply the owners of the business, that is to say publicans, consumers and suppliers, the decision would almost certainly have been different. This kind of thinking was refreshing, although for Vaux it was clearly too late. I had the impression that a brewery is like a coal mine: once shut it is impossible to reopen. So much for that theory then, but nice try.

Although unprepossessing on the outside, within seconds of entering it is clear that Blackburn Cathedral should become recognised as a third reason for having heard of the town. Although not really a lover of church architecture, which I usually find to be constricting and dark, even morbid, this example was a complete revelation. Only granted cathedral status in 1926, the church's fabric is only a hundred years older than that, betraying the town's own relative youth, although, as is often the way with these things, a case can be made for the site having been a place of worship since the year dot.

The immediate ambience was one of light and space, so much in contrast to the usual experience. Over the altar stood the freshly restored Lantern Tower, which as luck would have it was due to be officially reopened the next day by the Princess Royal. This coincidence meant that the place was in the process of being decked out with flowers, notably spectacular white lilies which were the perfect choice. The renovation of the Lantern Tower had followed a fund-raising drive locally to restore a structure which had only been completed in 1967 but, like so many of the concrete structures of that time, had experienced rapid deterioration.

If the mention of concrete conjures up the usual nightmares, dispel them now. This was a beautiful structure, interspersed with one of the most imaginative uses of stained glass, certainly modern glass, I have ever seen. This described a circle, with reds and oranges symbolising leaping flames merging into a calmer set of blues and violets representing flowing water. As the sun moved around the sky, different colours seeped into the cathedral, creating different moods at separate times of the day. At night the scene was floodlit, which in itself must be a sight worth seeing. The whole thing was set off with an aluminium spire.

The Lantern Tower was, in effect, a crown covering an equally engaging high altar, designed by the cathedral architect Laurence King in the 1960s, which has stood the test of time admirably. Even my untutored eye was able to appreciate that this feature was designed to represent a crown of thorns. Other details I particularly liked were an anarchic collection of organ pipes jutting out from the wall, as if giving a fanfare, and the sculpture *Christ the Worker* by John Hayward wrought entirely from aluminium and black iron, proving that what might be termed industrial art need not be abstract.

The whole effect of the cathedral was of cleanliness and purity and, dare I say it, of holiness and genuine worship, rather than the sometimes ostentatious display of wealth over taste sometimes on display in the older showpiece churches. I was reminded of our recent visit to St Mark's in Venice, which for all its age and veneration I would pass over for the chance to visit Blackburn any day. There, take that for a recommendation, and while you're about it take a pat on the back, Blackburn, shout about your cathedral as loudly as you do your football club! At least one of them is Premier League!

Because of the official opening the next day there was an exhibition detailing the church's history. This showed details of the original plans for a much more grandiose structure, ambitions which were fortunately suffocated by the post-war inflation. This just went to show how the best results are as often the product of chance as they are of planning.

Funnily enough, although it has a cathedral, Blackburn remains a town, not a city, although the council was in the process of putting a case together to be granted this status. This, I thought, would be fitting. One of the most pleasing aspects of our visit had been the clear demonstration that the renewal of the church had been achieved through a collective effort, involving a cross-section of the local population including individuals and businesses, who, through their individual efforts, had made this community effort. How much better this was, I concluded, than simply being handed funds on a plate from someone like the National Lottery or the European Union. There was a clear sense of commonly held pride and ownership which the helpers in the cathedral wanted to share with you in a way which went beyond normal C of E enthusiasm. All in all a timely counterpoint to the more depressing thoughts of earlier in the morning.

Having feasted our eyes, we decided it was the turn of our stomachs, and as we didn't fancy either fish and chips or a kebab, which seemed to be all that was on offer in the high street, we entered the ubiquitous shopping mall and a Debenhams in-store restaurant. Thus, in a single stroke, we destroyed any opportunity of happening upon any regional delicacy. Inside the controlled atmosphere we both went quiet, not so much with contemplation of our recent visit to the cathedral but with tiredness. Gradually conversation dissolved into yawns, which as night turns to day would have moved on to sleep. We had to get out. So, having naturally taken advantage of the facilities, we went on our way. This phenomenon of sudden somnolence henceforth became known as the Debenhams effect.

Retracing our steps, we both found ourselves feeling a rocking sensation, our heads confused with this strange concept of terra firma. Withdrawal symptoms were clearly beginning to kick in so we made rapid tracks back to the boat. After Alan's dire predictions it was good to see *Florrie* in one piece, her bow rope fender slightly askew, emphasising her prominent nose by giving her a drooping Poirot-like moustache.

Given the intensity of the warnings we'd been given we'd taken every precaution to secure her, checking and double-checking the padlocks, closing the curtains and hiding away valuables in discreet places. It came as something of a shock therefore to discover that we'd left the key in the ignition. Later I was to discover that Blackburn is also home to the Institute of Professional Investigators, which may have gone some way to explaining the apparent law-abiding nature of its citizens.

I never did find out anything more about the holes.

Chugging to Chorley

Blackburn had made a real effort with its locks, with little plaques signalling that they had been the subject of a regeneration project in the mid-1990s. They had held their looks since then, being both well kept and remarkably graffiti-free, more evidence for the 'honest Blackburn' theory. In fact we had liked all we had seen of the town, which admittedly was only a small slice, but such was the nature of this sort of travelling.

As we wended our way down through the heart of the town I could sense some twitching coming from the Lockmeister who knew that a further half dozen locks stood between us and our mooring for the night, taking us a further fifty-five feet closer to sea level. As the weather was so good and we had gained both nutritional and spiritual sustenance, there was nothing for it but to press on. We duly completed the mini-flight completely solo, developing a routine whereby I hopped out once *Florrie* was in the lock, moored up loosely and closed one of the back gates before starting one of the paddles on the front and jumping back on board before she'd fallen too far. The Lockmeister seemed to have perfected a little run and jump as he approached each narrow walkway along the top of the lock gates, a mannerism with echoes of a high jumper which I don't think he was conscious of.

For me, this was good experience to gain as I was conscious that the time I had spent operating them myself had, up until then, been minimal. The temptation to leave it to the expert had been irresistible. Unfortunately on the next leg of the journey the crew would be looking to me for advice, so I needed to know more than simply theory. Moving around also gave me a wider perspective on what was actually going on during the boat's descent.

I watched as small whirlpools formed in the water, the funnels of which were under water as the paddles sucked water out from the lock and into the canal below. Strangely adaptable forms of plant life clung tenaciously to the lock walls; spending half their life under the surface they were deprived of light and looked bleached and pale. Where they gained their sustenance was anyone's guess, and how they retained their footing in the mortar between the bricks was a further mystery. Occasionally I pulled one free, out of devilment. Although I justified this as a contribution towards the conservation of the lock, I always felt slightly guilty afterwards, as if I'd exercised my greater power in a malevolent way.

Once through, we agreed that we were now running well within our schedule and began to contemplate a mooring for the night. All around was built up, however, and although we had seen no evidence of possible trouble (quite the opposite), Alan's warnings continued to resonate and we agreed we would prefer somewhere a little quieter. There seemed little point in tempting fate further after the keys in the ignition incident.

In the end the best we could get was the suburb of Cherry Tree, the alternative being to press on and bite into the next day's cruising, something we were loath to do. By now the end of this leg of the journey, unthinkable three days before, was becoming a tangible reality and we wanted to delay it as long as practicable. We therefore moored up without incident at what seemed like a quiet spot and, as canal etiquette dictated, placed some empty bottles over the otherwise barely visible tops of our mooring pins, indicating we were set for the night.

For the first time at an overnight stop we were overlooked by houses as we lifted the engine hatch and turned the tap on the stern prop shaft gland. This was neither open fields nor inner city. We were in suburbia. On the opposite bank three young boys were fishing with nets whilst another shouted across the water asking for advice on how to make a raft. Perhaps he was planning to escape. The housing around confirmed that this might be a possibility, as it was another example of the sort of ugly development we'd seen earlier when entering Blackburn.

Amongst a phenomenon marked more by its lows than its highs, these were an especially bad example. The brickwork in particular seemed noticeably poor, with different types of bricks being used in a haphazard way, so that the overall effect was of a wall infected with a particularly nasty disease. This effect was accentuated by apparent attempts to create geometric patterns within them, attempts which had generally been abandoned halfway through, making them look as if they had been constructed by Picasso on an off day. Even the mortar was inconsistent, varying in shade, leaving an overall impression of extremely poor workmanship.

I remembered reading that there was currently a shortage of skilled construction workers due to the economic boom taking place in Ireland, with much of the itinerant labour having returned home for richer pickings. These houses seemed to be a physical embodiment of this, and would remain as a semi-permanent reminder of the compromise in standards that had flowed. This theory was in part confirmed by a sign I saw when out shopping for supplies, which was asking (pleading?) for bricklayers at the estate's entrance as a further phase of the development had recently been approved. I sighed in despair and walked on.

There was a steady flow of traffic along the footpath, the canal here clearly being seen as a recreational resource. Most of those walking along it had dogs, most of whom left their usual calling cards. There was even similar evidence of horses having used the path, although almost certainly they hadn't been towing boats.

One particularly irritating adolescent was using another form of horsepower in the form of a trail bike that he used to buzz us, coming from nowhere like a low flying jet to scare the hell out of us. As we were putting away the boathooks for the night (everything movable was brought in once the sun had fallen), we lingered. An alternative use for them was forming in our mind, one which would have involved making sitting down on anything extremely painful for a few days, if not weeks. In the end a gathering chill sent us in to change out of our shorts and into something a little more suitable for wandering the streets of Cherry Tree. At that moment a leather jacket and knuckledusters seemed like one possible option.

In other ways the mooring was fine. On the towpath side there was clearly a tennis court hidden by a high hedge, and our evening meal was accompanied by the gentle plopping of tennis balls, reminding us that back in the real world Wimbledon was still on. Listening to the radio later though, it turned out that rain had made play impossible all day in London SW19, which gave us a rather smug feeling.

This was our first real taste of a non-city, non-honeypot location, just a plain ordinary place where people simply lived, worked and existed. It was also clearly an area in transition, and had two or three 'exciting new developments' juxtaposed against more traditional terracing and sixties-style housing. Although the Nicholson suggested there was a good range of shops and takeaways here, we found the majority of them had closed and been boarded up since the guide had been published. Whether this was for redevelopment or because they couldn't survive economically it was difficult to tell. Their fading signs spoke of a time when there had been a sufficient demand for a butcher, a florist and a newsagent, but despite the promised new housing these had all now gone.

We eventually found a single mini-market, but it was on its own and sited next to one of the new developments, an odd island in a sea of what can best be described as 'dwellings'. It was busy, and clearly provided a vital service, I guessed as a gathering point as much as anything. Looking around, it didn't take a genius to work out that before long it was likely to be faced with the need either to sell up or to grow significantly, as I suspected one of the chains would move in.

I restocked with essentials and made my way back to the boat. The view as I did so was dominated by a huge ugly red warehouse, which I took at first to be a DIY shed, but in fact turned out to be a fashion warehouse, something which to my mind is a contradiction in terms, but there you go. That this now constituted the view out of the back bedrooms of one of the new developments seemed to offer some kind of poetic justice.

Over dinner we agreed that our progress over the three and a half days we'd been moving had been steady, eventful and fruitful, not only in terms of distance covered (we were on course to complete fifty miles), but also, we felt, in terms of experience gained. Our basic skills in locking, mooring and passing, as well as with bridges and tunnels, now all had a solid foundation. What was more, the whole experience had lived well up to expectations, and indeed had even exceeded them. Our skin, especially on our faces, had taken on a healthy-looking weather-beaten sheen and even the Lockmeister's legs, which in normal circumstances were rarely if ever exposed to ultraviolet, had caught the sun. We'd eaten and slept well and found a routine that had worked admirably. I wondered if things would be as relatively effortless with different crews as *Florrie* and I made our way south.

The next day marked the start of the final push on this leg. *Florrie* was booked in for her holidays at the White Bear Marina where we'd left the car what seemed like an age before, the passing of time being another thing which we'd learnt to recalibrate. Because of our good progress – we'd been averaging seven or eight hours a day on the water – we were able to take this day steady. We therefore kicked off with some basic chores and routine maintenance. One of these was to double-check the diesel level, another the thankless task of putting a hand into the weed hatch to test if the prop shaft was clean.

This was something I'd been putting off, not so much because of the task itself, but because of memories of a frustrating afternoon spent during my only other experience of narrowboating twenty years before. That time it had required a combination of kitchen knives, boathooks and sheer bloody hard work to free the shaft after it had had an argument with some weed. Mercifully *Florrie*'s prop was as clean as a whistle, the metal cold and smooth to the touch. Finally we had a clear out of old paint and odds and sods of varnish, as well as stiffened brushes and irregularly shaped bits of wood we'd found in the hold. I'd been getting whiffs of white spirit from below my bed each night and had had enough of it.

Once under way the back gardens of Cherry Tree took on a whole new aspect, allowing us to adjust upwards the opinion we'd formed of the place the night before. The gardens we passed were on the whole immaculately kept, something which, judging by the people we saw in them, could be put down to the high proportion of the apparently retired. Even early in the morning these people were out putting in the hour or two of cutting and pruning necessary to achieve the standards we were now able to take pleasure in. One or two even had moorings, and one a narrowboat of its own. These were clearly decent people.

Through the stretch before us we experimented some more with steering, gaining a deeper appreciation of the effect of momentum, and using it to our advantage, and trying to gauge where the pivot point was on our boat. This fulcrum exists between a third and a half down from the bow of a boat, but varies on each craft. Knowing its position is vital as a boat does not steer like a car, with the front end going one way and the back the opposite when the tiller is turned. In executing a turn there is a period when half of the boat is going one way and the other half the opposite. This we had learnt intuitively, but it was good to experience and to be able to predict it at first hand.

As the gardens petered out we returned to a fully rural scene, although the distant rumble of the motorway was never far behind. In particular we plunged into some kind of demi-forest, which was as pleasant as it was unexpected. This was comprised mostly of mature beeches and sycamores, some of which had fallen into the water and had been left to rot, something which was going to take a long time. Thankfully the canal was sufficiently wide at this point and they represented no hazard to shipping, which probably accounted for why nothing had been done about them. The overall effect was sombre and almost secret, and it probably would have been spectacular if a low sun had been filtering through the leaves, highlighting the different shades of green. Instead it was overcast but dry, which was an improvement on the forecast so we felt disinclined to feel too bad about it.

In line with our plans to take things steady, I spotted in the Nicholson that we were approaching a small model village, Withnell Fold, built to house workers at a canalside paper mill. The book painted a picture of picturesque cottages grouped around three sides of a square, with the fourth side occupied by a set of stocks for outsiders. It sounded intriguing. I thought this might be interesting both for its own sake and as a comparator for some of the more recent attempts at estate building we'd seen alongside the canal around Blackburn. Besides, I was just in the mood for a little excursion.

By the time we'd agreed that this was a good plan we'd missed the official visitors' moorings, but saw that the towpath was reinforced beyond and therefore presumably dredged. We pointed the bow towards it and slowed down, the F-in-L up front, rope poised, like a cowboy ready to lasso a steer.

Schlurp! You could almost hear the mud as we slid on to it; you could certainly feel it. We were stuck again, and this time not simply inconvenienced, but stuck good and proper. Luckily the stern was still in open water, but the engine was no match for the powerful suction of the mud and it was unable to dislodge us. We paused for thought, feeling exposed, frustrated and not a little stupid.

Hopes of a tug out were slight; we'd only seen two boats the whole of the day before, and they were going the other way, not that that would matter. We needed to think more laterally. From the front it was just possible to leap ashore, so I did so with the boathook in hand and, in the absence of a better strategy, tried some good old-fashioned brute force. It soon became clear that my efforts were definitely a case of a resistible force meeting an immovable object. Our next tack was to use some cunning in the form of leverage. The whole episode had begun to take on the characteristics of a management course initiative test – one we were failing. The F-in-L threw the stern mooring rope out and I hooked it round a tree, pulling with all my might while we tried reverse once more. Nothing. Nice idea though, three points.

It was at this point that the statutory gongoozler came along, full of advice. The ability of these characters to turn up just when you didn't want them was at times uncanny.

'You don't want to moor there,' he informed us, 'it's nowt but mud.'

'Really?' Then, as if encouraged, a voice came from up high, via a house with a balcony a full fifty feet away. Another one and, what was worse, one on permanent station. These gongoozlers clearly hunted in packs.

'Aye,' he added helpfully, 'they normally come down t'other side.'

Thanks, I thought, just about resisting the temptation to say it, that's useful to know.

We reassured them that contrary to impressions we were not completely stupid, we were just not from round these parts and were a little light in the clairvoyance stakes. It was good to know that the good folk of Withnell Fold had lost none of their traditional goodwill to strangers. Back on board, we regrouped.

It was then that I remembered another trick, which by then was beginning to look like the final throw of the dice – rocking her off. This was something I'd read about, but never seen done. The F-in-L stood on one gunnel at the side of the boat gripping a handrail, me at the other, our bums sticking out like outriders on a racing motorbike. Gently at first, but with little expectation of success, we began to rock see-saw style, in opposite time with each other's efforts. Once the boat was swinging I kept up the momentum while the F-in-L pushed her once more into reverse. This time, as if she had completely capitulated to our superior intellectual capacity, *Florrie* slipped off the mudbank as if she was tired of playing that particular game. The whole incident had taken less than twenty minutes but had seemed to last for ever.

Once free, we gunned up the engine to show her who was boss, and on turning a corner immediately faced a further obstacle in the form of a massive British Waterways maintenance barge sat stationary under a bridge, which the men aboard were busy painting. They looked like they were in for the duration, and not really that bothered about letting us through. By now the wind had got up and our patience had worn thin, so it was with no little annoyance that we lost the decorum and lessons of earlier in the morning and got into a complete mess trying to hold a steady course. Despite the width of the canal at this point we managed to bump into both the towpath at one end and the overhanging foliage at the other. It was impossible to know what the professionals on the maintenance boat were thinking, but thankfully they soon took pity on us and pulled out of the way.

After these two episodes the locks just before Chorley were going to be light relief, and although I suggested to the Lockmeister that we stop for a bite before tackling them, as a successful passage was likely to require the thick end of two hours, he predictably didn't seem keen. I knew when I was beaten and dropped him off on the towpath. Even using the routine established the day before, two hours was what they ended up taking, although it didn't really seem like it.

As we emerged from the final lock we came across an impressive sixty-footer, decked out immaculately and suspiciously clean. It didn't take long to twig that this was an example of the phenomenon of the 'boatel', a boat operating as a floating hotel. This one seemed particularly exclusive, with one couple running the boat for another paying for the privilege, joining in if they felt like it. Normally a boatel will take six to eight guests, so I hated to guess what this trip was costing them. The basic concept seemed to me to be flawed, although I could see the superficial attraction of it. Surely more than half the fun of being on the canals is having to respond to crises as they occur and planning the route? That had certainly been our experience. Take that away and you were simply in a moving hotel room. Still, horses for courses.

Chorley itself was now looming up fast and I decreed that we would have another go at the idea of an excursion. The chosen destination, for no real other set of reasons than it was there and that it was an old mill building and I was quite keen on seeing the inside of one, having seen enough empty ones, was an edifice called Botany Bay. This was a strange place, at once bringing together the British obsessions with getting in their cars and 'going somewhere', buying things, anything loosely connected with heritage and finally eccentricity. It was the last of these which was first in evidence, with a collection of old tanks, fire engines and helicopters littering the forecourt, forming a life-sized representation of an average schoolboy's bedroom floor. In the depths of my imagination I saw a giant training shoe flying across the scene, scattering all before it.

We moored up on the bankside conveniently made available for the purpose and approached with not a little trepidation. Botany Bay is what its proprietors liked to call a themed shopping village. This was another term for a high-class car boot sale, with a plethora of the usual crafts and curios available from traders who'd rented a pitch from which to sell. All that was missing was the hubbub from the traders themselves and, significantly, from possible punters.

We wandered around all five floors of the place, fulfilling that obligation which is driven by the belief that the next floor might just have that something you've always been looking for, a belief which I supposed kept the place going. As we crept steadily higher we found we were following a salesman who was attempting to lure a potential prospect for one of the pitches. His patter was interesting, not least for passing on an understanding of how the prices for different floors and different pitches were calculated. It's got a lot to do with footfall from the stairwell and routes to the tea shops and toilets by the way.

Indeed, once inside we had ourselves agreed that a brew was a good idea and had headed for the first floor tea room. Unwittingly, by doing so we fitted perfectly into the expectations placed on us by the people who ran the place. It was only on leaving that we realised that the whole point of Botany Bay was not to come and buy at all, but to look and drink cups of tea. In all the time we spent there, about an hour and a half, I didn't see a single person buy anything – other than tea, of course, oh, and cakes. I can only assume that those behind this venture have an endless supply of people wanting to pay rent to display their wares, an entirely possible scenario, or, like the pubs, they make their money at the weekends. As soon as we settled with our tea, we found ourselves succumbing to the Debenhams effect again, so before it had even had a chance to cool we were forced to drink up as fast as possible and get the blood moving again.

As is often the way with these places, the best way to get through it is to have a competition to see who can find the best item. Our winner was an old car from a 1950s' funfair ride, a spaceship in the Gerry Anderson mould, all tail fins and wide glass-covered cockpits. Great to look at, but would you really want it in your front room? The F-in-L also liked some of the old school desks, but I managed to drag him away before he spotted the canes.

The best that could probably be said for Botany Bay was that its creation had stopped at least one more massive mill from falling into disrepair, and this was quite a lot to have in its favour. That and the fact that wandering around had made the F-in-L feel quite sprightly compared to the vast majority of the other punters.

The ticket's declared aim was to become the number one retail attraction in the north-west. It is probably some way off yet.

Back on board we knew that with every passing minute we were chugging ever closer to the White Bear and we even contemplated going straight there and spending the night in the marina. Somehow this seemed like cheating, and spotting a line of boats moored up a mile or so later we decided to join them. The spot was conveniently near a bridge and the presence of other boats suggested a good depth of water and so it proved to be.

In fact, as we approached them I was struck by the extent to which the boats we were approaching comprised a representative sample of narrowboats on the L & L. First, there was the smaller, unostentatious weekender boat, very rectangular and functional, with only a couple of windows down each side. Its ropes had been tied very slackly, with one turn round the pins, as if it didn't really mean to stay very long. Painted a muted yellow and red, this was functional, but clearly loved.

Next to it was a longer, more elaborately done-out boat, complete with shiny brass ventilation mushrooms on the roof, which also sported a series of highly decorated buckets, watering cans and pots. The boathook and poles were also heavily painted, there more for their contribution to the overall effect of the boat than to be used. It was pointing towards us and its bow had the traditional white streak either side of its rope fender, which hung slightly too loosely by its chains. The front doors were obscured by a screen that had a sequence of red, yellow, blue and white diamonds going down its middle and a cascade of painted roses either side. The screen also sported the boat's headlamp, which looked enormous compared to our meagre offering, and was covered with a protective jacket which only served to emphasise its importance. The windows on this boat were also made of brass and were square rather than round, something we did have in common.

The third boat was a converted butty, one of the old cargo-carrying boats. Only half of this was actually cabin space, the remainder being covered in a loosely draped tarpaulin which was a dull grey and looked like it had seen better days. As if to make up for this drabness, the cabin itself was almost startling in its use of colour, and the doors were something else. These had been left open which allowed us to see that they were of highly varnished wood, in the centre of which had been painted a miniature rural scene. Most spectacular of all, however, was its high curved tiller, also made of wood and decorated in red, white and blue. This was attached to a wide rudder, which started above the waterline, offering an opportunity for yet more effective use of strong primary colours. All that was missing from the scene was the floating bar type of boat, which was a blessing.

We approached with circumspection and glided to a spot at the back of the line. As we killed the engine birdsong reasserted its natural dominion in the air and we immediately became part of the scenery. Once tied up we dutifully and routinely lifted the engine hatch to grease the stern prop shaft gland. As we chatted I twisted the tap and felt a slight crack, after which the tap head spun free. Even at the last, it seemed, *Florrie* still had some surprises to pull. Closer inspection revealed that we'd run out of grease and the split pin had gone in the tap head.

Luckily we had more grease, thus defying Sod's Law which would normally have stated that we would have thrown this out with the old paint tins earlier in the day. We effected a temporary repair, but I made a mental note to bring more permanent materials with me on the next leg of the journey. I was beginning to wonder where this myth that a canal holiday is restful and nothing much happens had come from.

It being our last night we decided we'd earned the right to eat out. The only problem was we had no idea where to go. Emerging from a bridge we noticed a thirty speed sign straight ahead with a road leading up a hill, and reasoned that this would take us into a built-up area and, in all probability therefore, a pub. Left and right looked less promising, being a busy road stretching out in both directions for what seemed like miles. Just to confirm our suspicions, we stopped a local who was walking by with his dog, who agreed that a pub did indeed exist up the road, and, what was more, it was one where they served good food.

It was only as he ambled past that I noticed that he looked decidedly down on his luck and smelt much the same. He was wearing a raincoat which looked like it had been picked out of a bin, and he had an unfortunate skin condition down one side of his face, causing one ear to look as if it had a mild dose of elephantiasis. He was also sporting two days' growth of beard. It's probably best not to linger on the condition of the dog. It was at this point that I considered the general rule which links the quality of advice with the status of the giver of that advice. His idea of 'good food' was likely to be very different from ours, most of his meals presumably coming from the same source as his coat. Ignoring the F-in-L's mutterings about the possibility of brawn sandwiches, I decided to chance it and we proceeded up the hill anyway.

There was indeed a pub when we got there. It even seemed to have a dining room. But as soon as we entered it we knew from the lack of cutlery and the wiped-clean blackboard that our luck was out. It was the weekends only syndrome again. We asked the barmaid and the customary solitary customer for advice and were pointed towards an Indian restaurant in a converted church – 'Ten minutes' walk down the main road, you can't miss it.' We agreed that it didn't sound like the sort of place you could miss and set off.

In fact we ended up in a pub next door to the Indian called the Spinners Arms, which had swept its commercial viability up into its hands and taken the chance on serving food midweek. In doing so it had found that, yes, there is a thing called demand which exists outside Friday to Sunday. What was more, the food they offered was both good and highly reasonable, although I resisted the one concession to local cuisine, the black pudding starter. In fact, we returned there the next day after liaising with our respective wives. It turned out that the ten-minute walk had been more like twenty and the pub was but a hop, skip and a jump from the marina, but we didn't mind. The point of the exercise was not to be efficient, but to collect experiences.

Once again, dinner was a good opportunity for reflection, away from the throbbing of the engine and the ever-present prospect of another crisis. The previous night we'd considered our progress with the boat, this night we pondered on what we'd seen. We agreed that the area we'd passed through over the past four days had surprised us. Both Burnley and Blackburn seemed to have a spirit, a positive feeling about them which we'd latched on to and enjoyed. The clichés had lived up to expectations, but not in a depressing way, with the possible exception of the large mill buildings, almost without exception bricked up and dying on their feet, an image I'd found a little unsettling. It wasn't so much the fact that they were closed, after all, they were the victim of world markets, more their desperate state and the seeming lack of any prospect of redemption. Large spaces, often in the centre of major areas of housing, had effectively been abandoned.

The cobbled streets and terraced housing belonged in the cliché category, but compared to what was replacing them probably still had a lot going for them. Likewise, the zigzag roofs of the industrial buildings, like monster's teeth in a child's drawing, were a distinctive feature. Many of these though were very much alive, the machinery inside giving a buzz of confidence. All in all, we were left wondering if we hadn't tasted a nuance of some kind of rebirth of the Calder Valley.

Back at the mooring we met and greeted the couple on the boat next to ours, who turned out to be yet another of these pairs who spend the summer roaming the canal system. Ralph and Janet were from Surrey and were clearly enthusiasts. During their months on board they eschewed television, preferring instead to wallow in each other's company and brushing up on the art of conversation. Although fine in theory, we found that this could rebound upon any poor unfortunate soul who bumped into them, especially Ralph.

Half the art of conversation is listening to what the other person says. This is the half Ralph had lost. Soon we became the victim – there is no other word – of his stories and advice on alternative routes. Clearly telling him our plans was the one thing we had said which had sunk in; unfortunately he had taken it as a contention upon which to build a thesis rather than a statement of fact. Ralph was the canal equivalent to a bus or train timetable bore, reeling off lists of acronyms and place names as if they should mean something significant to us. He talked with his hands thrust deep into his pockets, his body slightly hunched over, conspiratorially.

On our third or fourth attempt we managed our goodnights,

although Ralph insisted on coming down to see *Florrie*. I'll admit his complete silence on seeing her hurt a little and it was no great loss when he melted back into the night, muttering something incomprehensible as he went.

The short mile into Adlington the next day gave us a chance to prepare *Florrie* for the next stage of the journey. We topped up with diesel, replaced the Calor gas and, for it could be put off not longer, had a toilet pump-out. Being a serial alliterator, I had earlier christened the hold hidden within the hull the Turd Tank. Although we had been sparing in our use of the on-board facilities, there was unfortunately no way of knowing when this vital task had last been carried out, or indeed how long the contents had lain in their chemical bath. Luckily this was something the boatyard staff did for us. A bargain at a tenner.

It was unfortunate to say the least that the pipe that did this work had, at its business end (literally), a transparent section, which made it possible to track the contents of the tank on their way out. This proved to be an unedifying although somehow fascinating sight, a little like watching your laundry spin round. There was also a distinct whiff, but the lad doing the work assured us that he'd just come back from the Glastonbury Festival and was used to it, causing us to reflect that it was strange what some people did for fun. When he'd finished and put the hose away, he generously gave us a bottle of 'blue' – disinfectant and deodoriser in one – on the house. Perhaps, we wondered, his air of indifference had been slightly feigned all along.

This vital task completed, there was just one more chance to display our newly found virtuosity in manoeuvring the boat as we were required not only to turn her round, but also to reverse her into her temporary berth. This we achieved without mishap, the only disappointment being the absence of gongoozlers to watch us get something right.

The first phase of the journey was over and had been a success. It was only once we were home that I remembered that I'd left a half eaten loaf of bread in the bread bin. I'd also forgotten to find out what a drumlin was.

Part Three
Chris and Tom

From Nightmares...

'Thar's a bluddy Lister in't it?'

The remark was delivered in a way that summoned up images of some kind of skin condition that had died out years before. Up until then we'd been so focused on staring into the engine compartment that we'd completely missed the approach of this particular gongoozler. Although at first apparently superfluous, his announcement marked him out as an informed gongoozler, one able to identify the source of our motive power not so much by sound, which was the usual and incontrovertible way, but by sight. For himself, he had the added virtue of appearing halfway respectable, certainly compared to some of the types you generally find hanging around boatyards, being dressed in a shirt and trousers rather than overalls, although it has to be said that the shirt had seen better days.

He didn't wait for any kind of response to his introductory remarks before delivering his *coup de grâce*. 'You've gar yer bluddy valve lifters pointing the wrong way, you know,' he indicated, pointing a bony ET-like finger down towards the deceptively simple-looking mass of blue machinery below. 'You'll never get tha bugger to star' like that.'

He was right. Getting the bugger to start had eluded us for the past half hour, and for a further few minutes three hours before that – the time it had taken us to realise that the main battery was as flat as a battery can get. It turned out that the independent switch to the fridge had been left on when we'd left the boat five weeks before. Naively, it seems, the F-in-L and I had thought at the time that turning the battery isolator off would have removed power to all things electrical. We'd been wrong. A final legacy from the first leg it seemed, the battery had probably been halfway drained before either of us had got home.

Once reunited with *Florrie*, it hadn't taken too long to diagnose the problem. The expected hum hadn't followed when I'd shut the fridge door, after having restocked it with essentials such as lagers and milk. Intuitively, I'd known at that moment that something was wrong, but as had become my habit I'd rationalised it away. It was only when I'd turned the ignition key and not even the light had come on that I'd known we were in trouble.

It had been at this point that I'd offered thanks to my personal Deity for the prescience that had made me leave *Florrie* at a boatyard, within easy reach of our salvation: the required supercharger. Duly located, this had been hooked up and left to do its work while we'd nipped out for a late lunch and a spot of sightseeing with sufficient grounds for optimism to buoy us along.

The first semblance of real panic had only began to ferment in my stomach when we'd returned and found that, despite having poured the electrical equivalent of gallons of juice into the battery, things still weren't happening as they should. There was life, but not as we knew it. When we turned the ignition key angry metallic noises issued out from the engine, clashing sounds rather than the sweet harmony of moving parts lubricated with oil. Clearly departures were something of a problem for *Florrie*; perhaps she didn't like change.

The whole incident was unfortunate in more ways than one. Not only did it inconvenience us practically, but it also had the effect of reinforcing doubts that had begun to creep in on a more psychological level. After such a successful first leg, it had come as a bit of a shock when, in the days leading up to this stage of the journey, I'd become aware that my preparations were being complicated by the steady accumulation of often conflicting, and generally poorly articulated, emotions. These had gathered like protean gases over the intervening five weeks, their final form unresolved, and had an impact upon not only my personal feelings, but also the very enterprise itself.

In attempting to come to terms with these feelings it had been relatively straightforward to recognise that some of the gloss had been taken off my initial idealism by the very fact that the first leg, despite its ups and downs, had been so successful. Less acceptable had been the gnawing thought, somewhere deep in my subconscious, that I was beginning to regard the whole journey as less of an innocent adventure and more as a project, if not yet an actual job of work. Although further reflection might have suggested that this could be a healthy shift, it wasn't something I necessarily welcomed.

Virginity had been lost somewhere in the Lancashire hills, and as with all successful deflowerings the question had remained whether it would be as good, better or worse the next time round, and subsequent occasions after that. Against this backdrop, the notion of the exercise becoming merely a project, functional and devoid of romance, was wholly unattractive. With the gloss of expectation now removed there was a growing suspicion that an essential dullness might be revealed beneath the surface.

Away from *Florrie*, the steady chug of her engine and the constantly changing landscape, I'd begun to wonder if the second leg and the ones after it would become increasingly less satisfying, in time becoming routine, a sort of law of diminishing returns. Two trips were planned over three weeks, giving plenty of scope for overfamiliarity to set in.

What was more, these had originally been planned on the assumption that August would be quiet, but in reality a number of pressures had begun to mount, not least the prospect of some real work and with it, some income. I'd also begun to feel guilty about leaving the family again at the beginning of the school holidays. Was I being selfish? Was I being fair? These concerns were reinforced as Annette took on more and more freelancing commitments to keep the family coffers topped up. Were her encouraging noises heartfelt or were they simply polite?

At home, with two days to go, I found my preparations became clandestine, my attitude more devil-may-care, as if I was about to go away on an unwanted business trip which, given the chance I would rather avoid. All these were mechanisms to assuage my growing sense of guilt, but at the same time to retain a sense of practicality. After all, my mission (I was increasingly struggling to come up with appropriate terminologies) would not go away. To paraphrase the great Magnus Magnusson, I'd started, so I had to finish. Besides, I'd bragged to too many people about what I was doing to renege on the deal now. This was a tactic I'd found myself employing more and more, as if by doing so I not only burnt my bridges but laid the land behind me a radioactive wasteland at the same time.

And yet the doubts persisted. I felt like a showman who had performed a magnificent trick, only to be asked to repeat it. Would it work again the second time round? Anyway, why should it matter – after all, hadn't I shown I could perform it? For *Florrie*, commencement of the next leg would also provide a true rite of passage. For the first time she would slip her metaphorical bounds and emerge into waters new to her. For her, the negotiation of the Wigan flight of locks would be the equivalent of digging a tunnel, preparing false papers and crossing the border unchallenged all in one. How would she take it?

It was with some relief therefore that I met up with my brother Chris, along with his son Tom, and journeyed once more up the M6. We had spoken, albeit briefly, about what lay ahead, although in truth I had taken their participation and co-operation a little bit for granted. A miasma of anticipation fused with the discordant sounds emanating from the car stereo as we made our way north, but I comforted myself with the knowledge that at least it was action at last.

As with the F-in-L, it was difficult to imagine circumstances in the ordinary run of events which would have otherwise thrown the three of us together into such an intense environment. It would be fair to say that Chris and I had never been what you would call close, even though, over the course of a lifetime, we'd shared a bedroom together for longer than I had with Annette. Despite a relatively slender age difference of six years a sort of generation gap existed between us. This had been forged in the heady days of the 1960s, which had been Chris's formative teenage years, but which for me had been filled more with everyday boyhood pursuits such as riding my bike or collecting worms.

For Chris, the love of his life is, was and ever shall be, it seems, music. Even when we shared a room his record collection seemed to dominate, and even though the records have got smaller, the proportion of wall space they now take up in his house remains much the same. At a time when most of my peer group have started to sound like our fathers, complaining that they simply don't write tunes like they used to any more, Chris is right up there, and probably before his own grown-up children, when it comes to picking up on the latest vibe. One of his greatest concerns in planning this leg of the journey had been the on-board facilities for 'sounds'. Thankfully we'd agreed that the best option was probably a Walkman and lots of batteries.

Whilst Chris had grown up to a proselytising soundtrack of the Beatles and the Stones, my teenage years had rung to the more cynical rhythms of glam rock. This was something I suspected he would always see as an advantage that his education had had over my own more formal learning.

Our lives since those days had largely taken different directions, as befitted our individual circumstances, and what made him tick these days was probably as much a mystery to me as my meanderings were to him. In truth, Chris was probably slightly too young to get the complete benefit of the days of peace and love, and has probably been chasing the mirage of what he'd missed ever since. It occurred to me during the trip that he was probably the same age then that Tom was now, something I found hard to appreciate.

If Chris was a mystery, Tom was its sequel. Whereas I'd been around when his two older sisters had been growing up, allowing me to observe and at times share their formative years, Tom fitted a different phase of my life. The essence of it was that we didn't know each other that well. His role as a convenient childminder for his younger cousins whenever we'd gathered as a family meant we'd rarely chatted. This then was an opportunity to play catch-up, and perhaps to gain at least some appreciation of what makes a fifteen year old adolescent tick in a world of computers and drugs. This was a subject where my knowledge was lamentably lacking, and one where a little research might not go adrift; I'd already begun to detect signs of incipient teenage nonchalance in Peter, our own eldest son, and some early tips might come in handy.

Once we'd diagnosed the problem with the battery, there'd been nothing for it but to find something to do for a few hours while the supercharger did its work. As we were but a skip away I suggested a visit to Wigan Pier. When I'd first started planning the trip I'd thought we'd be going past the pier on the water, but closer inspection of the Guide had shown that it was on a different arm of the canal, and as such it represented an optional extra. As we were effectively losing half an afternoon because of the battery problem, it was clear that such luxuries would have to go, so my logic was accepted by all involved.

None of us really knew what to expect though, which was probably just as well as it saved us from disappointment. Wigan Pier was essentially an unloading platform, a kind of dock. Although the wooden slats which formed its core had clearly benefited from a no doubt expensive renovation, once we'd clapped our eyes on it and read some of the information boards there was not a lot else to do. It was easy to sympathise with the man who'd made it famous, George Orwell, who, on a visit to view the pier after writing his famous book, had failed miserably to find it and had subsequently concluded that it no longer existed.

Wisely the local authority had recognised this singular lack of distinction and had made the Pier a focal point for a range of attractions, including an historical 'experience'. However, our general air of anticipation over what kind of experience we were in for that evening didn't put us in the mood for such structured diversion, although Opie's Museum of Memories did look intriguing and, given more time, we may have been tempted by it. Examples of old pumping machinery and even an old narrowboat were scattered around the site, impressive but redundant, like a series of follies. More usefully, I was able to dispense a brief lecture-ette on how to work a lock, using as my demonstrator an example that sat outside the pier.

A need to know our fate, coupled with the fact that the boat-yard was due to shut at five, drew us back to *Florrie*. Whilst waiting for one of the mechanics to help us, we had time to sort out the stuff we'd brought with us, not knowing if we were destined to stay the night somewhere or feel the movement of water beneath our feet. Somehow moving in was a way of defying the Fates, not to do so an act of surrender. Only Tom, in his adolescent innocence, dared to voice the dreaded 'What if…?' question, but we adults chose to leave it unexplored.

Inside, *Florrie* was exactly as I'd remembered her. Even the interior lighting worked, this being run from a separate battery (something that had initially fooled us when diagnosing the ignition problem), and some of the doubts of the previous few days instantly begun to dissolve. Luckily the half loaf of bread we'd left in the bread bin had simply turned black and petrified, just before the unpleasant odours and all-purpose bug-trap phase of degradation. It went into the boatyard skip, along with a dozen cans of out of date Yorkshire bitter we'd found in one of the holds. On her outside *Florrie* had gathered more cobwebs than Miss Havisham's dining room, and while we continued to wait for a mechanic I went round her with a broom to clear the worst of them away.

It had taken half an hour of frustration – of the engine nearly working, of perhaps wanting to work – before the gongoozler had arrived and provided us with the solution we all knew had to exist. With the simple expedient of throwing the valve lifters forward *Florrie* started first time, as if she'd merely been playing a trick on us. The throaty roar of her engine as it finally caught could almost have been a laugh.

It was only an hour and a half to the top of the Wigan flight, but we reasoned it would be worth getting it under our belts if for no other reasons than to get the battery back into working order and to give us all a feeling of progress. Whilst the engine idled, proving its virility and giving Chris and Tom their first taste of the awesomeness of its chugging capacity, I decided to quiz the gongoozler further. This man I now regarded as a thoroughly decent sort, and asked his opinion on the best places to moor for the night.

His advice was simple: go straight for the top lock and eat at the Kirklees Hall pub. Here, he advised us, in his inimitable patois, we would find 'right good food'. Having been caught before on this one, I raised my eyebrows in an encouragement for him to continue. 'Right good food,' he repeated with a nod, stressing the word 'good' and putting his hands out like an angler describing a fish an indication that good equated to big. We were happy to go with that, thanked him profusely and engaged the clutch. The water churned up white behind us and we began to move forwards.

As if to make up for the false start I executed a perfect 180-degree turn out of the marina which I could see impressed my new crew (or, in Tom's case, as much as it's possible to impress a fifteen-year-old) and sent us on our way. The old magic was still there. The stretch before us was uncomplicated and I used the opportunity to give Chris and Tom the chance to get a feel for the tiller and to learn the art of making yourself heard above the engine. Within minutes they'd both retreated to the front to enjoy what had turned out to be a pleasant summer's evening.

The topography on this stretch was disconcertingly flat, deceivingly so given the twenty-three locks we knew lay before us. Being that bit taller than my brother (and just taller than my nephew) I was able to see over the hedges and view the precipitous drop we would be negotiating the next day. From what I saw I decided to keep this knowledge my exclusive preserve for a little while longer. In the meantime, however, the canal clung tenaciously to the line of the contour, its banks lined with tall grasses and a profusion of yellow lilies, their eyes beginning to close as we passed, as if they were getting ready for bed. Brambles in the hedges were laden with reddening fruit, two or three weeks off being ready for picking, and in the water random bubbles, presumably of methane, rose to the surface and broke.

Stranded at the stern without the Nicholson, I had no idea when the top lock was due and took what I thought was likely to be the last few hundred yards extremely steady. I was particularly anxious not to have to suddenly throw the boat into reverse and suffer the inevitable loss of brownie points I'd earned by steering us out of the Marina so immaculately. In the event the mooring was telegraphed well in advance, and once successfully roped up in the queue for the locks the next day, we set off without further ado to find Kirklees Hall.

In the event the pub was easily distinguishable by its ersatz-Tudor exterior and its position adjacent to the second lock down the flight. Everything about it shouted 'Come in,' so we did. Inside, the menu was indeed extensive, as well as being stupefyingly cheap, and we prepared ourselves for a feast, reasoning that we'd earned it, even though we'd already had a pub lunch.

Once inside, the only obstacle to enjoyment was making ourselves understood. For some reason the barmaid, who was short and more than a little chubby and had one of those faces that send out signals saying 'Please speak slowly,' had trouble understanding simple English. Chris and Tom managed to get through on their third attempts, but for some reason we got completely stuck on the word 'cod' when it came to taking my order. After half a dozen attempts I'd formed the distinct impression that I'd wandered into a Victoria Wood sketch and contemplated changing my choice, when all of a sudden it clicked. I don't know what did it, but suspect that something within her internal clock had caused the necessary cogs to slip into place. It had been fast approaching seven thirty and, when I returned to pick up some cutlery, she was completely engrossed in an episode of *Coronation Street* on the widescreen TV.

The culture shock for Chris and Tom was palpable as we ate silently, surrounded by families composed entirely of very large people, clearly frequent patrons of Kirklees Hall. With the exception of ourselves, everyone sported at least one highly impressive tattoo, as if members of a secret club. They also deployed accents which, to my crew at least, and by and large to me too, were completely impenetrable.

The food finished – the gongoozler at the boatyard had been spot on in his review of the place – we sat in a contemplative silence enjoying a last drink while some children jumped into the lock. This was of course completely contrary to the advice (and indeed regulations) of both British Waterways and the local Public Health adviser, as well as obviously ill advised to anyone with half an ounce of brain. Weil's disease, a particularly severe form of jaundice caused by rat's urine, was known to be a hazard in the canals, making prolonged contact inadvisable under any circumstance. For the moment though they seemed to be enjoying themselves.

We took the opportunity to take in our coming challenge, to 'walk the course,' or the beginnings of it anyway. At first sight it seemed benign enough, but on turning the first corner it became possible to appreciate the true scale of the flight. As they staggered down the hill, one lock pretty much merged into another, the chequerboard blacks and whites of the lock gate balance beams marking out staging posts along the way. The sheer size of gates themselves was revealed in an empty lock, great solid blocks of wood reminiscent of a medieval castle's doors and seemingly just as impregnable. I knew from experience that our descent would share many characteristics with a mountain climb, with constant optical illusions promising an end. As we progressed, each peak, or in our case each lock, would seem to be the last, but beyond it we would suddenly spy another, then another, then...

The culture shock of being so far north was less acute for me. Although I knew I would see little of the town itself this time round, Wigan was not completely unexplored territory for me; my personal map did not carry a warning of the 'here be dragons' variety. Not all my memories were good. One of the biggest nightmares of my professional life had taken place in this town, a day which had begun with an early alarm call and a dash up the motorway to make a hotel for a half past nine meeting. The meeting was to be the culmination of six months' work and the local great and good had been invited to feed on the crumbs of wisdom I was to scatter before them in a beneficent and techno-logically inspiring presentation.

That at least had been the theory. In practice, I'd been beyond Birmingham before I'd realised that although I'd sensibly put trainers on for more comfortable driving, less sensibly I'd failed to put my black brogues in the car as well. Hurried calculations had suggested that if I put my foot down (with its comfortable arch support and latest in basketball technology) I would have time to dash into a shoe shop to remedy the situation, although it would be tight.

The next two hours had been preoccupied with constant recal-culations of miles left against time remaining, a sort of 'run rate required' which oscillated according to performance over the previous few minutes. Despite my efforts, these figures varied by only a few decimal points all the way up, but remained reassur-ingly in my favour. Eventually I made it just as the shutters were going up in the high street, ran into a shoe shop (aided by the air-cushioned springiness of my soles) and bought the first pair of black shoes that vaguely fitted. Much to the assistant's dismay, I took them as they were, dashing out of the door as I pressed a twenty pound note into his hand. The quickest – and possibly earliest – sale he'd ever had.

'You believe in cutting it fine, don't you?' my client had complained as I'd parked in the disabled bay near the entrance to the hotel, his smile fixed to his face with raw determination. Little did he know. Luckily a lorry had very publicly shed its load, a phrase which I've always personally found particularly disgusting, a few hundred yards from the hotel, and although this had taken away a few more precious minutes it had also furnished me with an excuse for my lateness.

Heart thumping and feet aching from the blisters which were already forming as a result of my half-size too small new shoes, I listened to the introduction to the event and eyed up the agenda, which naturally, given my status at the proceedings, I headed. Only half listening to the chairman's remarks, I rummaged through my slides in an effort to reorientate myself and get into the swing of it all. It took all of thirty seconds to realise that my secretary had printed off a version of the presentation that was at least a week old. From awe-inspiring and technologically stunning I had drifted into winging it. Although not a unique experience – my secretary at the time had had a habit of doing this sort of thing, although not normally quite so comprehensively – prayers commenced at that point for some kind of natural disaster, or at the very least an unfortunate heart attack.

My moment came, and I sauntered down the length of the room to the accompaniment of polite applause, trying not to limp too much. The clapping died down and I turned on the overhead projector, fully expecting it not to work. The sound of it whirring and spluttering into life is with me still. I asked for the lights to be dimmed in a shameless effort to waste more time, and my orders were immediately obeyed. I asked if I could be heard at the back and an answer chorused back in the affirmative. I toyed with the idea of asking everyone to stand up and to follow that up with 'Simon says scratch your head,' but thought I might be pushing it.

'Thank you, Mr Chairman,' I started instead, 'and thank you

for inviting me here today. In your introduction you rightly drew our attention to—'

But that was as far as I got. It was at that point when my prayers were duly answered. In professional terms it was nothing short of a miracle, but its agent was not so much an angel but more a balding thirty-something in a rather sad-looking red and gold braid uniform. This man knocked determinedly on our door and barged his way in before we'd decided who had the authority to answer him.

'I'm afraid I'm going to have to ask you all to leave as fast as you can,' he announced confidently, in a way designed to generate rather than dampen down any possible threat of panic. He then added, almost nonchalantly, 'There's a bit of a bomb scare on.'

This last piece of information, which suggested different degrees of bomb scare (I'd always taken the view that a bit of a bomb scare was like being a bit pregnant), was delivered almost as an afterthought, but had the desired effect. Chairs scraped across the parquet flooring and an excited babbling filled the air. The sight of the respected burghers of Wigan taking the opportunity to display their true Lancastrian grit filled the room.

In all the commotion, I was forgotten. One second the centre of attention, the next yesterday's news. Because of my position in the room, I was the last to leave and for a moment I contemplated making for the back exit, or possibly through the kitchens, like in a Hollywood film, something I'd always wanted to do. I decided not to risk it, however, and made for the car park with everyone else, making a good fist of my regret and annoyance when all I was really feeling was relief.

Later we learnt that rather than being one of the routine false alarms around at that time, when the IRA was active on the mainland, there had been a real threat. An unexploded Second World War bomb had been displaced in some building work and had worked its way down the river the hotel stood by. It was one of three apparently, and one had already gone off. The image of hundreds of pounds' worth of explosive somersaulting past us in the current, waiting to hit the right spot to detonate, only came to me later.

I never did give that presentation, and I was actually rather glad that the hotel itself was not on our route, as the canal takes you round the edge of the town. I can still picture the annoyance on my client's face at the time, as my conclusions were to provide the basis for a bid for promotion. The thought of him rushing out and grabbing me and demanding his pound of flesh has been a recurring nightmare ever since.

The next morning we remembered that despite having time on our hands the day before we'd failed miserably to do any shopping. While this was not a complete disaster for either Chris or myself – we had bread and marge and could make toast – it was more concerning for Tom, whose eating habits were, shall we say, still settling. For him it was Shreddies or nothing, so unfortunately it was nothing. In fairness he had recently acquired a taste for takeaway curries, and one of the challenges Chris had set for their holiday was to expose Tom to the full experience of an Indian restaurant, which for some reason he had reckoned would be more authentic in the north. This lack of sustenance was a shame given the work that lay before him, but he was, at that stage, still largely oblivious of this, so I was able to assuage my guilt when I prepared a third slice of toast. Besides, there was no time to worry as we were at that moment approached by a woman from another boat in the lock queue who was looking for partners to go through the flight with.

'Ten minutes?' we asked, raising our cups of coffee that were still only half drunk. She seemed to acknowledge our request and walked back to her boat. It came as something of a shock therefore to see her a minute later chugging past the corner on the way to the top lock. We had little choice but to sling what remained of our coffee into the canal and get going. We were anxious not to lose the opportunity to go down together, the alternative being an entire flight set against us. Suddenly it was action stations and we unhitched our ropes and began to pray that the engine was going to start. Thankfully it did, a sweet, sweet sound, and as the rain began to settle in nicely for the day we pulled out and turned the corner ourselves.

The lock was waiting, full of water and half full of boat, its gates akimbo. As soon as we entered the still water it was as if I'd never been away. As we began to fall I felt the refreshing feel of a light drizzle upon my cheeks. The old routine returned, the constant checking for the position of the boat and making sure that the crew had done everything right, the texture of wet ropes and, most of all, the nauseating choking of diesel fumes bouncing off the lock wall and into my face. Each of these sparked happy memories. Slowly the boat descended to an accompaniment of rushing water and the shouted instructions from the four busy workers manning the locks as they calculated the most efficient division of labour – one going on ahead, two working the lock and one mopping up.

I stood at the back and chatted with Gordon, half of the pairing which made up *Gordann*, the name of our partner boat. They were based in Darwen just outside Blackburn and, pretty much inevitably, spent the summer cruising the system. At that moment they had his wife's widowed sister with them. They were clearly old canal hands and Gordon was keen to know where we were headed, the staple opening question of any canal conversation. I told him what we were doing and where we were going and he was visibly impressed.

'You'll find the locks very different further south,' he suggested, pausing while he found the right word to describe them. After a few seconds he offered the single word 'Snug', as this seemed to sum them up. He was full of helpful hints about these single locks, such as when to lodge the boat against the back of the lock and using the engine to open recalcitrant gates. Although I'd heard most of these suggestions before it was useful to have them confirmed and I was an attentive listener.

Our passage through the locks was steady and unrelenting. Roman numerals chiselled into the outgoing wall told of our progress, which at first seemed surprisingly rapid, until I got round to checking my watch. We were averaging ten minutes a lock, which constituted excellent progress, but I didn't dare tell this to Chris and Tom, who clearly wearied as we went on, driven forward by the enthusiasm of our helpmates and the absence of alternatives.

After the first half-dozen or so the novelty had clearly worn off, but they didn't complain, not that there was much chance for communication, or even encouragement, as the well-oiled rhythm they had developed propelled them forward. Only once did they lose their momentum, and that was when the early morning traffic made crossing a road nigh on impossible. Below on the canal we simply chugged on regardless and wondered where they'd got to, slightly perturbed by the interruption.

Although the routine was the same each time, every lock seemed to have its own quirks, making any kind of complacency out of bounds. One might have a gate that didn't work, another a sticky winding mechanism, another still a certain piece of detritus to look out for inside the lock. Improbably, some seemed smaller than the others, with the *Gordann* at times struggling to fit in, it being the maximum sixty feet. After a while this fact led to a variation to our routine, with only the gate closest to our partner being opened on exit. This allowed me to use the extra sixteen feet at my disposal to manoeuvre *Florrie* through the gap, saving on opening and closing one gate and therefore a minute or so on each lock.

As we passed through the flight it was difficult to gain much of an impression of the area or indeed to get a feel for Wigan itself, and I was glad we'd caught at least a glimpse the day before. It seemed improbable that this area had once supported a thriving coal and iron industry employing up to ten thousand people, with ten blast furnaces roaring throughout the night and 675 coking ovens sending their showers of sparks up into the sky. Now it was quiet and nondescript, as if all that activity had been a dream.

At last we reached the junction with the Leigh Branch of the Leeds and Liverpool, the turn that meant we would not be going past the pier. As half a mile separated us from the final two locks the workers got back on board and I decided to give Chris the opportunity to take the tiller whilst working the last two locks myself. Up until then there simply hadn't been the chance to swap over. For Tom, the ordeal was nearly over and his face showed his relief. It had taken just under three and a half hours to work our way through and he'd managed it without so much as a bowl of Shreddies. In later conversation with old canal hands it was generally agreed that this represented pretty good going, a fact we owed in part to the good folk of the *Gordann*.

That evening we spotted in the Nicholson that the Kirklees Hall offers an embellished certificate to all boaters who have completed the ascent. None of us could face the prospect of either going back to claim our prize, even if we did, trying to make it clear what it was we'd come for once we got there.

...to the Theatre of Dreams

The sheer tenacity, spiced with a more than a hint of self-righteousness, of the average canalside fisherman is a wonder to behold. They seem to enter a kind of state of grace, oblivious of their surroundings, their gaze drawn permanently to the small tip of luminous orange, yellow or red in the water before them. The concentration they display is total in a way that is only ever seen elsewhere in chess. Their kit carriers, oblong and functional, like cool boxes, provide a place for them to sit, motionless except for the brief punctuation of activity that is a fresh cast. This action is itself invariably over almost before it has begun, an aberration in the normal course of their (non) activity.

Although rarely explicitly articulated, a tussle seems to exist between these fishermen and boaters over the issue of primacy over the water. It is a battle the banksiders cannot win by sheer dint of the truism that the boats are on the water while they are merely dabbling in it. Despite this fact, for fact it is, the fishermen do not concede easily. Although throughout our journeying we had displayed due courtesy on approaching fishermen by slowing down, and therefore reducing our wash, the usual response from them was to maintain a fiction that we didn't exist, that despite the obviousness of our approach they hadn't noticed us. Only at the last possible moment did they move their rods away, and even then some deigned only to raise them just high enough to let us pass – and woe betide anyone lying invisible on the roof, for any hook would surely catch them.

In fact, as we were to discover, they knew only too well of our approach, and only partly because of the noise of our engine. In the course of an ordinary conversation two people standing at the stern tended, despite themselves, to raise their voices more than a few decibels. As a result, their discussions would carry across the water and arrive at the canalside with amazing clarity. This was proven to us when we first encountered the phenomenon of the fisherman's rod that reaches almost to the opposite bank. An almost obscene and certainly curiously disproportional device, such rods appeared on first sight to be dysfunctional – surely they were too heavy to support? This led in turn, in the true spirit of tillerside rumination, to a debate on what they were made of. Bamboo perhaps, or maybe carbon?

The answer was provided by a fisherman himself as we rounded a sharp bend. As our backside swung out towards him he grunted 'They're carbon' at us, timing his comment to perfection, in that by the time we'd worked out where the voice had come from we were too far away to quiz him further. The only explanation was the obvious one, that our voices had carried over the water and he'd heard us, and from that moment on we learnt to keep our counsel when there was the prospect of bankside company.

These core characteristics of fishermen were displayed amply when we moored up a couple of miles into the Leigh Branch for a late lunch after our efforts through Wigan. The clouds above looked ominous, their blackness spreading across the sky like a stain into a carpet. We were suddenly grateful for our forced early start. Locking in a thunderstorm, now that would have been a true baptism of fire.

Within seconds, the clouds soon began to empty, sending solid globules of water rushing towards us as if they were worried about the time, and for good measure threw in a rather spectacular combination of deep resonating thunder and sharp tongues of blue lightning. The canal at this spot was open, the stretch from Wigan having been unusually straight and raised up, a result of continuous shoring up after years of subsidence. Appropriately, this had been achieved using mine spoil, as it was the underground workings that had caused the collapses in the first place. As a result, we had a front row in the stalls view of the storm, including the ferocious bolts of lightning which momentarily lit up the sky and gave a loud reminder of the power of nature.

Throughout this spectacle the fishermen fished away stoically, as if nothing was happening. If we'd stared long enough we might have noticed one or two of them huddle grudgingly towards the centre of their umbrellas, but none of them gave up or took shelter. Their response was all the more remarkable for the danger it placed them in, reports of death by lightning attracted to the pointy bits of fishing rods and umbrellas may be rare, but they do happen. Naturally, nothing was caught during this time, but there again, it was an unusual sight indeed to see any of them catch anything anyway.

It could be argued that they had little choice, other than we were moored up right outside a pub which could have easily provided a not unwelcoming berth from the storm. Although, as we were to discover, this didn't offer food (much to our chagrin and contrary to the advice from the Nicholson). It did, however, provide a roof. It also offered coverage from the test match, something Tom appreciated while Chris and I supped a quick pint, although we drew the line at *Neighbours*.

For a fisherman, however, to accept shelter appeared to represent a flagrant disregard of the rules, as if such an act would be to concede ground to the fish, who meanwhile sank a little lower and presumably chuckled away quietly to themselves. It was from that moment, I think, that my initial frustration with fishermen (who had been strangely absent on the Leeds and Liverpool) began to gel into a kind of qualified respect. As a minimum, it always makes sense to give a madman plenty of space.

Back at the boat, the rain had given *Florrie*'s paintwork a wash over and added a quality of glossiness that hadn't been there before, but I knew it was only a deception. As all traces of the storm rapidly evaporated patches of blue sky began to peek over the horizon, as if to check if it would be okay to come out to play, and within an hour we were basking in a truly glorious English summer's day. Traffic on the water remained amazingly light, with less than a dozen boats recorded over the rest of the day. As a result we were able to enjoy the countryside in splendid isolation as we passed through a wildlife sanctuary established on redundant minefields. It was as if the whole scene had been laid on for our benefit. Waterfowl dipped into the man-made lakes and insects hovered over the water, making faint buzzing sounds I could only hear when they flew past my ear, oblivious to my presence.

In the distance an old shaft-head, which marked the position of the Astley Green Pit Museum, was a reminder of what had once stood here and why the canal had been built. The land on either side of us was generally fallow, with straw-like grass but destined never to be harvested, the farming rights presumably having been lost when the area was coalfields. That or, more likely, the land had been poisoned by the effects of industry.

The canal stretched before us in long straight sections, a kind of pre-industrial equivalent of a Roman road, and for the first time on the journey I found I was experiencing the vision I'd had in Skipton the first time we'd seen *Florrie*. One hand on the tiller, the other gripping a bottle of beer, the sun on my back (we had even reverted to using sunscreen), and silence all around (with one obvious exception): this, I realised, was the idyll I'd been chasing since setting off. It felt good.

The connection made, I gathered up a conscious effort to wallow in the experience, slipping into a state of autopilot, resting on the tiller rather than actively manipulating it. As we made our passage, lilies either side of us were sucked under the surface as we passed, folding themselves up slowly as they did so for neatness, like a piece of origami. Their action was mesmerising, both in its simplicity and its tempo, the effect being like watching a stop-frame nature film, only in reverse. A blur of unrealistically large turquoise dragonflies held their station impatiently, waiting for them to return.

In the blue above us light wispy clouds came together to form different shapes, of faces or the outline of countries, whilst the straight lines of aeroplane vapour trails cut a path through them a few thousand feet higher. One set of clouds in particular suggested a woman's profile and it struck me that this could be used as a kind of alternative ink-blot test. This thought was enough to make me avert my gaze and concentrate on the water. Too heavy.

For once there was no event, no happening, no sudden crisis to destroy the moment. This state remained for over an hour until we approached a swing bridge, which was in fact a mechanically operated lift bridge, controlled by traffic lights, a reminder of approaching urbanisation. This turned out to be Leigh, which the canal passes through the outskirts of. More importantly, Leigh marked the end of the Leeds and Liverpool and the commencement of the canal oddity which is the Leigh Branch, technically of the Bridgewater Canal, which we officially joined at Bridge (rather than route) 66.

The Leigh Branch was dug to link the Bridgewater to the Leeds and Liverpool, and therefore to join together the two metropolises of Manchester and Liverpool, a feat that was achieved in 1820. The single-mindedness of its purpose is reflected in its routing, which retains the theme of long straight stretches, as if nothing was allowed to get in the way and the builders wanted to get it done as soon as possible.

Cruising along this stretch started a yearning for more bends, an element of challenge for the helmsman and the prospect of fresh scenery for those up front. Soon, however, we were hemmed in by trees and deprived of any view at all, and the realisation dawned that our wish was not going to be granted. At this point, the challenge became seeing how long the straight sections could last, with some exceeding a mile in length – which is more than even the misnamed Burnley Mile had managed.

Although the Leigh Branch was important in canal terms, its achievement was eclipsed more than slightly by the completion of the world's first passenger railway service, which also linked those two great cities, only ten years after its completion. Although it took some time for the railway to usurp the canal's dominance, once it had become established the process of one technology passing the torch of progress to another became inexorable.

I'd been looking forward to the Bridgewater, which appealed on a number of levels. Not only was it new territory, my first new canal, affording an opportunity to inspect whether different canals had different characters, but it offered a number of sights which I was keen to see, having read about them beforehand. The first of these was Worsley, an otherwise unprepossessing small town, more of a village really. However, if anywhere can claim the honour of being the birthplace of the canal system in the UK, then Worsley is that place.

It was the prodigious output of the mines at Worsley that encouraged Francis Egerton, the third Duke of Bridgewater, to investigate the potential of water transport against the then cumbersome system of turnpike roads. By doing so, the duke is also generally according the title of father of the system, although the first duke (his grandfather presumably) also has some claims. It was he who had been the guiding force behind the idea of making Worsley Brook a navigable cut way back in 1737. He even went so far as to get an Act of Parliament passed allowing him to carry out the necessary work, but nothing was ever done.

As with most inventions and discoveries, shining the spotlight on a single individual can be an iniquitous business. For example, the duke's uncle, it being a small world, Lord Gower, had had a possible route surveyed from the Mersey to the Potteries. The duke's blood, however, was bluer, and in such matters a duke is always more likely to win out than a mere lord. It is known that the third duke had seen and appreciated the potential of inland waterways during his Grand Tour travels in Europe, and he was certainly active in his promotion of them in England. For this dedication it seems reasonable to award him with the honour. The Bridgewater is also remarkable for having but one lock, the one which connects it to the Manchester Ship Canal, a feature which I felt my crew were going to appreciate over the coming two and a half days.

The eventual impact of the Bridgewater was remarkable, both financially and psychologically. First off, it cut the cost of coal in Manchester in half to 4d per hundredweight, which must have been a kind of reverse 'oil shock' of its day, with industry in those days becoming as dependent upon coal as the west was on oil in the early 1970s. Secondly, the sheer physicality of the canal, both whilst it was being built and afterwards, when the boats started to ply its length, must have been breathtaking in its day.

A further factor marking out the Bridgewater is the involvement of James Brindley in its execution. A millwright and mill drainage expert, Brindley was the man who had surveyed Lord Gower's proposed Potteries canal and his name has passed into waterways legend, being for ever associated with canals in the same way that Capability Brown's has become synonymous with landscape gardening. Rare indeed is the canal which does not claim some connection with Brindley, although ultimately it was his capacity to spread himself too thin amongst the various projects which now claim his input which was to kill him. More on this later.

Back in real time, approaching Worsley was an experience in itself, starting the Bridgewater off in style. The water soon ran to a dirty brown colour, a legacy of the local iron ore deposits. In time, as we approached closer to the mines, this turned to a deep gold. The effect throughout was heightened by the brilliant bright sunshine, which added its own particular lustre and caused deep threatening shadows to be cast from the mature trees lining the bank.

As we turned a bend, the first sight to hit us was the steps of the Packet House, which led down to a small wharf from which day trippers used to board their packet steamers, hence the name. The Packet House itself smiled out at the river, with a half-timbered frontage that was perfection itself. Dark black beams criss-crossed in balanced symmetry. Squares on the chequerboard were filled in with different patterns on each storey of the house; the whole thing topped off with a grand brick chimney that looked too heavy for the more modern-looking tiled roof.

At the time of our visit the house sported a FOR SALE sign, although a later inspection of the local estate agent's window did not reveal a price, which made it perfectly clear which league it was in. To the left of the Packet House lay the entrances to the mines themselves, the very *raison d'être* of the canal, although these were low and partially hidden by the lower branches of the trees which had grown up around it. The entrances could only really be viewed by foot, so, as this was something of a place of pilgrimage, and because it was getting on, we decided to stop for the night.

This decision was mine, and was made at a time when I was at the front of the boat taking photographs. I turned round to communicate with Chris who was at the helm, and realised at that point that he too had been taken in by the view and had done the one thing you can never afford to do when responsible for steering, namely lose concentration. Within a matter of microseconds *Florrie* was heading straight for the bank, something which wouldn't have been too bad in itself if a fairly decrepit cruiser with a wooden cabin hadn't occupied the space we were heading for. Further inspection revealed that the cruiser had a bad case of wood rot. The instrument that was *Florrie*'s high-fronted rammer was homing in on a particularly vulnerable portion of the boat's superstructure with all the precision of a laser-guided weapon. I leant out as far as I dared, the strange colour of the water hardly inspiring a dip, and prepared to fend off with my hands, but *Florrie* seemed determined.

The sound of sodden wood taking the strain of a powerful force hitting it can be a curiously satisfying one, combining as it does the squelch of moisture being squeezed out with a muffled cracking sound. This effect is made all the more rewarding if amplified by an empty space behind. The capacity of wood to bend without actually breaking can also be surprising, a capacity I was especially happy to observe on this occasion, as I managed to deflect the continuing momentum of our vessel away from the unfortunate object of our attentions. Our bacon more or less saved, we momentarily considered whether to press on, but the historian in me overwhelmed the pragmatist and we moored up successfully just opposite the barge house, built by Lord Ellesmere to accommodate Queen Victoria's royal barge for her visit to Worsley in 1851. Beside us on the shore lay part of a tree rescued from the canal, its branches dyed a deep orange, its leaves gilded as if painted for a stage set, a pantomime perhaps?

Taking advantage of the late evening sunshine, I went for a wander and aimed for the mines. Close up, the entrance belied their magnificence, being a series of low-slung arches beyond which all was dark. Each arch was blocked off with a thin wire mesh and overgrown with luxuriant foliage, although water still ran in and out of the mines. One of the original reasons for the canal was to provide a drainage system for the workings, and although the needs of man may have moved on, those of nature, it seemed, had remained.

Behind the mesh there was in fact a highly complex system of forty-six miles worth of underground canals existing on four different levels in order to work the coal seams. Special craft used to ply these underground waterways, roughly the same length as *Florrie* but only four and a half feet wide, their prominent ribbed sides earning them the nickname of 'starvationers'. Incredibly, these were pulled five at a time by horses, with each one capable of holding fully twelve tons of coal. Men, women and children would chip at the coal in these cramped and inhospitable conditions, working fourteen-hour shifts.

The heyday of the mines, and of the boatyards beyond, was the latter half of the eighteenth century, when the scene would have been one of heaving activity. Although those days are long gone – what was the boatyard is now the local green – Worsley remains proud of its role in the development of the canal system and has erected a series of informative boards around the village. Walking around is to experience the epitome of the English village, and it is difficult to imagine both what the scene would have been like two hundred years ago and the degree of risk that building the original canal must have represented. Indeed, as an example, the *Manchester Mercury* at the time had been particularly scathing of the idea, suggesting in a sarcastic tone that 'the canal will be of very great use as an ornament.'

One aid to the imagination remains, in the square fountain on the edge of the green, which was the base of the boatyard chimney, now topped off with a decorative balcony. Inscribed round the fountain is a verse in Latin, which one of the boards helpfully translated, and I found it particularly evocative.

> A lofty column breathing smoke and fire
> Did I the Builder's glory once aspire
> Whose founder was the duke who far and wide
> Bridged water through Bridgewater's countryside.
>
> Stranger! This spot, where once did never cease
> Great Vulcan's fear, would sleep in silent peace
> But beneath my very stones does mount
> That water's source, his honour's spring and fount.
>
> Alas! That I who gazed o'er field and town
> Should to these base proportions dwindle down
> But all's not over, still enough remains
> To testify past glories, duties, pains.

One final story which I liked. The bell that now hangs in the parish church of St Martin's belonged originally to the boatyard.

To this day it strikes thirteen times at 1 p.m., as the workers used to explain their tardiness in coming back to work after lunch by the fact that they couldn't hear a single strike. The then duke's solution had been simple, and new excuses had to be found if a yardman was to be late.

That night we dragged ourselves over the road to the Bridge-water Hotel for dinner. Unusually for this trip, this turned out to be a pub that was busy midweek, Worsley clearly being a honey-pot location for reasons other than its historical associations. After an adequate meal, straight out of the standard pub chain menu, I was astounded to discover that Tom was ignorant of the family card game of Pest, so without further ado we marched back to *Florrie*. After the familiar chorus of padlocks being opened and chains rattled I led the way in, smashing my head against the hatchway as I went down. I hadn't done that for a while, and was reminded that it was an experience best avoided.

Although Chris knew he'd played Pest before, he'd forgotten the rules, our heyday of family games having coincided with his rebel phase. I prepared myself to clean up, but predictably was beaten hollow by the novice and near novice, reinforcing the family maxim that victory in Pest is never secured until the game is finally over.

For years the ingeniousness of the Bridgewater set it out as a standard-bearer amongst canals, and it was only in 1974, nearly two hundred years since its opening, that commercial traffic ceased on the canal. Its absence of locks and winding contour-driven course became trademarks of the Brindley approach. It also demonstrated a generous use of aqueducts, although it is thought that Brindley was not a great fan of this technique.

That said, the Bridgewater was daring in its use of these, nota-bly the one at Barton where the canal crossed the River Irwell. At the time aqueducts were seen by many as the work of madmen, and when the one at Barton was first opened people turned up to it in anticipation of it failing, much as some people used to go to motor racing to watch the crashes. Before building could even start, however, the great man had to convince people that it was possible at all, so he constructed a model – out of cheese. History does not record which type of cheese he used, or if he ate the evidence afterwards in case it turned out not to work after all.

An aqueduct remains at Barton, although these days it passes over the Manchester Ship Canal, which subsumed the Irwell. To this day the Manchester Ship Canal is also the owner of the Bridgewater, although holders of British Waterways licences are allowed seven days' consecutive passage. The bright weather of the previous day continuing, we were able to make this journey in brilliant sunshine, which served to accentuate the contrast between the two verticals of this rectangular cocoon, which were painted in a stark black, and the horizontal, which was a bright, freshly touched-up white. Scarlet latticework formed a roof and laced the sides in an architectural style clearly influenced by the growing dominance of railways at the time of its building, just before the turn of the century. Whilst not long, the views from the aqueduct were spectacular, although the Ship Canal was devoid of seagoing craft when we passed over it, making it seem like more a marvellous engineering feat rather than something of practical value.

The story of the Bridgewater is in many ways the story of the canals. After a reasonable period of immense success, a protracted but always doomed battle followed with the railways. In the Bridgewater's case, the building of the Manchester Ship Canal added a quirk to history. Although for a time the Bridgewater was owned by an alliance between two railway companies, the Midland and Manchester and the Sheffield and Lincolnshire, who bought it for the princely sum of £1,115,000 in 1872, this phase in its own particular history was to be short-lived. The Act of Parliament which authorised the Manchester Ship Canal in 1885 also allowed the new corporation to purchase the Bridgewater. Amalgamation of the two was to have two immediate and disastrous consequences for the older canal. Firstly the original Barton Aqueduct, hailed as one of the wonders of the system, had to go, and secondly the new company had no interest in small collieries, leading to the closure of the Worsley mines in 1887. In the end, canal did for canal as surely as the railway would elsewhere.

Things went fine until the First World War, with the transport of coal, especially over the Leigh Branch, continuing to provide a good income. When the boats were returned to their private owners after the war, however, few could afford the necessary maintenance to bring them back up to scratch, hastening the underlying trends which were heading towards the use of road and rail for the movement of coal. The rest, as they say, is history.

Passage across the Manchester Ship Canal signalled the imminence of the city itself and, for Tom at least, the highlight of this leg of the journey. This was to be his haj, his pilgrimage to the holy of holies. He was even dressed for the occasion, with a red shirt bearing the name of a Japanese electronics manufacturer on the front and his own surname embossed proudly on the back across his shoulder blades.

Whereas Chris's conversational topics tend to be dominated by music, his son's, much to his despair, focus almost entirely upon sport, in what may be his version of rebellion against his father (he also abhors the use of alcohol, another of Chris's little hobbies). For myself, although no expert on sport, I know enough to keep a discussion going for a while, at least, on most sports. The one exception to this is rugby league, a fact which carried no little irony as we were at the time going through a part of the country where even the road signs seemed to be displaying some kind of rugby league results table – Sale 6, Warrington 24; St Helens 14, Wigan 10; and so on.

The object of our attention was, of course, Old Trafford, not just for the football ground, which was to be the focus of the trip, but the cricket ground, as an overhead TV blimp signalled that the test match we had viewed briefly in the pub during the thunderstorm the day before was in progress. As we approached the appropriate junction we took the sharp left hand branch towards Manchester, the fishermen raising their rods in both tribute and, I suspected, understanding. We motored gingerly towards the centre of the city, anxious that we did not miss passing the ground itself, which the map promised was right next to the canal, but also aware of the dire warnings of vandalism in this neck of the woods which still rang heavily in my ears. The landscape was bleak, heavy with large industrial plants, with the delicate scent of cornflakes emanating from a huge Kellogg's factory – a cruel reminder of our continued failure to procure any Shreddies for Tom yet. I wasn't sure he'd have been able to eat that morning anyway.

Chris was allocated the tiller as we got closer, seeming to take an age to pass by the immodestly named World Freight Centre. Over the fence we could see cubist mountains of containers piled improbably high, like a Lego tower built to impress a child, but one which looked like it had insufficient foundations to stay up for long. Then we saw it, the stark plain font that spelt out in red block capitals the words MANCHESTER UNITED on the top of a recently completed stand. The white cobwebs of the cantilever supporting it were echoed along the side where yet another new stand was in the process of being erected, a testament to the recent astounding success of this once sleeping giant of English sport.

The final mile and a half into the city centre was probably unbearable to Tom, a case of so near yet so far. He had the comfort of knowing that we had a booking for a three o'clock tour of the place; all we had to do was get there. Our route took us alongside an extension of the Metrolink tram service, my last memory of which had been the traffic chaos it had engendered in the centre of the city during its construction. That it was being extended seemed to be a heartening sign, as was the evidence of some imagination being used in the architecture of the new stations. In fact, pretty much everywhere we looked we could see evidence of building, or conversions, especially alongside the canal. This was clearly a place to be if you were in the construction trade; the city seemed to be undergoing a boom.

Our target was Castlefield Junction, not only because the Nicholson referred to it as 'excitingly restored,' but because there didn't seem to be anywhere else. Excitingly restored it may have been, but when we were approaching it some clues as to when it might be coming up would have been helpful. Not only was the alternative to start the run of locks which marked the beginning of the Rochdale Canal, something which my sensors perceived would at that moment go down like a manure vol-au-vent, but our map indicated a sharp right-hand turn would be required. Unfortunately, the area was littered with potential sharp right-hand turns into small basins. With the locks clearly visible in front of us and a British Waterways barge blocking the underside of the bridge ahead, I took a last minute executive decision to hang a right at a corner where some new flats suggested an area of gentrification and exciting restoration.

Big mistake. Just at the point we were committed it became clear that a barrier was blocking the basin off and despite correcting action we hit the freshly laid concrete of the corner full on, sending a shudder through the boat and leaving, we discovered later, a neat white dent on the very front of the hull. To using a sporting parlance that even Chris would understand, following the incident with the cruiser at Worsley that made it one–all. The men on the British Waterways barge opposite looked up, and then returned to their work in the nonchalant way they all seemed to have. It was just possible they were the same men who'd seen me perform so incompetently when with the F-in-L.

The Castlefield area lived up to its billing. Not only was it convenient for the city centre but it also seemed to offer a modicum of security. We therefore moored up and, after a lunch from a decidedly yuppie menu in a decidedly yuppie pub, we split up; the sports fans for Mecca, the remainder on a search for second-hand record shops.

As predicted, the Metro delivered us simply to Old Trafford, where we were able to peek over the fence at the scoreboard to see that England were all out for 199 against a weak New Zealand side. Walking past the ground we were surprised by the lack of atmosphere inside, until we realised that it was still the lunch interval. Ten minutes' walk took us past the Red Devils fish and chip shop and similarly named emporiums and we reached our objective.

There can be no doubt that Old Trafford football ground is an impressive spot. In my time I have visited a number of the major grounds in the country, but to date this one had eluded me. I was aware that stadium design had moved on in leaps and bounds during the fifteen years since I'd regularly attended football matches, as indeed had the game itself in the place it occupied in the nation's psyche. The sheer scale of the change, however, came as a surprise, if not a shock.

Earlier religious analogies were not out of place. The impression that people were there simply to be there, even though, or perhaps because of the fact that, the start of the season was a week away. Having visited both the Superstore and the Megastore, both of which sported imaginative ways of transposing the Manchester United logo onto items of everyday use, we entered the museum. This was impressively laid out and loaded up with high-tech wizardry, and it was here that I saw Tom's breath literally taken away, and it was the simplest of objects that did it.

A tall, but still smaller than I'd imagined, silver cup sporting red ribbons stood behind glass, rotating on a perspex plinth. The European Champions League Cup, once more in the Old Trafford trophy room. I pointed it out to Tom and he froze in his tracks, his mouth opened and his awkward arms dangled down by the side of his body. At last, the veneer of teenage stoicism had been cracked. After that it was a relative disappointment to divert his gaze towards the Premiership Trophy and FA Cup, which together made up the treble of the remarkable by any standards season of 1998–1999 for this club.

The tour itself, when it came, was slick and well done, laced with a combination of statistics and easy anecdotes and just enough awe-inspiration and freedom to walk in the steps of heroes, even if just for a few seconds, to make it money well spent. There were about thirty of us in the party and, to my surprise, the vast majority of them were locals. Surprise because this was somewhere which has become for many the very antithesis of regional pride. Manchester United was more of a national – nay, an international – icon, rather than an institution which might actually tell us something about the area we were passing through. Our guide herded his flock with a practised ease. It wouldn't have been too great a leap of imagination to hear him yelp 'Come by, boy' at us as we obediently wended our way through the labyrinth beneath the stadium. Occasionally we bumped into other flocks at different stages of their tour, at one point cutting through them with all the precision of a marching band at half-time on Cup Final day.

I had booked the tour as a treat for Tom rather than as an opportunity to pursue my investigations, but was happy to be proved wrong. The club presented an image of success coupled with a pride in that success. Rather than complacency, the prevailing air was one of continued progress, of a story not yet concluded as it continued to build to consolidate the position it had won back through hard work and not a little skill. These were also qualities we picked up about Manchester as a city during our brief time there. Horror stories of vandalism proved to be unfounded, and the place seemed to be looking towards the future, building on its past rather than resting on it.

Reunited at Castlefield Junction, we picked up the signals that said this being Friday night this joint was going to rock. As we were worn out by our respective pilgrimages (Chris had found a rare CD and a book on Led Zeppelin he'd been trying to find for a while), we decided to rejoin the main line of the Bridgewater. It turned out later that our instincts had been right. Unwittingly, we had been in the area of Canal Street, which in turn had become the focus of the local 'gay village'. We had, it seemed, not noticed the signs, upon which some locals have scratched away the C of canal. Whilst not disapproving, we somehow felt we were unlikely to share the values about to be displayed.

As Tom related the tour to his father inside, the latter listening patiently, I opened the throttle and pushed us just outside the city into the outskirts of Sale where we moored up just beyond the first vaguely welcoming pub. It turned out we were a week too early, however, as the Bridge Inn at Sale was due to hold its annual summer party and boat rally the following weekend. This promised to be an event not to be missed, with live music and the prospect of a hog roast and at 3 p.m. on the Saturday a pie-eating competition.

This, we agreed, would have been a sight worth seeing, as judging by the local population concerns about the effect on one's heart of overeating were pretty low down the priority list. One of the tables outside in particular held court to two of the fattest most tattoo-encrusted men I had ever seen. Furthermore, as if they didn't have enough weight to carry, each wore the equivalent to a small country's gold reserves in jewellery. The sight of them dashing in when it began to rain was not a pretty one.

From being heaving, the pub cleared suddenly around nine, as if there'd been a cue that we, as strangers, had missed. Everyone, it seemed, had somewhere else to go, and so did we, to the boat and more games of Pest which Tom, fittingly, for it was his big day, won.

That night he went to bed in his MUFC top, a thin line of sunburn on his neck complementing the red of his shirt.

Saturday Night in Runcorn

The prospect of a break from pub food and the pursuit of a decent curry now dominated our thoughts. In a rare piece of route planning, we consulted the Nicholson to agree a place to aim for. In doing so we agree that a guide to the best curry houses would be a worthwhile addition to the unfailingly useful (if not always accurate) lists it already carried.

Viewed from a purely practical point of view, Runcorn seemed the only reasonably populated area within a day's travel, there being little in the middle between where we were at that moment and there. None of us knew anything about the place and none of us had ever been there. That sealed it. Even though Runcorn represented another detour from the main route of the canal, we decided to make it our target.

From the wider perspective of the trip, Runcorn offered additional advantages, it being the end point of the canal. As we'd already been through the Bridgewater's starting point at Worsley, it seemed somehow symmetrical to round things off by going to its end. Not that Runcorn was the originally intended finish point. Fired up with the success of the first sections of the canal, the Duke of Bridgewater had altered his original plans to allow it to continue on to Runcorn so that it could connect up with the Severn. This, he'd reasoned, with ever an eye on the main chance, would provide an alternative route to the sea from the existing Mersey and Irwell Navigation, which as its name suggests is mainly river rather than an artificial cut.

Before we got going, I decided to use the bike I'd had brought up at the end of the first leg and explore that bit of Sale I could reach before getting either soaked (the rain had once more returned) or tired (I was not in the peak of condition). As the town began to show signs of waking up, first impressions were unspectacular. Small local businesses in old houses were juxtaposed with international brand names atop spanking new red-brick offices. The shopping centre was the usual pedestrianised precinct, intercut with main roads, neither of which seemed that friendly to travel by bike.

I caught up with the canal about a mile further down and found what looked like a more upmarket pub than the Bridge Inn. Hard experience had told me that appearances can be deceptive; anyway, as I've hinted, we were beginning to get more than a little tired of pub food and the ubiquity of the menus, especially Tom with his rather more eclectic tastes. This said, I was keen to check, but was thwarted by the closure of the towpath at the necessary point, so I was forced to go back the way I'd come to rejoin *Florrie*. Making a virtue of this necessity, I took advantage of the fact that the bakeries were just beginning to open and, in the absence of any obvious local delicacy, bought some croissants for the crew.

Once under way we were immediately confronted by a two-mile stretch of strait, with occasional permanent moorings on the non-towpath side. These were invariably highly protected with razor wire, closed circuit TV cameras and boards placed over the exposed windows of the boats. It seemed as if there might have been some truth after all in the warnings I'd been given on random vandalism. On exiting Sale the canal once again began to meander, which made steering more interesting to the helmsman of the moment. Then, all of a sudden, in a way that only happens with canals, the landscape switched from being heavily urban to utterly rural. Although it was difficult to give a reason why, the impression remained that this was only a temporary blip. Never during this stretch was one left with the feeling, often felt earlier in the trip, that you'd never see bricks and mortar again.

As we went through these stretches the full scale of the endeavour associated with cutting a canal once again came through to me. Armies of men armed with pickaxes, shovels and wheelbarrows, dependent upon their raw energy and ingenuity, working in all weathers to dig a channel sufficiently deep, with robust sides, often against a deadline. And that didn't take into account the building of locks! It seemed a crime and an insult to their memory that so many had been filled in.

The noise they must have made, the sheer social impact on local communities as they passed through. I remembered some work I'd done in Folkestone a few years before which had revealed a rocketing rate of single parenthood, which could be ascribed directly to the influx of transient workers during the building of the Channel Tunnel. Would that have happened two hundred years ago, or did wives and children travel with the workers? The art of canal building in the UK was learnt largely through experience, although some tips were learnt from the continent, where the inland waterways were much more developed, there being a much stronger tradition of river transport there. Because these men were building routes for navigation, they became known as the navigators, shortened in time to the modern day usage of 'navvies' for construction workers.

There would be no more talk of single mothers from that point on however, as we were firmly in Cheshire, and as if to prove it we moored up in the pleasantly middle-class town of Lymm for lunch. This even had a thriving Conservative Club, a rarity almost anywhere in the country, and certainly north of Birmingham. If only it had been sunny the scene would have been pure picture postcard, with the canal running through the heart of it and shops selling horse tack and fishing gear. It also had an impressive delicatessen, where I picked up some local Cheshire cheese, some Stilton and Guinness pâté and some marmalade (another favourite of Tom's, although it took him two days to notice it in the fridge). Largely through habit, however, we succumbed to yet another pub meal for lunch, although for once we had no trouble in making ourselves understood. We could almost have been in the New Forest.

An island of twee and tweed in an otherwise arid landscape, Lymm offered an oasis of calm. We suspected that the town was the natural focus for the county set; horses were certainly a big deal there judging by the shops. People seemed to know each other, openly greeting each other on the streets, and the notices in the shop windows spoke of a world of community events, jumble sales and whist drives. Comforting though these were, there also seemed to be a kind of antiseptic safety about the place. It was uninspiring and unchallenging, for all its niceties. For us Lymm was an aberration, not, I rush to add, an unpleasant one, but it seemed a place out of context. We saw nothing like it either before or after on this leg of the journey. It was as if it were a dream sequence, possibly in colour, in the middle of a gritty 1960s' film. Not real life as ordinary folk would know it.

Memories of Lymm were soon banished by our departure, when we had our inevitable but so far avoided tangle with dog dirt on the mooring rope and, in time, on our shoes. Is there anything worse than getting dog shit out of the grooves of a pair of trainers? I don't think so. Scraping away I found it difficult to fathom the kind of mentality that allows these animal owners to let their dogs defecate in such an obviously inconvenient place when all they have to do is direct them away from the water's edge. As I heard an American who suffered the same fate later in the journey say, it made you want to shoot them. Such was his anger that it wasn't clear from his tone if he meant the dogs or their owners.

The canal took us through the outskirts of Stockton Heath, tantalisingly close to views of the Ship Canal, and then through another openly rural stretch before the turn to Runcorn. The water here was clear, and as I peered into it I could see a healthy sized fish wiggling its tail gently in a shallow, holding its station against the mild current in some weeds. It had nowhere to go, and being on the opposite shore was safe for a while from the attentions of any fishermen, no matter how long their rod might be.

By way of contrast we had a rendezvous. Traffic by this point had picked up with weekenders, despite the miserable weather, and it was a relief to enter the relative quiet of the Runcorn branch. After the first fifty yards, which led to a busy marina, we were on our own. The lack of company was ably demonstrated by the increasingly dense weed covering the surface of the water. As we swept through, *Florrie* cut a path, like a breaker through ice, as she passed. The water lilies in particular seemed to thrive on this branch, at times threatening to colonise the entire surface of the water, starting on both banks and reaching out to touch each other in the middle. Where there were clear stretches the fishermen were out in force, stone-faced and at one point openly angry with us, despite the fact that you'd have thought they might have welcomed our lily-cutting contribution.

Branches overhead were noticeably lower in the middle of this stretch, requiring foresight from the helmsman if he wasn't to damage either himself, the bike padlocked to the roof or anyone unfortunate enough to be sitting up front. There was a growing sense that we had embarked upon an expedition to penetrate the heart of a jungle. I began to feel like Kurtz in *Heart of Darkness*, there was no knowing what lay in store for us ahead, but there was a growing belief that it might be life changing.

It came as something of a relief therefore when, after an hour of chugging, the dead end of the canal loomed suddenly like a full stop. In the absence of any viable alternative, we moored as close as it was possible to get to the blank brick wall that now stands where a flight of ten locks used to take the canal down to the Mersey. We could now truly say that we had cruised every inch of the Bridgewater, or what remains of it. A sign told us that the locks had been removed in 1966, long enough ago for any trace of them to be eradicated. Instead, the local transport landmark had become the huge turquoise Runcorn to Widnes road bridge across the Manchester Ship Canal, a triumph of later engineering.

The sign also told of how locals used to be so desperate for fuel that they used to fish bits of coal which had fallen off the boats out from the canal. This nugget of history should have told us something about Runcorn. You couldn't imagine people doing that in Lymm. At the time we were simply pleased to have reached our destination and weren't open to warning signals. The light was falling and our stomachs were grumbling in anticipation of the meal to come. We'd had a long time to warm to the idea of food.

A quick reconnaissance on the bike, however, brought reality firmly to the fore. Repressed first impressions were confirmed. Runcorn was not the centre of the universe. In fact, it seemed to be a bit of a hole. We were committed to stay, however; there wasn't enough light to go back and even if we did there would be nothing waiting for us. We entered a phase of damage limitation. Although Chris and I had a pretty good idea of what we were in for, Tom, in his innocence, did not, so the pair of us put on a brave face moving *Florrie* a few hundred yards downstream and moored up in what we hoped would be a safer and quieter spot. There was one consolation: I had spotted a curry house on my travels, and it looked fully capable of living up to the expectation of offering the full Indian restaurant experience.

Our instincts no doubt dulled by our time on the boat, we routinely followed our habit of falling into a pub for a pre-meal appetiser. Mistake number one. A large-screen TV was showing a sports competition which even Tom and I were unable to identify, whilst simultaneously the loudspeakers were blasting out dreadful acid house music at a volume which might have been necessary, just might, if the pub had been packed to the rafters. As it was there were just the three of us, a quartet of youths who looked and sounded as if they'd been there since lunchtime, and a woman in a miniskirt with a young child of indeterminate sex. The child was clearly highly familiar with the inside of this particular pub and treated it like its home. We drank up and left, a mutual decision that required no consultation, even if conversation had been possible.

After the pub the curry house was a haven of normality, the familiar surroundings placing us in practically any town in the land. Red fabric lampshades, even flock wallpaper, and the familiar twanging strains of the sitar on the sound system. All set the scene well for what was to follow. We began to relax. Our choices made, the waiter came over and took our order. There was some hesitation from the waiter as Tom requested a prawn jalfrezhi, accompanied by a warning that it was quite hot. Both Chris and Tom assured him that hot was fine, so he didn't press his case and the moment passed. As far as he was concerned he'd fulfilled his duty to the customer.

Mistake number two. Never ever go for hot in an unknown Indian restaurant. Although the starters went well enough, a second after Tom took the first mouthful of his main course it became clear that the whole reason we'd made the detour and subjected ourselves to the experience that was Runcorn on a Saturday night had turned out to be an unmitigated disaster.

It was hot all right, hot veering towards 'take that, you cocky English teenager, you asked for hot, you got hot' hot. Even though we diluted his dish down with my more medium-strength prawns the damage, both physical and psychological, had been done. His fork didn't travel to his mouth more than four times the entire time we were in the restaurant, which was once less than the number of times that he made it to the Gents. All in all, the whole event was yet something else to take from the day which we could only chalk up to experience.

Still, if he had it bad, Tom's experience was nothing compared to the suffering of another punter whom presumably he got to know quite well during his visits to the loo. His problem was a disastrous, choking cough, of the kind which made you fear for his life, such was the intensity and length of each bout, to say nothing of the frequency. Whether or not this had been caused by the food it was hard to say, but it certainly did something for the general ambience, sending out signals which shouted out the single word 'Avoid!' to any passing stranger.

Back at the boat uncharacteristically early, Tom decided to stay outside and try his hand at fishing, using a rod we'd found tucked down the side of one of the bunks. Although the evidence of the afternoon suggested that this stretch of the canal might have been a favoured spot, inevitably he got nowhere. It had become clear some time before that this was not going to be his night, but it was good of him to try. I made a mental note to challenge him to Pest later.

While he sat on the bankside taking deep gulps of the fetid local air, I decided to get on the bike to locate a phone box and check in with home. Our whole experience of Runcorn had provided a desperate contrast to the comfort and love of home and I was missing them. I also couldn't wait to share the story of the Indian restaurant with someone who I knew would appreciate it.

The feeling of movement and effort was a good one, and I took what turned out to be the long way round back into town. Once there it became clear that in the hour that had passed since we'd left the town centre the place had come alive. High skirts complemented low cleavages as the local talent came out to play. The busiest places on the high street were the cash machines as wallets were stocked up for some determined fun seeking. From the anonymity of my telephone booth, it was possible to observe initial skirmishes taking place in the battle of the sexes as more pubs and nightclubs started to boom out music in a modern example of heavy artillery fire. At least Tom had been protected from this scene, despite the fact that some of the girls looked no older than him.

The gathering atmosphere wasn't threatening as such, but neither was it comfortable. There were rules here which I didn't know or understand. If this was the future for those left behind by the new economy, then perhaps this was one thing George Orwell had got right.

Back at the boat I noticed that some mad fool had moored up alongside us, presumably in the misguided belief that there was safety in numbers. She was about the same size as us but considerably better decked out. Unusually, but wisely, the occupants were nowhere to be seen. I felt a combination of comfort and a sense of brother-in-arms comradeship, flavoured with a dash of guilt that we might have lured them to us.

Outside, the midges were biting, no doubt attracted by the stagnating water found at the end of the canal, so we went inside and turned to the promised Pest and a bottle of Chilean red. As we played, Tom's lucky streak remarkably stayed with him, his fortunes advancing in time with the steadily growing booms of the so-called music outside. Even Chris, with his catholic tastes, was ready to concede that this was less true music than a soundtrack for chemically induced mood alteration. By the time we were ready for bed mistake number three had become all too apparent.

Where we had tied up was a case study in how not to choose a mooring spot. The high wall on the opposite bank seemed to be acting as a giant receiving dish for all the 'music' from the surrounding nightclubs. Once the signals had been collected, the wall bounced them back in some kind of mangled code straight towards us. For a time Chris was able to counteract the effect with tapes from his not inconsiderable collection, played on our small battery-operated radio cassette. When the time came to turn in, however, the only question on our minds was how long the steady thump-thump-thump, with occasional muffled counterpoint from a DJ, could go on. We weren't optimistic.

In fact, we reckoned it all stopped around midnight, which was an extraordinary stroke of luck, the first we'd had in Runcorn. In the meantime the Chilean red began to have the anaesthetising affect it is renowned for and we balanced between sleep and some kind of disturbed consciousness. It was in this state, and under the protection of darkness, that a fresh set of unwelcome sounds started.

At first they were short poots, suppressed and somehow cut short, unnatural somehow. They were irregular at the beginning, but in time became more liberated, as if their source was becoming more confident, more devil-may-care. The finger of suspicion during this time pointed quite naturally, and incontrovertibly, at Tom, he being the one amongst us who was surely suffering the most. No doubt he thought it was one of us.

In time the poots became parps, more throaty and determined: they had something to say and they didn't care who heard it. All three of us kept our counsel, certain that sleep wasn't far away and anxious not to enter a game of claim and counterclaim, even less a battle. After all, who was to say that there was only one source, or indeed that any one of us might not, in time, welcome a cover for our own contribution?

Sleep, however, was impossible under these conditions. It was not so much the fact of the matter but the longevity of each bout and, in time, the other-worldly, hardly human quality of them. Full-throated raspers flowed with the ease of mercury on glass, continuous raspberries which seemed to defy ordinary capability. Any respite was only temporary, and was always cut short with a real cheek burner, perhaps accompanied by a counterpoint of high pitched screamers. One second the note would be bass, another decidedly treble, petering out in time to a couple of full stops.

Questions detached from their answers plagued my mind. How could anyone keep going that long and with such intensity? What was likely to be the cumulative affect? What if the fumes hit the pilot light? Goddamnit – were the windows open?

It was then that it dawned on me. These sounds were beyond the capacity of man to produce. With a hint of triumph, I announced my discovery to the assembled company. 'It's the boat outside,' I told them. 'It's rocking on rubber fenders – really,' I added belatedly, lest I had been thought the culprit. But answer came there none. Both father and son had fallen asleep. I didn't trust myself to speculate on the content of their dreams.

Once again the first to wake, I decided to give Runcorn a second chance. Mistake number four.

Daylight did little to enhance the impressions formed the night before. My first stop was to see if it was possible to trace the previous line of the canal, beyond the road bridge. I found a way through via an underpass and lined myself up with what I thought must have been the course of the canal. Through an effort of highly focused concentration it was just about possible to imagine its original course. A line of white terraced cottages clung incongruously to the top of the hill, their position possibly signalling the top of the ten-lock flight, and a road beyond headed off in a straight line slightly downhill in the direction of the river. All there was to see was a rather run-down housing estate called Dukesfields, which was hopefully named after the Duke of Bridgewater. The presence of a local called the Duke of Welling-ton rather denied this hope, however, although I was pleased to see that a Brindley Street still existed and wondered if this was a better indicator of the course of the canal.

This part of my quest complete, I wandered back into the town centre, at a little more leisurely pace than the previous night. My wanderings confirmed that we had indeed been in the centre. One possibility that had been voiced the previous evening had been the thought that we had somehow stumbled into a particu-larly unsavoury area on the edge of town. Nope. The local shops were dominated by funeral directors, solicitors and insurance brokers, a more dissolute band of brothers it being hard to imagine. Otherwise, retail outlets were either selling cut-price goods in permanent sales or had given up altogether, their windows boarded up protecting nothing but glass.

Some attempts were being made to invest in the area, mainly with European money, but one was left with the impression that it would take more than a few fresh railings and smoother roads to revive the place: it needed an injection of confidence. Runcorn was at the end of the line, in more ways than one. Only the imposing road bridge linked it to the real world, but even that was hard to find, judging by the motorist who stopped me and asked the way. To be fair, the streets were surprisingly free of debris from the night before. The towpath was not, as we'd feared, littered with used needles, and I didn't sight a single condom, but these were pretty backhanded compliments. As I turned round and headed back to *Florrie* a shop alarm went off and for a moment I feared a sudden cavalcade of police and being hauled in for questioning, being the only person on the streets at that hour. No one took any notice, however, and it continued its insistent clanging, fading only when I turned a corner. I knew the silence had been too good to last.

Back at the boat everyone was up, so we cast off and left Runcorn and its canal to its clan of gathering Sunday fishermen, arranging their kit as an efficient secretary might sort out her desk at the beginning of the day. As we pulled away, one of their number rather rapidly reclaimed part of the towpath we'd been moored up against, suggesting that Tom might have had some luck if he'd persisted the night before. That or we'd infringed some ancient squatting rights.

The trip back to the main line of the canal was slow as we passed through more and more fishermen, who seemed to gather like flies round a piece of rancid meat. At one point a row of around twenty rods stretched out before us in a straight line, and it rose in a wave as we passed below, like the swords at a guard of honour, albeit a reluctant one rising and falling in a wave. The likely presence of fish was confirmed by the presence of whole squadrons of herons lining the banks. On the outside sedate and beautiful, I watched from the front as one of them suddenly took off in our path and chased off a troublesome magpie. Whether this was for sport or from a defensive necessity I didn't know, but what was clear was that strangers were not welcome. It was a cue we were happy to accept as we gratefully passed Preston Brook Marina at the head of the branch and took a sharp right-hand turn to resume our delayed passage south.

Heartbreak Hill

I'll concede that the entrance to Preston Brook Tunnel comes up on you quite quickly, but, let's face it, it is on the map and is, therefore, predictable. All you have to do is look. And maybe I'm old-fashioned, but in my book the presence of a red light usually means you have to wait. From the relative calm of the front of the boat, where I was catching up on the omnibus edition of *The Archers*, I had taken comfort in these two considerations. I was therefore more than surprised to find ourselves ploughing merrily into the tunnel's mouth where I could quite clearly see the lights of oncoming traffic in the murkiness ahead.

I stood up and shouted at Chris, who, to his credit, immediately appreciated his dilemma and began to reverse, which inevitably threw the boat into all sorts of trouble. Within seconds we were describing a perfect forty-five-degree angle and chugging backwards fast into the side of a particularly shiny blue seventy-footer with a couple of likely-looking lads playing chess at the back. Either they hadn't seen us or they wanted nothing to do with us. I decided to be charitable.

Whatever the truth, we were clearly on our own and it was with a combination of fending off, forward and reverse chugging and heaves on the rope from the shore that we managed to moor up in the only available space, at the head of the queue. All this was achieved with what could only be regarded as a reasonable dose of opprobrium from the boats emerging from the tunnel. Frankly, it was embarrassing. At the first opportunity I slipped off from the front for a nose around and a leak, preferring to leave any mopping up and mollifying to the character who'd brought it about. It seemed that not even *The Archers* was sacred when you're the nominal skipper.

The ground above the tunnel was wooded, with the occasional house tucked away. A little way into what would have been the course of the tunnel I spotted the first black and white iron milestone of the Trent and Mersey Canal. On the left it proclaimed PRESTON BROOK on the right SHARDLOW 92 MILES. Shardlow on the Trent marks the end of the canal, but our course wasn't going to take us the whole length. These milestones were to be our constant companions for a few days.

Once the red light had turned green I regained charge of the tiller without any challenge and waved the other boats in the queue through, tucking in at the rear of the procession which resulted. Preston Brook Tunnel was by far the most hair-raising of any of the tunnels we'd so far encountered. It was not as straight as Foulridge, or indeed anything like as even in its proportions. Even with the advantage of a full set of lighting, and craft to follow, the concentration required to negotiate a passage was absolute. Despite our best efforts, the bike, still padlocked to the roof, took a bit of a hammering from the low ceiling. As with most collisions, each crash sounded worse than it actually was, the acoustics of the tunnel amplifying its effect.

Back in the daylight we paid a price for our enforced courtesy at the other end of the tunnel, as we waited in the resulting queue for the shallow stop lock which marks the official beginning of the Trent and Mersey. This lock was even more seemingly pointless than the one at Hawkesbury Junction we'd done on my Inland Helmsman's course, with as much water lapping in over the top as came through the paddles. I was glad the Lockmeister hadn't been there to see it: to operate it would have been below his dignity.

The presence of a lock at all, however nominal, was of course a novelty after the lock-free days of the Bridgewater. In cricketing terms, however, this was but a loosener for the thirty plus to come, the section into Stoke which some used to call Heartbreak Hill, and after our experience some still will. Furthermore, of the seventy-six locks on the Trent and Mersey, sixty-nine of them are narrow, providing a fresh experience for us. In theory at least, narrow locks should be easier, the boat being effectively wedged in, but as we were to discover this is only true if your boat is full length. We were about to learn a whole new art.

The Trent and Mersey, or T & M, is the canal most associated with James Brindley, although, as now seemed to be par for the course, he died before it was completed. The T & M no longer joins the Mersey, but it is ninety-three and a half miles long – enough to justify its original name of The Grand Trunk. This title reflected the original ambition to join up the two sides of the country, as well as the fact that the canal eventually linked up with no fewer than nine (count them!) other canals or significant branches.

The Grand Trunk was in itself part of an even grander plan to create a Grand Cross linking the four main navigable rivers of England: the Trent, Mersey, Severn and Thames. Once again, the ambition and ability to get things done of this pre-industrial age says a lot about the people and prevailing confidence of the times. The T & M epitomised the potential of canals to boost trade and reduce prices, and in so doing their critical role in providing the motive force behind the industrial revolution. Benefits ranged from the ability of the Potteries to access china clay from Devon and Cornwall (brought by sea to the Mersey) to the ability gained by farmers to gain stable manure from the cities (I wouldn't have fancied being behind a convoy of boats carrying that), as well, of course, as irrigation.

The T & M was also literally the cause of the death of James Brindley which I promised to talk about much earlier. This took place in 1772 when he was carrying out a survey on a branch line to Leek and Froghall. He got wet in a heavy storm, slept in his wet clothes, woke with a chill and died a few days later. It seems somehow fitting that water was his undoing. At the time of his death he was involved in literally dozens of canal projects, largely because his was the only show in town. It's difficult to think of a modern equivalent of James Brindley, which says much about his role in establishing the canal system. Some comparisons can be made perhaps with Isambard Kingdom Brunel and the railways, but the modern age doesn't seem to have thrown up a similar personality. Possibly a case could be made for Bill Gates and the computer industry, but we were using the word personality here.

The canal was completed in 1777, although there were various branches added to it over the years. It was enormously successful. After fifty years this success bred competition, which in turn brought forward a response, with a major upgrade of the locks of

Heartbreak Hill and the cutting of a fresh Harecastle Tunnel, supervised by Thomas Telford in the 1820s. This was built in only three years, an incredible achievement considering the technology of the day. Both of these landmarks were on our itinerary over the next two days.

Our immediate experience of the T & M was of a canal much narrower than either the Leeds and Liverpool or the Bridgewater, as well as a lot more undulating, certainly more than the latter – a classic Brindley characteristic. These two features made steering much trickier than before, with turns disguising surprises, especially as the traffic levels seemed to swell, mainly with holiday hirers, and I was reminded of Keith's advice about three classes of canal user. The early stages of the canal were also quite high up, the prelude to Heartbreak Hill itself, giving good views of the River Weaver below. This was a much more substantial waterway, with the locks to prove it, capable of taking seagoing craft.

The landscape also became noticeably more cultivated, as we hoped the people might be after Runcorn. The canal itself certainly seemed tidier somehow, with low-slung, picture book white stone arched bridges, the sort of image which if reflected perfectly in the water made an ideal photograph.

Two more tunnels followed hard on each other's heels, the Saltersford, 424 yards of twists and unpredictable roof heights, and Barnton, which although longer at 572 yards was much easier to negotiate. With both of these there was no policing, the only option being to plunge in and hope that anyone coming the other way would hear you coming. With our Lister we reckoned we had a natural advantage. With each there was a queue waiting to come through at the other end, so presumably our tactics worked, with most of them probably surprised to see the size of *Florrie* as she emerged, certainly relative to her noise. The thought of having to reverse out of either of these had not been one any of us had wanted to contemplate seriously. Reinvigorated after our recent travails, we began to relax again. Most alluring of all was the prospect looming after Barnton of an opportunity to see one of the highlights of the canal system: the Anderton boat lift.

The Anderton boat lift is one of the marvels of the canal system, with old canal hands falling into two categories: those who've done it and those who haven't. Like people who've climbed the Leaning Tower of Pisa, the former are currently a declining privileged class as the lift is currently out of commission pending a major restoration, funded in part by lottery monies, in my view just the sort of project these funds should be directed towards.

The lift links the Trent and Mersey with the Weaver Navigation, and was constructed to ease the trade in salt and pottery (raw materials south, finished goods north). Anderton was a transhipment centre for these cargoes, a role which required a heavy investment in salt chutes and tramways. Partly due to increased demand, and partly out of fear of the threat of potential competition from the railways, the Weaver trustees settled upon the notion of a boat lift as a way forward. Although the idea was not unique, the execution of it was, and it took three years to build.

The lift was completed in 1875, but its fate was sealed by an accident just seven years later when one of its cylinders burst and a tank with a boat in it fell into the river, thankfully without loss of life. The chain of events this accident set in motion was to prove fatal, however, although it was to be a slow, lingering decline, a bit like the action of the lift itself. The steady action of the corrosive effect of the alkali plant opposite the lift, coupled with the constant presence of salt while the lift was out of operation, had a damaging effect on its hydraulics.

These were eventually replaced, with an electrical system put in the place of the original steam engine, and further enhancements were made, allowing the lift to carry on providing an improved service for commercial traffic right up until the mid-1950s. Thereafter, as with the canals as a whole, pleasure craft took over, and it was an accident with just such a vessel in 1981 that precipitated its eventual closure in 1986. Since then, much of the original structure has been removed to relieve the framework of the weight, and although it retains much of its original majesty, it currently looks somewhat emasculated.

I'd written these words on the back of research carried out before we'd set off and was pleased to find that none of them were contradicted by the story of the lift given by the enthusiasts who manned its visitors centre. This was based out of an old cargo container, possibly one on 'permanent loan' from the World Freight Centre. In fact, my version was more backwards looking, focusing on the history of the piece rather than its future which, given developments in the intervening few weeks, they were naturally keener to emphasise.

Although the words were never actually uttered, it was clear that the enthusiasts were within a hop, skip and a jump of reaching their target for matching funding. This, combined with the monies from the National Lottery, British Waterways and English Heritage, would see them realising a dream which many of them during their association with the lift must have despaired of.

Their confidence was palpable, with a date of Easter 2001 being given as the time when they hoped to be carrying vessels down into the river once more. I hoped they were right, for their sake and for the sake of the canals as a whole; a working lift would be a major attraction. I was more sceptical as to their timing, and suggested to Chris that making these dates would represent almost as great an achievement as building the thing in the first place. His response was not to be so pessimistic, or words to that effect, so we agreed to differ. Time will tell.

As for the structure itself, it's difficult to say. The description of it as emasculated seemed a fair one, although it is difficult to know having never seen it in all its virility. It is certainly an impressive sight, reached by a clamber down a steep and, in our case, rather muddy bank. It brought to mind something out of a science fiction story, *The War of the Worlds* perhaps, or one of those giant walking things with gangly legs from *Star Wars* (an AT/AT, my son informs me), such was its other-worldliness. It was impossible to get close enough to it to gauge its state of repair; we just had to take the enthusiast's word for it that it was structurally sound, although a cynic could doubt it.

A better view could be had from the top, where the two tanks were clearly visible, one full of algae-ridden green water, with both sporting a degree of pond life that in normal circumstances would probably be protected by a European directive. Chris and I were just considering how it might work and how many craft you might get in each tank when Tom demanded the key and rushed off. I looked at my watch – four o'clock. Manchester United's first game of the season was about to kick off. I bought an Anderton boat lift tea towel for *Florrie* as my contribution to the fund-raising effort and we got on our way.

The rest of the afternoon was spent meandering through what turned out to be salt country. We failed to spot any of the nodding donkeys pumping out brine promised in the Nicholson, however, which was a shame as I had been looking forward to the incongruity of a Texan wildcatting scene in deepest Cheshire. Less obvious evidence of the salt activity was plentiful, however, with a number of pools created on the edge of the canal where the ground had collapsed. Navigation through these stretches was noticeably different, the water being much deeper, and the concentration required harder if one was to avoid being drawn towards the clearly marked dangers offered by the mini-lagoons opposite. Thoughts of bottomless pits loomed large.

Our early start now began to make itself felt in our legs and arms, and we consulted the book to find a convenient mooring spot for the night. Chris had offered to cook, so we didn't need to be anywhere within reach of civilisation, but we opted for Middlewich all the same. Our reasoning was sound, as this represented the start of Heartbreak Hill. His match over (it was a disappointing draw), Tom had consulted the book and gained some inkling of what was to come. A rest up and early night seemed sensible. Our previous strategy with locks of making a quick getaway having stood us in good stead, we wanted to be ready to plunge straight in in the morning.

One lock stood between us and Middlewich, unusually for the T & M a double, and as we approached we could see that it was occupied and that the gates were beginning to close. We blew our horn to stop them, but the gates kept on closing, so we blew it again twice, almost angrily until the folk up ahead finally clocked our meaning. Our new partners were rookies, going through their first lock, and they did not seem that happy at the prospect, especially the lady of the party, who had a bit of a face on her. Being old hands, we were happy to help, and soon both boats floated up an extra five feet one inch and exited without incident, or indeed thanks. Once through we immediately started looking for somewhere to stop.

With Chris declining offers of help with the cooking – like me he liked to operate a one-man kitchen – I once again got on my bike and went exploring. In common with the canal on which it sits, Middlewich came across as a neat and tidy sort of place, with subsidence from the salt works having restricted development over the years, something which may well have worked to the town's advantage in many ways.

I quickly realised that Middlewich had also been quick to exploit its position at the beginning of the next flight of locks by becoming the focus of a lot of hiring traffic. This was perhaps only fitting, seeing as it was the place where the cutting of the Trent and Mersey Canal began. It also lay at the heart of the popular Cheshire Ring. Taken together, these facts, coupled with its obvious picturesque qualities, meant that it was something of a magnet for narrowboats.

Historically Middlewich had always been the epicentre of the local salt industry. This began before Roman times, but kicked into gear when they colonised, even calling the town Salinae, meaning salt works. They also apparently paid their troops in *sal dare*, which is reckoned to be the origin of the word 'soldier', and who am I to argue?

After a brief exploration I stopped by the boat to check progress with the meal and then walked up the canal to assess the lie of the land before the next day's obstacles. Forewarned was forearmed. The first sight to grab me was that of our companion of an hour or two before in the double lock, apparently stuck on the exit of the first of these locks. At first we thought he was stuck on mud, but it soon became apparent that his position was more precarious, both physically and personally. The middle of his boat was pivoting on the cill. He asked my advice ('Get the hell out of there, even if it means reversing'), but luckily he didn't start to follow it as the water bailiff arrived. In his mid-thirties and accompanied by a young child, he seemed to ooze confidence. The muscles on his right arm were testament to regular windlass duty. He radioed on ahead to a disembodied assistant further up the system, and between them they gauged the situation.

'It's not your fault,' he reassured the hirer, 'this sometimes happens if the water gets low. The fisherman down there' – he indicated somewhere below the lock with his thumb – 'reckons it's been gushing out all day. Just sit still and we'll soon have you out.' Despite his air of confidence I could see that the lady of the boat remained distinctly unamused, and she said so.

'Never again,' she muttered. Her husband kept a practised silence, they'd clearly been married for some time as he knew when to keep his mouth shut. You didn't have to be Einstein to work out whose idea a boating holiday had been.

'Oh, don't say that,' replied the bailiff, slightly offended, or was that my interpretation? Either way, I don't think it helped when he added, 'Believe it or not, you wouldn't be the first to sink in that lock,' adding as if as an afterthought, 'but don't worry, you're a way off sinking yet.' The problem was, no one knew how close 'yet' was.

Not much liking the sight of blood, I took my cue to glance down at my watch and make tracks, leaving strict instructions for them to make sure they'd sorted it all out before the morning. We never did see that boat again, but we made it through the first lock the next day without scraping against anything unusual below. Before returning to my warming supper, I treated myself to a peek round the corner to assess what was to come, and was immediately struck by a sense of déjà vu. The balance beams merging together, the winding gear, the challenge, the pain. As I took in the scene a mallard emerged from the water and waggled its rear at me with exaggerated hip movements and obvious disdain.

In the event, our own progress through these locks the next day was itself depressingly slow, our first real experience of congestion. Eventually it took us two hours to get through four locks, a situation not helped by various manoeuvrings by boats in and out of a dry dock between locks one and two, at the elbow of a sharp ninety-degree bend. Not only did this mean waiting, but it meant fresh boats coming in and disrupting the natural order of things and upsetting the water levels as the dock swallowed and disgorged water. Somehow, it didn't seem cricket.

These locks, like those that followed, were singles, cutting down the possible rate of progress by half. Our policy of trying to be at or near the front of the queue had paid off, however, as by the time we finally got through there was a line of eight boats waiting.

A stuttering progress followed, with more evidence of salt and its importance to the area, something I'd never previously appreciated was such a big deal. A steady drizzle once more set in, obscuring our view of the local landscape and establishing a vision of streams of brine sliding down the hillsides. A pause to get through Rumps Lock just outside Middlewich afforded a spectacular view of the British Salt Works plant. Two alpine peaks of the stuff dominated, one outside, exposed to the elements (begging the question: why doesn't it simply dissolve?), with a dirty brown tidemark about a third of the way down, the other hidden under cover and noticeably cleaner. I hoped that it was salt from this pile which eventually made it into my water softener at home.

The descent into Kidsgrove was slow but never tedious as we worked our way steadily through the locks of Heartbreak Hill. Although they were all singles, they came in pairs, even though at times one of the pair was damaged. The drop on some was precipitous, on occasions up to ten feet, nearly double what we'd got used to. A sign on the first of these pointed out that they were 'fast' locks and that due care should be taken, which turned out to be not so much a statement as an understatement. The rush of water from the gate paddles on these locks was extraordinary, forming a bubbling cauldron of water within the lock itself which would alternately push *Florrie* back and then suck her forward as it drained, making her uncontrollable at times. At the same time, the rush of air being sucked down the vents made a ghostly shriek, which must have been something else at night when the water was worked twenty-four hours a day.

The best approach we discovered was to keep her as close to the back and out of harm's way as possible. We couldn't afford to let the engine cut out in these locks as during our descents maintaining this position would require bursts of forward power followed by reverse. This technique was only discovered as a result of trial and error. In the first two or three locks we found the boat being sucked forward with such a grip that not even our Lister in full reverse could stop the forward momentum. At one point, Chris rammed the front gate with such ferocity that I momentarily feared for their hinges. If the gate had collapsed the tidal wave that would have followed would have swamped both boat and driver, either that or he'd have surfed the wave in some kind of surreal way. We later comforted ourselves with the consolation that basic hydrodynamics made this impossible, but as neither of us could claim this as a specialist subject the consolation was somewhat ephemeral.

On another occasion the gate was hit so hard that a chain went on the front rope fender, making it sag sadly, causing *Florrie* to start wearing a frown. As a Rammer is not a rammer without its rammer, we stopped and effected temporary repairs. At this point, Tom was so cold that he took a shower in order to warm up, something Chris informed me represented a red-letter day. It was during this stop that Chris came up with the idea of painting shark's teeth on the bow of the boat, a thought I filed away under 'possibles'.

For most of the descent, however, we were on our own, with only occasional meetings with people coming up the hill. On one such occasion someone described *Florrie* – with, I add, a hint of intended affection – as a 'bit of an old tub'. Whilst not an altogether inaccurate description, I didn't quite know what to feel when it was offered. Hurt, or perhaps a little proud. I decided I preferred to describe her as having 'character' and to leave it at that.

The canal's sides at this point in its course were raised due to successive reinforcement over the years, giving at times excellent views of the surrounding countryside, especially when the rain finally stopped. Purple swathes of rosebay willowherb waved us through along the canal to the next set of locks, which tended now to be grouped together. Chris stayed at the helm for most of them while I helped Tom work the locks. The canal boater's enemy slipped in on one, however, when I threw the windlass down on the ground in order to open a gate. The cruellest bounce imaginable followed as it landed on its head, jumped into the air, spun 270 degrees and leapt off into the lock in a lemming-like fashion.

That was the last I saw of that.

As luck would have it, we were only one lock away from a shop, and I jogged on ahead. Canalside shops are a retailing phenomenon in their own right, one yet to be fully researched. They have a sort of end of the pier quality about them, a curious mixture of things you didn't realise they still made and the highly practical, if somewhat out of place. The boating stuff, occasionally referred to as 'canalia', invariably included some brightly painted wooden spoons and corkscrews, as well as sets of Nicholson guides. Another staple was brass wall plaques saying things like DON'T FLUSH ANYTHING DOWN THIS TOILET THAT HASN'T FIRST BEEN EATEN or WORK IS FOR PEOPLE WHO DON'T GO BOATING (true in my case). There were also plaques for each of the canals or highlights of the canals, such as significant junctions or a tunnel, and I'd started to collect these, screwing them to the side of the airing cupboard door as a memento of what I called the Grand Trek South.

We moored for the night at Rode Heath, between Sandbach and Kidsgrove, the prospect of going on being an uninviting one. The next morning we would be staring down the hill confident that we had only twelve locks left to do, a manageable prospect. We had broken the back of the hill, but we didn't want to break our own by continuing.

The sight before us once we'd moored was that of Rode Heath Rise, an ex-brine works that had reached its heyday in the late 1770s, but had actually kept going until 1926. Any hope of reviving the works collapsed along with the pump house in 1932 and the area has since been reclaimed in a rather touching way by the local populace as a nature reserve. A sign nearby recounted how children from the local primary school had planted wild flowers in the fields, adding some colour and variety to the stunning views beyond. All this made it a greater crime therefore that the local dog owners felt it within their rights to let their animals defile the paths through the reserve and the towpath itself.

Having got so far, we decided we deserved a good meal and hoped that Rode Heath could deliver it. Our opening shot was disappointing, with the canalside pub's chef being off sick (we hoped not with food poisoning), leaving a choice of chips or chips, despite the sign outside which stated GOOD FOOD SERVED ALL DAY. Back to definitions of 'good' again. This not being what we wanted, we walked on and found the Royal Oak, an establishment that served one of the most professional pub meals I've ever had. While Tom was satisfied with scampi and chips, I had a delicious breast of duck and Chris a shank of lamb, a lump of meat so huge it made my digestive system gurgle in complaint just looking at it.

As luck would have it, a charity pub quiz began as we were waiting for our food, and despite his protestations earlier in the week that he hated such events, little mumbles started to be heard when we got to the music round. We were all tired, and I could feel the Debenhams effect coming on.

'Eddie Cochran?' came a mumble.

'What?' I asked, looking round, wondering where the voice had come from. My eyes once more grew heavy.

Two minutes later: '1969'.

'Pardon?'

'Jeff Beck,' came the mutter, 'it's on the B-side'. It was then that I put two and two together and turned to see the beginnings of a smile forming on his face. He was in his own world. Tom and I left him to it and discussed Watford's chances of staying in the Premiership the coming season.

'"Please Please Me".' Chris again, not a demand from the waitress (unfortunately).

With the meal nearly over, Tom noticed through the window that the Royal Oak's sign offered only food rather than the more grandiose prospect of good food at the pub down the road. While waiting for the bill this information allowed us to promulgate an inverse theory of marketing: the more preposterous the claim, the less likely it is to be fulfilled. Shades of Dr Goebbels. It was one worth bearing in mind for the rest of the journey. We called it Tom's First Law of Pub Food in his honour.

With food resting in our bellies and alcohol on its way to our livers, well, mine anyway, Tom and I came over all mellow and reflected upon what we'd achieved over the previous two days. Runcorn seemed like an age ago, literally another world. The locks on the hill had exorcised its ghost, with the rush of water on each acting as yet a further flushing away of memories which, we agreed, we'd look back on one day and smile at. Not yet, however. The journey since Middlewich had been hard, but satisfying, the scenery varied and interesting. We could see how the hill had got its name.

'Heartbreak Hotel' came the voice from the other side of the table, a smile of smug satisfaction on his face.

That was our cue to leave. We decided to take it.

Who Turned the Lights Out?

All three of us were sitting at the front end of the boat eating a sandwich lunch when the acrid perfume of the toilet sanitising liquid began to wash over us in dense waves. It resembled a cross between a highly concentrated form of deodorant and the sort of smell often associated with hospitals. It looked as if I'd been overdoing the advice of the youth at the White Bear Marina back in Chorley.

Although neither of these smells is repulsive on its own, when they are distilled down to their purest form and mixed together some kind of chemical reaction must occur, the end result of which is barely less offensive than the smell they are trying to disguise. It was clear that a trip to a boatyard was needed sooner rather than later; the alternative was to throw yet more liquid down, and there was a general consensus against this. So much for the proud boast in the boat's instructions that the turd tank will accommodate (nice word that) six people journeying for a week. Either we had been particularly prolific, a possibility after Runcorn, or the tank was shrinking – a horrifying prospect.

We had successfully polished off the remainder of Heartbreak Hill when this happened and were waiting eagerly in the queue for the Harecastle Tunnel. In a sense, we were now in forbidden territory in that we weren't meant to have got this far on this leg of the journey. Such had been our rate of progress, however, that I'd been able to revise our original plans to moor up at the Red Bull Flight three locks short of the tunnel and had phoned ahead to book a fresh resting place outside Stoke. In terms of distance this made little difference, but when assessed in terms of time these extra couple of miles or so had the potential to represent the best part of a day. Besides, three locks and straight into the longest tunnel on the system would have been a bit of a baptism of fire for Annette, the scheduled crew on the next leg.

Not only were there the intervening locks, which in themselves could be unpredictable, but the tunnel itself was an unknown quantity, with some element of queuing inevitable. Besides, our experience at the White Bear had reinforced to me the value of mooring at a boatyard in case of emergencies. When we made the mouth of the tunnel there were indeed queues, so we took our place behind three others.

The water at Harecastle had taken on a Worsley-like bronze hue, adding to the sense that what we were about to experience was something special, possibly something mystical. The Hare-castle's reputation had preceded it, with mentions of it made during discussions en route with fellow boaters usually being accompanied by a rueful grimace or a shake of the head. Not only is it the longest tunnel on the system but also, perhaps, the most remarkable.

The present tunnel isn't in fact the original, but it is no less special for that. Almost inevitably, it had been James Brindley who'd had the vision to build the first Harecastle Tunnel, a task which took eleven years to complete, although I don't think he did it on his own. Completed in 1777, the tunnel provided a vital link in the vision of a Grand Trunk across England. Once again, as with all the engineering marvels of this time, people came from miles around simply to look at the tunnel when it opened. Not that there could have been much to see, only a yawning mouth in the rock. At a time when the height of technology for the farmer in the field was probably a scythe, these feats must have seemed prodigious, almost miraculous, Brindley and his men either fools or geniuses.

As I said, the tunnel wasn't that much to look at from the outside. The entrance to the original tunnel was still visible, although choked with weed and sealed off with bars. It seemed inconceivably low, a kind of toytown tunnel, built to scale rather than to be of any practical value. Although it was tempting to speculate on average heights in the days before free school milk, this can in fact be explained by the slow sinking of the tunnel over time. This in turn was a result of the mining subsidence that eventually led it to be closed, although this was after it had seen in excess of one hundred years' service. Before then a second tunnel had been built, with the two operating in tandem, one for boats heading north and one for boats heading south, for the greater part of the nineteenth century.

The new tunnel's entrance was equally unremarkable, offering an oblique angle of entry with white painted stones ringing its mouth like ulcers and a sign with black writing on a white background telling you in bold capitals where you were, in case you didn't know. It stood less than twenty yards from its predecessor and was guarded by a lonely red and white lifebelt. This was presumably for the odd cow which might be passing. A slim striped pole was strung across the entrance indicating that entry was forbidden, something it struck us they could have done with at Preston Brook. To be fair, it was difficult to see what else you could do other than deck it out in neon. Like so many of the amazing sights on the canal system it was understated rather than exploited, which was, of course, a considerable part of its charm.

The second tunnel's progenitor was no less illustrious than the first, being the great Thomas Telford, who in 1822 was asked by the Trent and Mersey Canal Company to make his recommendations to relieve the considerable traffic congestion which had built up around the tunnel by that time. This had come about partly due to the success of the canal and partly because of the slow and cumbersome process of legging through the tunnel. At one and three-quarter miles in length this must have been an awesome prospect. Telford's conclusion was that a second tunnel was needed, and amazingly this was achieved in only three years.

The new tunnel had a towpath, since removed, which must have been a challenge in itself, leading a horse down in the dark along a narrow path with no apparent end in sight. This was to be our route, to be completed under our own steam without the assistance of either horses or the electric tug that did the job for you during the forty years up until 1954. We waited in ignorant anticipation.

These days over six thousand boats a year use the tunnel, mainly pleasure craft controlled by tunnel keepers who keep in contact by telephone and regulate the flotillas which go through together. To paraphrase the Falklands War reporter, they count them all in and count them out again. This is no doubt an improvement on the previous system, which was based on trust, traffic going one way from dawn to noon and the other from noon to dusk. This system must have generated a few anxious moments every day around lunchtime.

As we sat waiting our turn the sky lightened and, with a mischievous sense of irony, the sun found a patch of blue sky and shone down brightly on us. It was our first sight of it for over three days and we were about to go into a tunnel. We took bets on whether it would still be there when we emerged forty minutes later. As we did so boats began to emerge, their helmsmen displaying a range of emotions, from relief to insouciance. The one thing they shared was a need to shield their eyes from the brightness of the light. They were an odd bunch, including an old working butty and the usual assortment of hire craft. The last to emerge was crewed by a brightly dressed bunch of alternative types, complete with cat and a slightly perfumed haze which for a moment swamped our own lingering odour. They had clearly decided to heighten their experience of the tunnel.

Our cue came quickly, and we had to cast off in a hurry as the boat behind us was already gunning its engine impatiently. The tunnel keeper told us to keep our distance and then we were in, the last vestiges of light fading rapidly as the dark enveloped first the front and then the sides of our field of vision. The boat ahead was nicely visible, a target at which to point our bow, its cabin doors open, throwing out a decent beacon of light. Because of this it was impossible to see whether the end of the tunnel was visible or not, although I doubted it. As such, we couldn't gain any information on how straight or otherwise the tunnel was, let alone an appreciation of its length.

Wary of drips, one shower a week clearly being his quota, Tom stayed at the front and flashed a torch over the roof of the tunnel ahead. The lights from the cabin provided further illumination. Although weak, more of a faint and slightly eerie glow than a beam, this provided a useful third dimension of information to the helmsman, as I attempted to keep *Florrie* from bouncing against the edges. Even with the towpath removed, the room for manoeuvre either side was slight. How the boats managed when there was one was beyond me; they must have been drawn through the tunnel like a cork from an extended bottleneck. The light from the cabin was strong enough for me to make out a series of bright orange numbers, two feet tall, painted every twenty-five yards, which counted up our progress every few seconds or so. Although useful, this also helped to remind us that there are a hell of a lot of twenty-fives in three thousand when you're travelling at two miles an hour.

By prior arrangement, I took the tiller for the first few minutes, with Chris due to take over after a while. Once I'd settled into a rhythm of concentration I found the opening stages fairly easy to handle, although as always it was necessary to guard against complacency. Small kinks in the tunnel's direction, coupled with occasional drops in height and narrowings of the walls, meant that you couldn't afford to lapse into automatic pilot for a second, the tunnel having the capacity to catch you out at any moment.

Chris duly took over and I went forward for the view. This was the first time I'd had the chance to take in this angle in a tunnel and it had an eerie quality of its own, a bit like being in a moving cocoon. Before long though the boat started to weave around a bit, so I went back to check all was well. It wasn't. Chris was having trouble coping with the changing perspectives, something we later put down to his not having his glasses on, and he handed the tiller over with obvious gratitude. He promptly advanced to the front, where he helpfully stood up in the hatchway, thus obliterating my forward view. With the echo of the Lister against the tunnel walls it was impossible to tell him to sit down.

He went in when the roof fell by yet another few inches, and I soon found myself crouching to get a reasonable enough view to steer by. I had now struck a groove of intense concentration, like I had in the Foulridge an aeon ago, and, conscious of the boat behind me catching up, pushed the throttle forward without incurring any penalty. Almost despite myself, the metronomic chug of the engine vibrating against the tunnel walls lulled me into some kind of semi-catatonic state, and my mind began to wander. As the end wove into sight, the leading boat having disappeared some time ago, the tunnel seemed to assume a womb-like quality, our re-emergence into the real world a little bit like the emotion a baby must feel when being born. The

Harecastle would not have represented a difficult birth, however, merely a protracted one. The passage was in fact almost disappointingly straightforward, or possibly I was now becoming something of an old tunnel hand.

Perhaps it was just as well that the end was in sight, or who knows what further stray thoughts may have emerged from my deep subconscious. I made a mental note not to share these kinds of thoughts with my wife on the next leg, her knowledge of psychology may have made me a candidate for the couch.

As the numbers on the tunnel walls reached the high two thousands, I braced myself for the expected sunshine, only to be predictably let down. Although bright, so bright in fact that I later sought out my sunglasses, the sun was notable only by its absence. Normal service had been resumed. The sun had shined and we had missed it.

The tunnel's fascia at its southern entrance was even less imposing than that at the other end, a case of if you blinked, you'd miss it. The canal immediately straightened out and then looped around the industrial hinterland of Middleport. We were now entering the extended collection of towns usually lumped together as Stoke-on-Trent. Each of these is distinct, like London boroughs, but the names of them are usually known only to locals.

The landscape immediately assumed a more industrial feel, not unlike the mills in Lancashire, although not quite so imposing and with the important distinction that many of the factories were still active. Through open windows we could see unglazed pottery, line upon line of matt white dinner plates and bowls waiting to be dipped in glaze. I fancied I could also feel some heat from the ovens.

We were, of course, entering the Potteries, a much derided and rarely understood part of the country defined both by what it does (hence the name) and by what it isn't. It isn't, for example, Manchester, but then again neither is it Birmingham, although many make the mistake of thinking that it is. The Potteries has its own distinct history, local colloquialisms and culinary offerings (although delights was probably pushing it, if memory served me right).

Critical, in the context of my quest, was the fact that they were defined largely by their industry, which had been, and to a large extent remains, dominant. Many places in Britain are associated with a single industry, most of these because they sit on top of a natural resource, be it tin, coal or indeed salt. Rarer are the cases where the natural resource is more to do with skills, although examples do exist.

The Potteries is one such example, with the very growth of the canal system through this area led partly by the possibilities they provided to access the much better quality clays via the sea, although the availability of local coal cannot be discounted as a major contributory factor also. After all, it was Josiah Wedgwood who cut the first sod of the Trent and Mersey. The growth of independent potteries, congregating skills and resources into one spot, in many ways provided the blueprint for the later industrial revolution.

For these reasons alone I viewed the Potteries as a must on my itinerary. There was another reason too though, and that was more emotional. Annette and I had met at the local university and, although we'd both enjoyed our brief stay there enormously the early 1980s had not been a happy time for the area. Part of me was keen to know if it had managed to cheer up a bit, and another part was keen to revisit old stomping grounds and even go to places I'd always meant to go to, but which had somehow been passé to us as students. All in all therefore, Stoke was an appropriate and deliberate staging post on the trip.

We moored up in Longport at a boatyard just after a bridge which neatly divided the two pubs of the Pack Horse and the Duke of Bridgewater. It was also just after the first of the distinctive bottle-shaped kilns associated with the Potteries, which signalled our arrival into the heart of the area. Longport was the first of the six towns to develop around a pottery due to its position at the intersection of the roads between Newcastle (under Lyme, that is) and Burslem. This still exists today as the Price and Kensington Pottery, and, along with Spode in Stoke, is one of the earliest examples in the country of a fireproofed building, which may account for why it is still standing. This too was just the other side of the bridge.

At last, after the Harecastle, the canal started to go downhill, so to speak. In other words, Stoke represented its summit and the locks for us from now on would be going down rather than up, a process that would hopefully be much easier for the person at the tiller. For all these reasons, Longport was an appropriate point to end this leg of the journey.

When I'd booked the mooring by phone, I had no idea of the sort of yard it would be, and when we got there it was immediately apparent that our berth was in more of a boat-building yard than a marina as such. And not just ordinary common or garden boats, but the top of the range, luxury end of the market. Poor old *Florrie* looked a bit out of place, like a 2CV on a Jaguar dealer's forecourt. Some of the boats on offer ran well into six figures, with one including a full air-conditioning unit because the owner's wife didn't like the smell of the canal! Crazy.

In a later discussion with one of the boatyard's staff we agreed that these were boats for poseurs, and I was reminded of the boat we'd nearly rammed on our first day in Skipton. These were clearly a breed unto themselves, although thankfully a significant minority on the system, probably because they so rarely actually moved anywhere on the water. There were other boats in the yard too, in for restoration, a fate it was increasingly becoming apparent would have to befall *Florrie* in the not too distant future.

This became all the more apparent the next day when I gave her a wash and found some rust spots under rivets in the roof. It wouldn't be long before water managed to find a way through those and from there to inside the cabin. It was therefore interesting to see the sort of work being done and also to get a feel for costs. Our boatyard friend was happy to confirm that there was always a market for boats like *Florrie*, which was also a comfort, although the prospect of us ever getting rid of her was becoming increasingly distant with each passing day. It had become easier to appreciate Linda's reluctance to let her go.

We bade a temporary farewell to our host and he turned to go.

'That's a Lister two stroke she's got there, isn't it?' he asked, pausing – a statement more than a question. All three of us nodded knowledgeably in unison.

'Thought so.'

The one major drawback from being berthed in a yard rather than a marina was the news that the gates shut at six, although we were informed that there was a fish and chip shop over the road. We were also swiftly advised that there was nothing whatsoever to do locally even if we were to escape. The disappointment this news engendered was palpable, so I sauntered up to the office and put the question in another way, only to find that there was a huge entertainment and retail complex a mile down the canal towpath at Etruria. Furthermore, someone actually lived on site and could be roused if you yelled loud enough. All was not lost.

First, however, we made a slight detour to the railway station to check out times for Chris's trip back to Wigan to pick up the car. He was most amused to discover that he'd be obliged to hail the train to make it stop (this actually happened, the train driver blowing his horn in acknowledgement). Unfortunately, on the short distance to the station he spotted a second-hand CD and record shop and both Tom and I knew that to try to persuade him not to enter would be a complete waste of breath.

While he browsed, I walked back to the boat to pick up my glasses in case we ended up going to the cinema. Upon leaving, in my haste I clicked the padlock shut before I realised I'd left the keys inside. It was at this point that the strategy of always mooring up in a boatyard once more paid off, as we spent the best part of an hour with a borrowed hacksaw removing the hasp. By this time the light was threatening to fade, but a walk to Etruria had now become a necessity to buy a new lock.

What we had been promised was only a ten-minute stroll turned out to be more like a half-hour route march, distinguished mainly by the desolation of the towpath and punctuated only by the occasional sculpture and descriptive plaques supplied as part of a regeneration project. Inevitably these had been the subject of spray paint from the local youths and half were already illegible. The walk was also marked out by the presence of the huge and actually rather threatening Shelton Iron and Steel Works, which dominated the view on one side for more than half the distance into Etruria.

The works were a series of massive rectangular buildings con-structed predictably of steel. From these buildings weird screaming sounds emanated, combined with some spectacular crashes, all from a site that you could easily have mistaken from the outside as deserted. It was as if we were listening to the moaning of ghosts from a long-lost industrial past. I thought it looked the ideal spot for a prisoner exchange or a meeting of gangland bosses, but then wondered if the prospect of visiting the cinema was getting to me.

Our destination was the Festival Park, and it was only when we got there that it dawned on me that this would have been the site of the 1986 Garden Festival, one of a series of regular such events held in inner-city depressed areas around that time. The fact that Stoke had been included in the coterie of half a dozen sites said much about its condition at the time. Little evidence of gardens remained, however, if you excluded the massive sheds of the chain store retailers. So much for creating permanent beauty spots, I reflected, pragmatism and materialism had, it seemed, won the day.

After the briefest of perusals of what the cinema had to offer (Tom had seen most of the films and didn't want to see anything else Chris and I might be interested in), we agreed that all we really wanted to do was eat and get a taxi back. Bereft of choice, we settled for a Pizza Hut, which just about summed up the 'could be anywhere in the country' feel of the place. Even the waitress spoke without a trace of an accent.

Chris got going early the next morning and I got up to do some of the essential maintenance tasks, as well as to go on a short reconnaissance for oatcakes, a local gastronomic fancy that had been one of the mainstays of my diet while at university. Eaten hot or cold, as a pancake or grilled, sweet or savoury, the oatcake is a tasty and, when made correctly, versatile foodstuff. It was also in short supply. Well, I failed to find any and filed away in my memory the need to get some on the next leg. It also proved impossible to buy a broadsheet newspaper, from which I'll leave you to draw your own conclusions about the kind of area we were in.

Jobs done, Tom and I turned our eyes cautiously to the sky to check out the much heralded full solar eclipse due that morning, although we knew we were only in for a partial obstruction. Earlier blue skies had predictably evaporated. However, this turned out to be to our advantage as dark wispy clouds skidded across the sun and allowed a perfect view of the moon's shadow as it crept first into one corner and then moved slowly across the sun's face, so that at its peak over ninety per cent of it was obscured. As predicted in the papers and radio, it went eerily quiet, and although a surprising amount of sun managed to escape around the moon's shadow there was a definite feeling of dusk about the place, with street lamps coming on and a bit of a chill descending.

Soon the opposite began to happen and normality began to flow back. Chris had returned and was keen to start the journey home. Just as we were carrying the last of our belongings to the car and carrying out the final, final checks on the boat ('Have you turned the fridge off?' 'Yes!') a boatload of Americans cruised by.

'Say!' one of them yelled, in the insistent and arrogant way I suppose they must learn at their mother's breast. I looked up, my arms quite clearly occupied with carrying a rather heavy box which politeness, as well as a pain in my arms, now obliged me to put down.

'Say, when's this eclipse we've heard so much about due to happen?'

They'd missed the whole thing! Bless them! At this point we were presented with both an opportunity and a moral dilemma. If we told them the truth, there was a real chance that they'd demand a replay, in my experience it being a belief of Americans that they had a God-given right to an experience if they want it. I paused only briefly.

'This afternoon,' I yelled back, pointing nowhere in particular 'we're further north here.' They nodded their thanks as the stern of their boat drifted by and we finished packing, finally closing the boot and climbing into the car for the journey home.

As he turned the key in the ignition, Chris turned to me and asked, 'You're absolutely sure you turned the fridge off, aren't you?' My reply is not suitable for publication.

Part Four
Annette, Peter and Edward

Dead Cats and Ducks

Few places are as vilified in canal literature as Stoke-on-Trent. Perhaps writers have taken their cue from LTC Rolt, the godfather of the modern canal system. No one can know for sure, but when he sat down to write the relevant chapter of *Narrow Boat* (called, stingingly, 'Industrial Landscape'), either his bunions must have been playing him up or he'd just unearthed an unpleasant liaison between his wife and a potter. Whatever, when it came to Stoke, he did not hang back. His approach to the town, which was the direction we'd be leaving by, he described in most unflattering terms as desolate and sombre.

Rolt was a purist, however, railing against the undoubted ugliness of mid-century industrialism and the disorientation of a society that he and generations before him had felt comfortable in. This vision was not dissimilar from John Major's famous description of matrons riding past on bicycles drinking warm beer, or whatever it was. Ten years after Rolt's visit the Clean Air Act was passed, a measure which made a considerable difference to Stoke and its proliferation of inner-city factories, the smoke from which was said to have the capacity to blacken out the sky for days on end.

That said, the case against Stoke has lingered. John Liley, for example, in *Journeys of the Swan*, which gives a record of the canal system during its nadir in the late 1960s, never tired of describing the variety of junk that repeatedly fouled his boat *Swan*'s propeller in the town. The only good thing either had to say about the place was that these scenes were relatively compact and got through quickly.

I was ready to make up my own mind, however, even though, and it hurts me to say this, my own solitary experience of the canals in Stoke had also been unremittingly depressing, if not downright nauseating. This had been in the early 1980s when the canal remained a depository of filth and litter, a place generally to be avoided. I'd been given a lift into the city centre and was making my way to the station on a route which took me past the canal. Although the water was still in use, it was clear that progress was difficult, as I could see by observing a still working butty which was clearly struggling. The boat in question was manned both fore and aft by burly blokes, the former armed with a pole, which he was using to punt the boat down the water, the latter with a paddle which he was using to give some kind of steerage and momentum. This lack of assisted motive force was presumably to avoid the sort of propeller damage Liley had experienced twenty years before.

All of a sudden, the one at the stern dipped his pole athletically a yard or so wider than his regular rhythm, making an action like an American Indian paddling his canoe. At the time, the splash he made as he did so had clearly demanded my attention, and I found myself turning sideways just as he heaved hard and catapulted a dark spherical object down the length of the boat towards his colleague. A scream rent the air, hardly a male sound at all, as the object hit the side of the deck and seemed to cling for a second before sinking back into the water in a kind of cartoon-like slow motion.

The next two sounds defined a stark contrast of emotions as the perpetrator laughed a throaty chuckle and the victim added further to the general unpleasantness of the water's condition by retching his lunch into it, leaning forward on his oar to make sure he missed the boat's side. Meanwhile the dead cat, for that is what the object had been, bloated and maggot-ridden, continued its slow progress northwards. I hoped to God things had got better.

The case against Stoke therefore was a fairly compelling one, even if Rolt was amused by the sight of a warehouse full of chamber pots which I'm sure was hilarious. I'm glad it wasn't all misery for him, however, as the area carried many good memories for me during my time at university around there. On reflection though, these had little to do with the city of Stoke itself, which generally we had avoided. We'd used Newcastle for shopping and Hanley for entertainment. In fact, my overriding memories of Stoke were of boarded up shops, rain, people with heavy shoulders and unsmiling faces and grime, always grime. Not totally unlike Runcorn, in fact, and that wasn't an experience I was keen to repeat.

But Stoke was where *Florrie* was, and we had no choice now but to go through the place. The challenge therefore was to see how much it might have changed, to see how it had fared through the further depression of the rest of the eighties and the subsequently slightly better years that had followed. One thing was for sure – it couldn't have got any worse. Surely?

This leg of the journey, which was going to be broken into two parts, would be the last. This alone, I reasoned, as once more and finally we journeyed north, would alter its character, as the countryside and people would steadily become more familiar, less alien. More importantly, the nature of my crew would mean that this leg would be very different from the others. Up until now I'd been the undisputed skipper, the person whose suggestions had generally been accepted without dispute or argument. I had been both the agenda setter and the master.

Now I was going to travel with Annette, my wife, and after that with Annette and our two small children, Peter and Edward. The words 'fish', 'of', 'kettle' and 'different' all sprang to mind, although not necessarily in that order.

Annette. The same Annette whose only experience of a moving canal boat to date had been a mainly disastrous few hundred yards at Skipton. This total lack of experience was something which astounded those we got chatting to over the next few days. Their reaction led us to think that, yes, maybe this should have been something we should have considered further before buying *Florrie*, but at the time her purchase had been as much to do with making a statement about changing lifestyles as the practicalities of cruising. Unfortunately it was these very practicalities, partially tasted and tested, which were looming large. It all added to the frisson of excitement that was flavouring the anticipation of this leg.

When we arrived I could see that *Florrie* was exactly as I'd left her, the remarkably light cobwebs a reminder that it had only been a week. One day there's a lovely little research project for one of these quasi-academic institutions on the attractiveness to spiders of steel canal boats. On making our reacquaintance it became immediately clear she was listing quite alarmingly to starboard, something everyone at the boatyard seemed keen to point out to me. However, I happened to know the problem was less water in the engine compartment than a desperate need for a pump-out. The poor girl had been sitting there with her legs crossed for a week.

We unpacked and Annette set about rearranging everything inside the boat, replacing the perfectly logical storage system I'd evolved over the two previous legs of the journey into something much more opaque, but which she, and she alone, would understand. The net effect of this action would be twofold. First, she was going to assert her authority on the boat, creating a domain where she would reign supreme and, second, in a by-product of this, she would gain a position of power over me as I'd be unable to find anything I needed from that point on. I didn't stop her, however, recognising this as a female trait, fighting it would be to fight nature, and experience told me it was much better to roll with it.

In a highly gender-specific kind of way, I busied myself around the engine, pretending I was doing something useful. My good intentions were rewarded when, to my considerable relief, the engine started first time. The familiar sound filled my ears, followed two seconds later by the scent of diesel smoke. We let slip the ropes and pushed the tiller to the left. Almost immediately we were occupying the centre channel in splendid isolation and heading towards Stoke city centre. After a couple of minutes of fresh air, Annette seemed happy to go back down below and draw up a shopping list of things we might need. Unaccountably, the first thing she put on the list was polish.

As we made our way, memories lodged deep in my databank began to stir. These were buried much deeper than the superficial recollections of our hurried walk along the towpath a week before. Although Annette and I had known each other when at Keele, we had not really been in each other's social circles, let alone 'walked out' together. As such we each brought with us our own portmanteau of memories. Most of these we had shared over the years, although the traffic was necessarily one-way in the joy or frustration of recollection that they brought. As we were to discover, however, other memories were shared, notably the underpass to the centre from the railway station and the overall feel of the place which I've already described.

As we passed through the centre, it became immediately clear that mooring up in Stoke isn't something that crosses many people's minds, least of all British Waterways'. There were no obvious visitors' moorings and the couple of times we made a pass for the towpath we were rebuffed by shallow water. Within minutes we were in danger of reaching the by now familiar panic of passing right through the town, missing it altogether. After the build up we'd given it, this would have been a shame, so we took our life in our hands and, after one of the most inelegant approaches I'd ever performed (hardly a textbook example for my new crew), we roped up untidily opposite a complex of retail warehouses. We locked up, kitted up and prepared ourselves for a stroll down memory lane.

One of the first things we saw triggered an immediate shared memory, one of the unfortunately named PMT buses. Although this in fact stood for Potteries Motor Traction, a name which evoked quaint beginnings, this acronym had always stirred up visions of irritable buses, a sort of 'I said there'll be another one along in a minute – all right!' kind of reaction. Following its path, we were pulled into the town centre, something it's not always easy to know you've reached when you arrive by canal without the confirmatory comfort of road signs telling you when you're there.

Our first impressions were that the town's fortunes had indeed picked up since we'd last visited. Although to describe it as prosperous would be pushing the limits of credulity too far, it clearly wasn't anything like as depressed as it was during our time there. Second impressions were of the plethora of pie and cake shops, which seemed to occupy every third shop frontage. If we'd been deprived of our watches it would still have been easy to tell that it was lunchtime. Everywhere people were either buying or eating pies and pasties, often as they walked, or occasionally sitting down on a municipal bench. The variety of pies was astounding, not just meat but vegetarian, and not only standard English fare but tikka masalas, madras and stir-fry. As our own stomachs were beginning to gurgle, we had no choice but to join in the fun and settled for a sit down in an outlet of the Three Cooks chain.

All three of the cooks seemed to be there, one serving the takeaways, another the eat-ins and a third kind of milling around, on a sort of lunch break judging by her reluctance to get involved in the action. The news was bad. It was one o'clock and clearly there'd been a rush on pies. I had no idea that demand could have been so unpredictable. Only one was left, which I was deputed to eat, and jolly good it was too, even if I had declined the proffered gravy, which I'm now sure was part of the local pie-eating experience. It wasn't too large, but was certainly hot (too hot!) and filling, especially as it came with a mountain of chips.

On leaving I noticed a sticker on the door which stated that the shop was a member of a scheme to report truants from school, and this seemed to be a good summary of the sort of place the Three Cooks was. Somewhere you could linger in the warmth and switch off from day-to-day troubles surrounded by the always comforting smell of fresh baking and the sound of other people's chat. We left before the Debenhams effect took hold.

Wandering round the town we were also reminded of the impression we'd gained twenty years ago of the overwhelming friendliness of the locals. People were invariably polite, keen to please and helpful. Despite the inherent warning offered by the truancy sticker, throughout the few hours we spent there we never felt in any way threatened or uncomfortable, despite walking through some decidedly dodgy areas. Although their town might not have always appeared in the peak of condition, there seemed to be an inner pride in the place. Despite my fears, Runcorn it most definitely wasn't. Thank goodness.

After a while, I began to get restless, mindful of the fact that we'd completed only just over two miles and Stoke, for all its particular charms, was not a place we wanted to stop in for the night. We therefore made for the nearest supermarket, a Co-Op, and proceeded to fulfil as much as we could of Annette's shopping list.

It was when we had finished packing our bags and were receiving our change that it happened. The woman on the till passed me my coins, smiled and uttered the immortal words 'There you are, ducks' before moving on to her next customer.

Ducks, pronounced dooks, through pursed lips, a word which was almost whistled rather than expelled. Oh, how that word brought back memories. Only in the Potteries is it used so freely, a sort of local equivalent to the Scousers' 'chuck', the Geordies' 'bonny lad' or the Londoners' 'mate'. Every Tuesday morning at university a middle-aged woman would rattle her pass key ostentatiously in our bedroom doors and burst in announcing 'Do your room for you now, ducks?' regardless of who or how many were in the bed, for Tuesday was sheet-changing day.

Shopkeepers, bus drivers, in fact anyone uses it, with one exception: half the adult population, the men. 'Ducks' is a term of endearment reserved exclusively for the female of the species, although they use it freely to men and women alike. Not once have I heard a chap use it; it simply isn't conceivable.

As we retraced our steps to the canal, just when I thought I'd taken in all I possibly could of the Stoke experience, a final surprise lay in store. Somehow, on our approach, we had missed a genuine oatcake shop. Not just a shop, but an upfront oatcake manufacturing plant. An amazing machine was depositing three cowpat-sized splodges of mixture on a hot plate, moving up the line as it did so. Within seconds, before our very eyes, the mixture turned into the honey-coloured article and was scooped up by a white-coated and hair-netted baker. Incredibly, and it really was astounding how she'd managed it, Annette had never had one before, so we bought a round dozen (not a baker's dozen, to my disgust) and made our way back to the boat.

Once under way again, we worked our way through what was an undeniably industrial landscape, although no worse or better than many I'd seen on the journey so far. The only surprise was the paucity of bottle kilns, and I was glad I'd stopped to look at the one in Longport. I'd read that those that remained were mainly scheduled monuments, but there must have been a cull at some point before this ordinance, and we saw no more than five or six during our entire passage through the town. Some factories remained open, sporting famous names familiar from the china section of a department store. The fact that they were open and clearly providing meaningful employment, even possibly pleasure, to the final customer was, I thought, a source of credit to the town.

It didn't take too much chugging to ease our way back into the countryside. Our arrival was confirmed by a gaggle of threatening-looking geese who jerked up suddenly from their contemplations and honked their disapproval at us for disturbing them as we passed. Inside the boat Annette had moved from putting the shopping away to polishing. What she was polishing I didn't dare ask and put it down to some kind of instinct to mark her territory, like a cat. After all, this chugging lark was a new experience for her and she probably felt a need to create a familiar environment.

Back amongst the fields it was good to look at cows rather than bricks and mortar. At one point, a herd of elegant-looking Jerseys lined the bank, craning their necks desperately to get a drink of the chocolate-coloured water which lay just beyond their reach. Those that had realised the futility of this task were making do with scratching themselves on the barbed wire. Elsewhere, heavily laden elderberry bushes were dipping their heads in salute to the slow passing of both us and of summer itself.

I continued to toil manfully at the tiller, my shoes leaving a dancing manual trace of white footprints on the back of the boat, a legacy of the clay in the towpath soil back in Stoke. Already that landscape, so derided by Rolt and others, seemed a memory. For us the experience had been a positive one, and I am happy to register here one vote in favour of Stoke in the annals of canal literature.

Approaching Trentham, we once again had the opportunity to peek into people's back gardens, and Annette emerged to join in the fun. It felt good to be together on the boat at last. I'd grown tired of retelling all our adventures and began to feel less guilty about being the only one in the family to benefit from the investment we'd made together in *Florrie*. More enjoyable was sharing the experience without having to vocalise it, wallowing in that state of semi-telepathy that comes after a few years of marriage. Best of all was simply being with my wife, my soulmate and partner. It added a third dimension to what we were doing.

As we approached Trentham the views on a micro-level were

spectacular, with immaculate bowling green lawns and intricate terraced patios, each of which must have taken months to plan and build. Marking the point at which the gardens met the canal, a line (or whatever the correct collective noun is, possibly a tragedy?) of weeping willows draped the tips of their branches delicately into the water. Their roots had invaded the bank and formed Loch Ness Monster-type hoops on the surface of the water. Elsewhere, small skiffs were moored in a scene which, taken together, reminded me of a mini-version of the Thames in rural Berkshire.

Our immediate target lay slightly beyond Trentham Lock, at Barlaston. The Nicholson had insisted that a stop here was mandatory and we were not disposed to argue, for Barlaston is the home of the Wedgwood factory and visitors' centre. I deemed I was now over the experience of the visitors' centre at the Weavers' Triangle and was keen to see how a huge multinational in a prestige industry managed the tourist angle.

The trip was important also for its connection with old Josiah Wedgwood, a man who in his day was famous for more than simply his pottery. A polymath before the word was put together, Josiah was interested in chemistry, became active in politics and was a strong voice in favour of the abolition of the slave trade. He was also grandfather to Charles Darwin, but that's another story. All of this along with being one of the prime movers behind the establishment of the canals. What a man!

In many ways, the original Wedgwood factory at Etruria was the *raison d'être* of the Trent and Mersey itself. Original factory because the current factory only came on line in 1940 and was built because mining subsidence had made the Etruria works unsafe. Wedgwood is one of the few examples of a single family with a sufficiently robust gene pool to be able to continue producing men of the required calibre to keep the business thriving through the generations. Other examples might include the Cadburys or the Sainsburys, but these remain very much the exception, although in each case the line has just about run out.

It was late by the time we got there, and, perhaps because of the mode of transport we'd chosen, we managed to bypass the main entrance and found ourselves walking through the back corridors towards the focal point of the attraction. In true Stoke fashion no one stopped us; indeed, we were smiled at and waved on our way by the security guards, grinning like monkeys. For all they knew we could have been carrying a bag of explosives, or maybe even worse, a bull for example.

It was with something of a shock therefore when we emerged from a locker room and suddenly found ourselves in the midst of a series of demonstrations of the potter's art. A number of craftsmen and women were arranged around a square, quietly getting on with their work, but happy to stop and answer questions when asked. Some were working on the famous blue and white Jasperware, with its neo-classical portraits on unglazed pottery. Others were working on jewellery or hand-painting ceramics with an enviable dexterity. Along one side a potter was explaining how to throw a vase on his wheel. Although this was a trick I'd seen performed many times, it retained its mesmeric quality as his hands gently caressed a shape out of the light brown material which was really little more than treated mud. Also fascinating was the art of the woman who managed to fashion recognisable flowers out of strips of clay, the skill lying as much in the speed with which she did it as the knowledge of what to do and how hard to press.

It turned out that the centre was in its last hour of opening and, despite our trying to pay, approaching the cashier from behind, much to her consternation, we were told that there would be no charge. As we wandered, we noted particularly the attention paid to meeting the needs of Japanese visitors, who on the evidence of our own eyes made up a considerable proportion of the total. This included the translation of anything official into their native tongue, adding a layer of indecipherable hieroglyphics to every sign from the entrance to the loo. This was something I'd only seen once before at a tourist site in this country, at Haworth in Yorkshire, home of the Brontës, and it struck me that the two places seemed to share some common characteristics in a link with a kind of dreamland England. For me the most attractive ware was the more contemporary, and it was satisfying to see that the company is a sponsor for the very best in young design talent, the local college understandably being a magnet for budding designers from all over the world. The company was justly proud of its achievements in marrying art with commerce.

Rushing through the inevitable shop, or as much as it's possible to rush in a china shop, we were left with a final rather surreal image, that of a Japanese shop assistant whose grasp of basic English was clearly rudimentary at best. She was clearly there to learn 'on the job,' and the thought of her, a few months down the line, handing out change with a valedictory 'There you are, ducks' was more than I could handle.

It was five o'clock, quite clearly knocking off time at Wedgwood, so we tried, unsuccessfully it turned out, to retrace our steps, eventually finding the boat where we'd left her just past the Oldroad Bridge. As we left the grounds, the sides of the level crossing at Barlaston Halt came down and an electronic peep-peeping sound echoed all around. What seemed like two seconds later an intercity Virgin express train thundered past at over one hundred miles an hour, dragging us back into the last year of the twentieth century with its urgent rattle and Doppler 'neeee-naw' as it disappeared behind some distant trees. Little did we know then that this was to be the start of a long association with Virgin Trains.

Stoned Again

Oldroad Bridge the next morning was, quite literally, a picture, so I captured it on film. Brilliant blue skies above, verdant foliage hanging over the bank, and a perfect mirror image of the stone semicircle on absolutely still water. I took a few more snaps and watered the nearby nettles before opening up *Florrie*. We'd been joined during the evening by a couple of other boats, which we were to see much more of later as together we climbed through the Meaford flight of locks.

All forms of boat life were there, including a floating artist, who presumably specialised in watercolours. One or two hire boats were moored near to us, but further down were others which a few telltale signs betrayed as belonging to the breed which spend half a year at a time on the water. Solar panels on one of these seemed to blend in perfectly with other paraphernalia on the roof such as the odd log for the fire and highly decorated plant pots, one a painted enamel bucket.

The circular windows on one boat were protected by a star-burst of crochetwork, a sort of spider's web woven with wool, the total effect of which was of an intricacy it was beyond my creative capacity to even imagine designing, let alone executing. A roofscape of different ventilation devices pulled the eye down the parallel lines of the assembled boats – mushrooms, witches' hats, square tin tack heads, all shapes were there, releasing their invisible fumes into the air. We could have done with an extra one of them ourselves back in Runcorn, I mused quietly.

The air itself at that time of day could probably best be described as being crisp, and a few lungfuls were enough to kick-start my day. As always, however, once up I was keen and willing to get going. Things were different for Annette. In many senses the holiday was now starting in earnest for her, and she had yet to fall into any discernible routine. I could sense that she had entered the decompression phase of every break when problems of work and home life have to be cast aside and the more simple priorities for the day ahead have to be sorted out. From having to decide how best to juggle departmental budgets, Annette's most pressing decision had become which of the variety pack of cereals she should open. It was a tough one.

Once we got going she became determinedly restless, clearly looking for things to do, having moved on from simple polishing to the cleaning of windows, something I'd previously managed with a squeegee mop and some canal water. I knew that it was simply a phase she had to go through and left her to it. Besides, I concluded, somewhat conspiratorially, the Meaford flight of locks would soon give her something to think about. Up until that point the locks had come in singles and this was a series of four – a nice little loosener for the four which would soon follow in Stone.

We'd both slept like logs the night before, although we each recalled the noise of the level crossing going on through the night, accompanied by the rush of yet another intercity train. More pleasing had been the alternative dawn chorus we'd enjoyed, that of geese honking up above as they flew in their chevrons to goodness knew where.

As we moved through a series of meadows, the landscape we began to pass through was dominated by lines of threatening electricity pylons, accompanied by severe warnings to fishermen on the towpath to avoid casting their lines at the risk of death. A diagram of someone being struck down, apparently by lightning, although it could have been a malevolent fishing rod, vividly illustrated this possible outcome. We kept an eye open just in case. Despite their usual obstinacy, the fishermen seemed to have got the message as the banks were deserted. The stretch that followed was also marked by continued proximity to the railway line, which we seemed unable to shake off. Every now and then, obscured from view, yet another Virgin express would thunder past and scare the living daylights out of us, appearing from nowhere like a jet fighter buzzing the ground.

Despite a promising beginning, within an hour of starting off the sun had been swallowed up by thick fluffy clouds, which didn't augur well for the rest of the day. I made a mental note to make sure my waterproofs were on hand. For the third or fourth time that morning I asked Annette to pass up the Nicholson so I could plot our progress. Something about my apparently obsessive need to know where we were struck her as vaguely trainspotter-like behaviour, and from that morning she took to calling the guide 'Nerdy Nicholson' or Nerdy for short. I had the last laugh however as my consultation was confirmed as the familiar black and white checks of a lock gate hove into view. Annette dutifully armed herself with a windlass, but as it turned out we were destined to wait before making our way through.

Some weeds had got stuck in one of the gates, jamming it open and making progress impossible. These weeds were a good example of the sort of sub-rainforest-type vegetation that grew in parts of the canal, being thick and almost bamboo-like, with long whip-like lime-green leaves. Where they grew they proliferated, a telltale sign often being huge piles of them stacked up on the side of a lock, slowly rotting away where they'd been left after being fished out.

We waited patiently by the towpath, gripping *Florrie*'s centre rope gently and resisting the temptation to join the growing crowd of experts who had gathered to offer their version of the solution to everyone's dilemma. It was whilst we were waiting that we were able to make the formal acquaintance of our fellow travellers, the boat up in front and the boat behind. The latter was being piloted by a young Geordie couple, giving Annette the chance to converse with a compatriot in that strange lilting patois which is often imitated, but rarely completely successfully. They were on a week's holiday and were thoroughly enjoying themselves, it seemed, although the woman of the pair confided that it had taken them some time to 'chill out'. I could confirm that they'd seemed to be doing all right the night before, when the last I'd seen of them was them sitting on the back of their boat polishing off a bottle of white before disappearing into their cabin at a disgustingly early hour.

They reported a few mishaps, but then again too few to mention. Except for one incident when they'd managed to trap their boat broad beam across the canal. Extraction from this predicament had been made difficult by the fact that a huge branch overhung the middle of the boat preventing access to their boat hook. They never told us how they got out of it, which was a shame as at that point we were still hungry to learn any tricks going.

Luckily the boat in front had the answer, for it turned out they'd offered a tug out. Another couple, although considerably older, if not quite yet into the retirement arena, they spent quite a few weeks a year cruising the system, their boat being jointly owned with another family. I was curious to know how well this worked, as it was an option we'd considered, albeit briefly, for *Florrie*, and it seemed to be a fairly common arrangement. It turned out that it worked well for them. They had been in two or three consortia, as they grandly called the arrangement, and it was their view that they had a natural life cycle to them, usually connected to when someone sold on a share and disrupted the original balance, which seemed to make sense. We were reassured that we'd done the right thing by *Florrie*, to whom we were now beginning to feel quite protective. Certainly the notion of sharing her was one we found hard to entertain.

Just as we were all beginning to contemplate tying up and having a party, everyone was getting on so well, some idiot managed to free the weeds from the lock gate and it was back to business. We'd been waiting an hour, but it had been an hour well spent, these chance meetings being part of the serendipity of canal travel.

With a logjam of traffic well established, progress was slow and not improved by the fact that the locks had become singletons rather than pairs, as they had been on Heartbreak Hill earlier on this canal. Eventually, however, we passed through and, as was often the way, we lost our new-found friends in the system.

The approach to Stone, our next major destination, was reminiscent of that to Trentham, with more willows innocently tickling the water's surface. Of all the places we'd visited so far on the trek south from Skipton, Stone exhibited the greatest pride in its position on the canal. Our first inkling of this came as we entered the town, with a large sign placed in a spot where only canal boaters could read it, which proclaimed WELCOME TO STONE, BIRTHPLACE OF THE TRENT AND MERSEY CANAL.

This claim is based upon the fact that Josiah Wedgwood hosted the first committee meeting of the new canal company in 1766 at the Crown Hotel in the town, a meeting at which, you've guessed it, James Brindley, was appointed surveyor for the proposed canal, still known then as the Grand Trunk. On reading this I began to wonder if he wasn't so much a man as a franchise. Given their goodwill towards the canal and canal users, it seems churlish to dispute this claim, so I won't. Besides, the town lies at almost the exact midway point of the canal, and therefore, by reasons of geography if nothing else deserves some place in users' hearts.

Stone's prosperity over the centuries has owed much to its strategic location transport-wise. It lies on the road from London to Chester, on the canal of course, and also, as we knew to our chagrin, on the railway line. In the mid-nineteenth century the town was well known for its trade in shoes, employing sixteen hundred in the trade before a series of strikes and unrest following the introduction of new machinery sparked a decline. Perhaps one of Stone's most unrecognised claims to fame is as birthplace to the charmingly named miller Richard 'Stoney' Smith. Mr Smith it was who invented 'Smith's Patent Germ Flour,' which went on to become Hovis, so called from *hominis vis*, Latin for the strength of man.

It is possible that old Stoney would be able to recognise much of the place if he were able to come back. These days, the population of 12,500 support what appeared to be a busy market town, with the main high street a thoroughfare of both main-stream and more esoteric shops. Perhaps the open arms it throws open to canal boaters is explained in part by the fact that twice the town's population passes through it a year on the water. Small lock-up cabinets, accessed via a British Waterways key, carried useful booklets and maps and illustrated a town trail designed to encourage visitors to stop and spend some money. Hats off to them, we agreed; it was nice to be welcomed and also to reward effort directed on your behalf. We were happy to stay, a while.

The only blot on Stone's canvas was a drunk punk, shouting the odds from the towpath. He was well gone. Sloshed. Drunk. Bladdered. Stoned. Naturally everyone ignored him, except for one fellow boater who perhaps cruelly, but equally possibly correctly, suggested that today was clearly benefit cheque day. This scene was an odd one for two reasons, firstly because it was so out of character with the general air of gentility otherwise surrounding us, and secondly because I didn't realise that punks still existed. His torn shirt and cockatoo haircut looked so, well, passé.

Gradually, during our couple of hours in Stone he moved through the cycle which starts with abusiveness, passes through incoherence and ends in collapse. Eventually he was swept up by a posse of police cars whose inhabitants were either grateful for something to do in this otherwise apparently law-abiding town, or were anxious to remove any sign of dissent from the carefully created picture as soon as possible.

We had an ulterior motive for stopping in Stone, and had timed ourselves to reach the centre for lunch anyway. This wasn't the first time I'd been there. One night while at university, while waiting for a loo at a party actually, I had found myself idling flicking through the phone book, as you do. Much to my drunken surprise I had found someone sharing the family name, based in Stone. Although on the surface an unremarkable discovery, when you come from a close-knit family with an unusual surname such things take on an importance those with more ordinary names, like Stoney Smith, probably find it hard to grasp.

That night, still in my cups, I had written to this family to introduce myself, and a direct consequence of this was that two weeks later I found myself on the train to Stone for supper. The recipient of my letter had consulted the family oracle and keeper of the family tree and had found that we were second cousins, or at least I was with his daughters. Not ever having fully understood what a second cousin was, or indeed how to become removed from them, I had been happy to take him at his word on this.

It is only with hindsight that one can reflect upon the generosity and the viscosity of blood over water that brought this ordinary family to invite an awkward student whom they didn't know from Adam, and probably had little in common with beyond a shared surname, into their home. The evening itself turned out to be pleasant if unremarkable, with just a few tinges of surrealism.

The husband of the house, Stephen, had been older than my

own father, a portly and distinguished man who looked as if he had made a decent career in the civil service. We'd gone for a couple of jars while his wife had prepared the dinner, a move which was later to prove Stephen's undoing as he fell asleep soon after we ate, leaving the pursuit of small talk to his wife, with whom I shared even less in common.

The idea of the pub, although on one level appealing, had been a disappointment at the time, as Stephen was the father of two rather stunning looking daughters whom I was happy to remain in the company of. Although I knew sex with a relative was distinctly bad form (but wasn't it all right with cousins, be they first or second and regardless of whether they are removed?), the fulfilment of a little student fantasy had seemed distinctly on the cards. It wasn't to be, however, and once Stephen had been roused from his slumbers I was walked back to the local station for the last train home. On leaving, I was glad I had made the trip, but had known that this was probably both the first and last time we'd ever meet.

What an opportunity to prove myself wrong! If for no other reason than to see how the daughters had fared, even though I was certain neither of them would still be sporting the Corble name. Alas, it was not to be; there was nothing between Corbett and Cordell in the phone book, the only conclusion being that this branch of the family had passed into the history books. In more senses than one, they were Stone dead.

We took comfort by retiring to the Star Inn, which boasts a position as the oldest pub on the entire canal system, being able to declare fourteenth-century origins. As we were beginning to discover, Stone clearly had a very active PR department some-where. Indeed, the pub still carried stabling for twelve horses into the 1950s. We ate in the Canal Bar, which was both appropriate to our position and convenient for the door, as serious swaying had now begun to set in and the pub boasted that none of its various rooms were on the same level. We didn't fancy staggering around like two old sots, so settled down for a functional but perfectly pleasant snack consisting of soup and a sandwich.

After lunch we stocked up on essentials – and more cleaning materials – and did what we could put off no longer. The much delayed pump out. First signs at the designated boatyard were not optimistic, but we were reassured that our waste would be welcome if we cared to moor up beside a half-built boat covered in red oxide paint to protect it from rusting, and probably much more besides. At first we thought this belonged to the boatyard, which like most yards on this stretch also did a good line in hire boats (it was where our Geordie friends were heading, but we didn't see them), but not so. The craft was being worked on by a Welsh couple who were more accommodating than I think I would have been to having someone else's poo-pipe draped across their boat.

Like approximately half the Welsh population, this couple were perfectly charming, and enquired in their singsong accents where we'd come from and what we were up to, as had now become enshrined as the traditional canallers' greeting. Our story struck a chord and soon, as was so often the way on the canals, we were into a full-blown conversation while the tanker in the background made unpleasant-sounding sucking noises, pausing occasionally for breath.

The husband of the pair was waiting to see if he was going to be made redundant, something he had mixed feelings about. Left to his own devices, he reckoned he'd finish the boat in six months; forced to continue working and he was staring three years in the face. The project was a challenging one, and one I was sure they'd complete, but like all such tasks it was clearly begin-ning to feel quite daunting. As an example, the day before they'd taken delivery of half a street's worth of paving stones for ballast, but having placed them in the boat they'd come to realise they'd need around the same amount again.

Perhaps predictably, he'd spotted that we had a Lister and he was keen to show me his. As was the way with all of the more traditional craft, this was inside. So, thinking rapidly of suitably encouraging phrases as I went, I followed him into the shell of their boat, resisting the temptation to play hopscotch on his flooring, and was shown the Lister.

What can I say? It was made of metal and had lots of twirly bits on it like mine, except this one was green whereas mine was blue. I repeated my rehearsed lines of approval and was astounded to hear that he'd been given it as scrap and had restored it himself. To me, this was a feat beyond comprehension, and I was duly impressed. He had noted that we started our engine with an electronic ignition, and was proud of the fact that when they got going they would be starting theirs every morning the old-fashioned way – with a cranking handle. As we left I noticed that he'd left the valve lifters the wrong way round, but didn't have the heart to tell him.

Once we were ready to go it seemed as if most of the annual tally of twenty-five thousand going through Stone wanted to use the remaining locks at once, and for the second time that day we were forced to bide our time. As we were waiting, the sun found a way to outwit the clouds and soon we were back into shorts and dark glasses weather. Passing through, we passed a lock-keeper's garden which had been featured on *Gardeners' World* and this seemed to sum Stone up nicely. Neat and orderly, a place of good ideas and not shy in showing itself off to a wider world.

As it happened, Stone had a parting shot it hadn't been so willing to shout about: locks which were up to ten feet in places, which counted as deep. Annette, however, was able to demonstrate that she was more than up to the task. Like her father earlier in the voyage, she spurned my offers of help and seemed to revel in the lockside conversations with fellow travellers. She was only a Lockmeister's daughter, but she certainly knew how to...

Beyond the locks we emerged into more idyllic countryside, mirror-still water in front of us, our bow cutting a perfect V and sending out tiny ripples either side of us. Reflections of trees and bridges gave the scene an unreal aura, with the sun casting perfect black shadows which provided both contrast and relief from its heat. On the bank huge rhubarb-like leaves up to a metre across threatened to take over, but stopped short, as if they instinctively knew their place. The land was sporadically cultivated, although there was plenty of evidence of centuries of farming families, three-storeyed farmhouses being the norm, each sporting a beard of ancient ivy on their face.

Even the bridge names evoked a sense of olde England. Names like Long Meadow Bridge or Flute Meadow Bridge with Salt Bridge (actually close to a village called Salt) and Brinepit Bridge showed that we hadn't left that particular industry behind either, although we suspected that here it was conducted on more of a cottage scale. On one such bridge a gang of cows peered over the parapet, lazily chewing their cud and seemingly as surprised to see us as we were to see them. Now I'd seen it all: bovine gongoo-zlers. Occasional locks appeared, although by this time we were untroubled by traffic, the crowds of boats in Stone having once again mysteriously disappeared. These weren't in sufficient quantity to really trouble us, but enough to prevent Annette from starting a fresh round of cleaning.

Such was the perfection of the scene that we chose a spot at random and moored up for the night. It was time to spend some quality time together. Well stocked up both on provisions and sensations, we settled down for some peace and quiet. As the engine died and I lifted the hatch to reach down for the tap that would grease my nipples, the water regained its mirror-like quality. A shadow puppet reflection flapped across the surface, as if formed by two human hands. It grew larger as it approached and then, all of a sudden, a heron came between me and the sun, landing twenty yards away before tucking its wings neatly back and resuming its static position. We had become accepted, part of the scenery.

Surprises and Disappointments

Just ask Buzz Aldrin – there's nothing worse than being the second person to do something significant. By way of proof, hands up if you can say what George Anson was the second man to achieve? A clue: he was also an admiral. He was in fact the second Englishman to circumnavigate the globe, and is, as a consequence, largely an unknown quantity to everyone except history buffs and inhabitants of Shugborough Hall. We all remember Sir Francis Drake, but poor old George Anson, well…

Shugborough Hall? Well, Admiral Anson probably had some kind of premonition that he was unlikely to make it into the *Encarta Encyclopedia* two hundred and fifty years later, so he decided to take his reward on earth rather than heaven. He duly captured the beautifully named Spanish vessel *Nuestra Senora de Covadonga* whilst en route out east, having earned the gratitude of his country (and presumably a number of Chinese) by saving Canton from destruction and fire. The things people get up to when they're circumnavigating the globe.

Luckily this ship was loaded to the gunnels with treasure and bullion, and thus he laid the family's fortune by taking care of it for a while. In time, this passed to his brother Thomas and thus a dynasty was created. A considerable portion of the treasure was used to found what is now Shugborough Hall, home to the Anson family ever since, better known to us now by the title conferred upon the family head, that of Earl of Lichfield.

We came across the village of Shugborough quite unexpectedly, our ambient state the night before having precluded any serious research on what might be coming up. In fact, we were simply heading for Great Haywood Junction, where the Trent and Mersey meets the Staffordshire and Worcester Canal. Originally it was our intention to pass through, or maybe stop for lunch, but a busy lock meant we had to tie up alongside a boat moored on the forty-eight hour visitors' moorings.

Inevitably a conversation followed and it dawned on us where we were. Our new-found friend was most insistent that we stop and look around the hall. What was more, he added gleefully, there was to be a kind of proms concert that night with a fireworks and laser display, all of which would be visible from exactly where he was currently moored, he added, somewhat cockily. He was sitting and ready, and he wasn't going to shift. His boat was the canal equivalent of a towel laid out on the best sunlounger by the pool.

A house and fireworks seemed an attractive proposition, but with the children temporarily off our hands we had half promised ourselves a night at the cinema. To help us decide we asked him if there was a cinema in Rugeley, the next major centre on our route. He responded in the affirmative. He knew for a fact that there was because he'd been there himself. With this confirmation, we decided to go for the best of both worlds. A spot on the moorings had become free while we were chatting so we grabbed it as a prelude to touring the hall before pressing on for a wild night out in Rugeley. Oh, the joy of being spontaneous on the canal. Our timing was good, as by then the source of all this intelligence had moved off tourist information and passed on to the limitations his arthritis placed upon his lifestyle. Experience had told us that once these types got on to their health problems it was time to make your excuses and move on.

Shugborough Hall was reached via an exclusive footbridge over the Trent. This was just wide enough for two people, but not wide enough for a pony and trap, and had a number of triangular passing places cut into its side. Not having a pony and trap about us, however, we found it convenient. After this impressive beginning the turn into the park itself was actually quite easy to miss, although we managed to spot it at the last moment. Any thoughts of possible disappointment after this unprepossessing start were soon dispelled, as we were faced almost immediately with the impressive frontage of what is called the Mansion House. Mansion it certainly was, to describe it simply as a house would require the very best of English aristocratic understatement.

And yet, as with many features of Shugborough, it flattered to deceive, as it turned out that one of the main joys of the place was its lack of pretension. This was something we put down to the fact that the current Lord Lichfield seems a pretty laid-back, happening kind of dude, still living off his sixties wild days, oh, and the fact that he's cousin to the queen. That and the fact that a couple of untimely deaths at the end of the 1950s, when death duties were at their peak, meant that the house was transferred to the National Trust in 1960, with the park passing to the local county council at the same time.

As such, there is no attempt to over-glorify the family who, through accident of history and a bit of casual piracy, happened to live there for three hundred years. This, by the way, was the same family who at one point in their history evicted the entire population of Shugborough village so they could gain a little more privacy and erect an 'Arch of Hadrian' to commemorate George Anson's circumnavigation where the village used to be.

The current Lord Lichfield still has a flat in the hall, which he rents off the council, thus claiming to have the best council flat in the county. Some flat! It has thirty-six rooms, and not even our guide had ever been in it. We asked, but unfortunately he wasn't around, otherwise we'd have been pleased to pay our respects.

Our tour was brief, the house actually being rather compact, but we saw what we wanted to see in a little under an hour and absorbed an idea of what it must have been like at its peak without getting too footsore. My favourite feature was a door in the library which was actually made out of false book spines, something I didn't think I'd ever actually seen outside a film before. The garden too was beautifully maintained and indeed developed, with new features being added all the time; an impressive herbaceous border, for example, was less than two years old.

The real challenge to the feet came with the Museum of Staffordshire Life, which although fascinating in lots of ways was, to put it kindly, comprehensive. Every possible angle of life in this prodigious county over the previous centuries was covered, in many ways providing a more than adequate glimpse of life in rural, pre-industrial England. Exhibits throwing light on the Potteries, for which the county is surely best known, were few and far between, this not really being the focus of this particular museum. There were some photographs of the Stoke Rolt would have seen, and these did something to convey the overwhelming dominance of the small factories and the thick sulphurous smoke which at the time was more like a permanent fog. For me, these images only served to underline how much things had changed.

Although there was more to do, such as a rare breeds farm, we didn't have the time to do them, so after a break for an ice cream we decided to wander back to the boat. Besides, there's so many of these rare breeds farms these days that I seriously doubt if they can really use the word 'rare' any more with any authority. While I waited for Annette to emerge from the shop my attention was drawn to a metal ring in the courtyard. It had a diameter of three or four inches and was made out of metal about an inch thick. It looked uncannily like a mooring ring. I was about to go up and read the caption above it when an elderly woman sitting next to mè asked her husband to check it out. I gave my feet a few more seconds' rest and let him go.

'It's where they used to tie up their balls,' he shouted across the yard.

A silence descended across the courtyard. I paused to consider the implications of what I'd just heard. In the name of God, why? Was this the antidote to the rural idyll the museum had been projecting? Were the estate workers little more than slaves, punished with cruel and humiliating torture for the slightest misdemeanour? It was only after a few seconds' similar reflection that I realised he meant bulls, not balls. The relief was palpable. Despite this realisation my gait was sufficiently awkward after we set off to excite comment from Annette. As we recrossed the narrow bridge back to *Florrie* we saw a group of young boys cooling off in the river. The obvious power of its flow as they used all their young strength to keep afloat was fearfully apparent and we weren't alone in being worried for their safety.

Unlocking the Fort Knox's worth of padlocks and mortises that protected *Florrie* from unwanted violation, we nodded our hellos to Mr Arthritis. Annette and I looked at each other and shook our heads before going down below. Again using the married couple's telepathy, we'd agreed not to tell him that the fireworks were the following night.

From Great Haywood we were quickly into Cannock Chase, an official area of outstanding natural beauty, a phrase which always reminds me of an old *Private Eye* cartoon which had a motorist stopped in a lay-by ogling a huge sign which said in letters twenty feet high BEAUTY SPOT obliterating the view. Going through this stretch confirmed the growing belief that Staffordshire is a highly underrated county when it comes to rural landscapes. Although we knew our impressions were influenced to a considerable degree by the effect of the glorious weather (I suspected that many of the scenes in Lancashire for example would have been equally beautiful in similar circumstances), the essence of its charm would probably have shined through regardless. Even the railway line, which continued to haunt us, remained silent, as if the trains had been diverted, like the planes used to be over Wimbledon during the last two weeks of June.

Rugeley beckoned, however, and drew ever nearer, its looming presence signalled by the smokestacks of its power station. Although we weren't necessarily looking forward to being in an urban area again we were beguiled, the entrance to Rugeley being actually rather charming. Its distinguishing feature is an aqueduct over the River Trent, after which there is a stretch called Brindley Bank, which had housing on one side and the river on the other, providing a balanced contrast. There was little time to contemplate it however as the clock was ticking against us if we were to make a film. A glance at the Nerdy had told us that we were committing ourselves to a night in a town, Rugeley having a tendency to sprawl on a bit.

Although slightly apprehensive at this prospect – it always seemed to be difficult to know how to pick the best mooring spot in a town – we pressed on, fortified by the sure and certain knowledge that there was a cinema at the end of the rainbow. My concern was probably also fed by a nagging worry that we might be about to repeat the Runcorn experience. After all, it was another Saturday night and both towns had names beginning with an 'R'. Paranoia time.

In the end we moored up in a spot that overlooked a playing field on the far bank and was adjacent to an industrial estate on the towpath side. Although not pretty, this would, we reasoned, be quiet on a Sunday morning. Still a little concerned, and mindful of the fact that although it was late it wasn't too late to escape if we wanted to, I decided to do a recce on the bike. Once again, shades of Runcorn loomed.

One of my first findings was that there was no cinema in Rugeley. If our informant in Great Haywood had found out about the fireworks and had been inspired by our talk of seeing a film he was in for a double disappointment. I did find an arts centre and, more in hope than expectation, entered its open doors, chasing the distant signs of life coming from inside.

A boy was stacking chairs while a woman, very possibly his mother, vacuumed the carpet. I approached the boy.

'Excuse me,' I asked, 'could you tell me if there's anything on here tonight?'

He told me to wait in reception. Frustrated, I pressed on. It seemed a simple enough request. 'I just needed to know if there was anything on tonight,' I repeated.

'Reception,' he mumbled back.

'Wedding reception,' came a voice from the Hoover. 'Here. Tonight.' Her tone was one all of us usually reserve for the terminally stupid or foreigners, or in her case southerners. I passed on my thanks and headed into town. By the time I got back to *Florrie* with the bad news neither of us was in the mood to move on so, chancing fate to the limit, we settled on the idea of an Indian meal, as I'd spotted what looked like a reasonable place on my rounds. It was that or gatecrash the wedding reception.

The restaurant, it turned out, was excellent. The reputation of the Bilash clearly preceded it, because even though we arrived before seven o'clock we were lucky to get a table. Initial portents hadn't been good however, with an irritating woman announcing to the whole restaurant through her mobile phone that she'd locked herself out and would have to wait until the morning when her husband returned with his keys. Her most pressing concern was the fact that she wouldn't be able to switch the alarm on, thus extending an open invitation to anyone who knew who she was to rob her house that night. I half wished I had the address and a mobile phone of my own. There should be a law against use of these things in public places.

The meal when it came was first class, fully justifying the decision to stay over. What was more the whole ambience was soothing, once the dreadful woman with the phone had left. There was even a tropical fish tank gurgling away contentedly next to us. As we sat waiting for the bill we overheard another conversation, this time between the head waiter and the next table. This was occupied by a husband and wife and a post-teenage daughter, the first of whom was clearly something of a wine buff, while his wife was French. The issue which was perplexing them was how the restaurant chose its house wines. A reasonable question, and one I've often pondered, especially when it turned out, of course, that the proprietor didn't drink. The answer, by the way, is first, price and second, the look of the label. I suppose you deserve whatever you get if you drink wine in an Indian restaurant; surely lager is the only reasonable option?

We ambled gently back to the canal, taking in the sights and sounds of downtown Rugeley as it prepared for Saturday night. The most promising option (assuming you weren't invited to the wedding reception) seemed by a long stretch to be the disco at the Rugeley Progressive and Working Man's Club. Part of me said that the very idea of a progressive disco was intriguing enough to justify the entrance fee alone.

We witnessed a steady stream of couples in their late forties and early fifties, the men in suits and the women invariably wearing spangly tops, heading for the bright lights and growing rhythms inside the club, and half wished we were going ourselves. Only half wished though, for exposure to the open air, coupled with all the walking we'd done around Shugborough, and in particular around the museum, made bed a more inviting option, and so it was.

It being a Sunday, we started slowly the next day. I wandered into town to get a paper while Annette finished hanging a new set of curtains in the cabin before starting on the brasswork. By the time I returned she was busy sponging down the outside of the boat. I decided she was getting restless again and ergo it was time we were getting on.

Just as we were preparing to cast off, the unmistakable poop-

poop sound of a Gardner engine eased up on the airwaves, a form of motive power even more revered by the canal boat enthusiast than a Lister. Looking down the canal it was easy to see its source, a barely touched old butty, its front encased in tent-like canvas, its cabin area brightly decorated with the full array of roses and castles, the traditional canal boat theme. No one quite knows why this is, but it has become an emblem which today's boat owners seem perfectly willing to perpetuate, usually with very highly glossed paints. On a watering can balanced precariously on the roof a slogan had been painted that declared YES, IT IS A GARDNER making passers-by as well as the cognoscenti aware of the privilege they'd been allowed to share. It was as if a ghost had wafted out of the mist, an awesome sight which made my morning.

A Gardner it might not be, but our old Lister made a pretty reasonable fist of drowning out the weird noises emanating from the Rugeley power station that Sunday morning. Although this would disappear from sight from time to time, it seemed to hang around for ages, reappearing occasionally when we turned a corner, as if playing 'Boo!' Equally enigmatically, the railway occasionally reappeared, determinedly sharing the Trent Valley with the canal for as long as it could.

Annette also reappeared, apparently rejuvenated by her spell of cleaning. In a sense, the same could be said for her wardrobe, for one of the main excitements of this leg of the trip so far had been seeing which old clothes of hers I thought had been thrown out years ago would turn up next. Somehow, my old clothes always seemed to end up in the dustbin. Annette's, on the other hand, I decided, must be squirrelled away in some secret place, reappearing just as you were about to forget they'd ever existed.

According to Nerdy, the point at which we were finally to lose the power station, if not the railway, was the Armitage Tunnel, which, although located close to the village of Armitage, was a tunnel no more, its roof having been removed in 1971 because of the danger it posed. In every other respect, it retained the idiosyncrasies of a canal tunnel, in that it was extremely narrow and had a kink in it, so we couldn't see the other end and therefore if anyone was coming towards us. Furthermore, much of the sides of the tunnel remained high, further restricting our view. On this occasion, simply being loud wasn't going to be enough to scare away rivals, as no roof meant no amplification of the Lister. As elsewhere on the journey, in the absence of better intelligence, our only option was to press ahead with bravado as our guide.

More by luck than judgement, this proved to be a sound strategy, although on this particular occasion it turned out to be a close call. About three-quarters of the way through we'd spotted a river cruiser heading towards what was for them the entrance, but for us was the exit. We saw them before they saw us, however, and a peep on our horn was sufficient to put them in their place. Luckily this worked, although what the situation would have been if we'd been even a minute later simply wasn't worth contemplating.

After Armitage we homed in on Spode's Cottage, described in Nerdy as so good that booking was advisable at weekends. Although this seemed on paper to be a possible option for Sunday lunch, our recent experience told us not to believe a word anyone told us about possible places to go. We therefore felt no disappointment when a huge sign proclaimed that the restaurant was closed for refurbishment, appropriately due to flood damage. Indeed, we felt a slight air of smug self-satisfaction in our cynicism. This area was also distinguished by the presence of the famous Armitage Shanks factory, outside of which there were pallets upon pallets of toilet pans. How many times had I seen those famous words? I couldn't help but think that old LTC would have got a belly laugh out of the sight.

After Armitage three miles of pleasant cruising through heathland lay before us, interrupted only by a single lock, before our target of Fradley Junction. Soon we were to be leaving the Trent and Mersey, having completed two-thirds of its distance. I had enjoyed it as a canal, offering as it did both variety and ease of passage, even if some of the locks had been a bit hair-raising. I made a vow to come back one day and pick it up again to its conclusion at Shardlow, where the canal system meets the river system. Having watched the countdown to this mystical destination on the mileposts for so long, I thought it would be almost a betrayal not to visit it.

Once reached, Fradley Junction on a Sunday lunchtime was

mayhem. It became immediately clear that we were not going to find a mooring spot before the turn into the Coventry Canal and we therefore proceeded with caution, the traffic being bad and comprised mainly of hirers. With amazing foresight, someone had allowed a hire company to establish itself right on the elbow of the junction, allowing the thoughtful introduction of hordes of beginners into a situation already fraught with the potential for clashes. The scene assessed, we decided to proceed with caution, Annette taking up position in the front in an attempt to relay information.

As we approached the turn itself my prophecies of doom immediately materialised, with someone emerging from the lock ahead and executing the sharp right into the Coventry without any hint of what he was doing. As he swung his boat, his bow came into instant contact with another boat that was holding its position. This in turn was awaiting the return of a member of its crew who had hopped off to operate the swing bridge at the mouth of the Coventry, something that represented a further hazard to shipping.

I decided to sit it out and watch the fun unfold. Through a deft use of forward and reverse, combined with a by now intuitive use of the tiller, I was able to keep *Florrie* more or less stationary without the assistance of a mudbank below. This triumph was all the more satisfying because by now the tangle was capturing the bored eyes of the Sunday drinkers at the Swan, which was located directly opposite the junction. For once I had an audience for my skill, not my incompetence, but I was only a sideshow to a greater performance.

Words followed. At last my first real evidence of canal rage, and I was able to rise above it, an interested bit-part actor simply waiting for other really rather silly people to sort themselves out. As I knew to my cost, the experience of reversing an unfamiliar boat in front of a crowd of people is not one to be cherished. It was this that the perpetrator of the mess was now having to do, and, to my overwhelming joy, he was doing it badly. Eventually he managed to get the back of his boat lodged against the bank and some of the gongoozlers around the lock, the entrance to which he was by then blocking, kindly held him fast against it.

The boat that had been leaving the Coventry Canal then proceeded. The only word that can possibly convey its passage is 'majestically'. The boat was a seventy-footer fresh from a new paint job. Delicately petalled roses tumbled down the sides by the back window, a thick coat of varnish keeping them in their place. Nearly every rope on board had been neatly coiled, and those that hadn't had been worked into intricate designs, like the Turk's Head coil around the bow, a purely decorative touch without any function whatsoever. In fact, I estimated that unpicking it would take a minimum of half a day.

Like us, it was crewed by a couple, the wife up front and husband on the tiller. Unlike us, however, they were linked by a two-way radio mike set-up, akin to the sort of headpiece worn by a telephonist or call centre operative. Both were standing imperiously erect, the wife a stand-in figurehead, all erect and bosomy. All their communication was remote; not once did either gesture to the other by way of emphasis or to point something out for greater clarity. They were tuned into a world of their own, somewhere around fifteen hundred megahertz.

They looked, of course, complete and utter prats, and we later agreed that we wished we'd had a radio set of our own simply so we could have broken into their frequency to tell them so. What was wrong with using the hand signals everyone else used and broadly understood? These were based upon a universal language, the Esperanto of the water based on common sense, with every boat having its own variants or dialects. For example, on our boat an arm flapping up and down meant 'slow down'. A hand flicking behind your back meant 'reverse', and hands clasped to the head and violent rocking motions from the neck meant 'what the hell do you think you're doing, you stupid bastard?'

Meanwhile, the helmsman of boat stuck to the bank waved us through, a broken spirit. By now he'd probably given up maintaining any semblance of dignity and was probably contemplating a dash for the public bar. That or the Gents. As my stern passed within shouting distance of his he did manage to yell some form of thanks for my patience and I was able to be magnanimous back. I'd been there, I knew how it felt, and it didn't feel good.

In turn, we made our way through the narrow gap which was

to send us south-east towards Coventry. Although time was getting on, we motored almost as slow as we could without the engine cutting out, mindful of the procession of moored boats along the towpath, the majority of which were occupied. Then, quite out of the blue, I received a barked shout of complaint from the back of yet another immaculately presented seventy-footer. My complainant was the very epitome of the type we'd already come across: the poseur who had a boat not so much to cruise and have fun in, but to strut about in and invite people over to admire. Paranoid should someone so much as ripple the water or, horror of horrors, touch their boat, these people were a blight upon the canal. His clothes were as pristine as his boat, all that was missing was an admiral's cap. After my uncharacteristic display of patience and forbearance at the junction I was in no mood to accept admonitions from his type and let him know in good old Anglo-Saxon. With hindsight I can only think that he'd mistakenly equated volume for speed as we'd made our approach.

We moored up and made for the Swan. 'What did you say to that old fool back there?' Annette asked as we made our way up the towpath. I delayed my answer until we were alongside the old fool in question and repeated myself at an audible volume in front of his friends.

I don't know if he took my advice, but there was no sign of them when we returned so maybe he did.

The Dog's Bollocks

Our determination to get to see a film before being reunited with the children was undiluted, and by this time had become an all-consuming ambition. We consulted the map and, ignoring all published advice, made a judgement that Tamworth seemed the most likely spot. We therefore set ourselves the goal of reaching it before early evening. This decision was based upon a rational assessment of the available facts. Although as a target it looked demanding it was also perfectly possible, given a fair wind. There were no locks or other potential hazards, and if we pushed it I calculated that even making an average of three and a half miles an hour we should make it by six. Subsequently I pushed the throttle forward and made ready to dash through our first stretch of the Coventry Canal.

In retrospect I don't know what came over us. Clearly the urge to get a fix of modern visual stimulation had overridden our logic circuits. It took less than half an hour for the pure foolishness of setting deadlines and targets when travelling on the canals to be rammed home to us.

Frantic hand signals from the front as we were approaching a bridge told me to slow down. The signals had come late and the best I could manage was to wedge *Florrie* on a minor silt bank on the left hand (that is to say the wrong) side of the canal. As a consequence I found myself waving the oncoming boat through and sitting it out. Valuable seconds were being lost, but these soon escalated into minutes and in turn to noticeable segments of the clock. The first boat to come through was followed by another, rather too close to its tail, with closer inspection revealing it was in fact being towed.

This unusual sight led to another, namely a procession of craft following through like a funeral cortège, each dutifully keeping a respectful distance between themselves and the boat in front, each progressing at a snail's pace. The gap was always just enough to induce a sense in me that I might be free to proceed, but never quite enough to make a manoeuvre possible, bearing in mind I had to get off the silt first.

I lost count of how many boats passed by as my engine chugged quietly away in neutral and I folded my arms and rested the tiller against my hip in an attitude of forbearance. In this pose I adopted the role of passive spectator, studying the variety of shapes and colours not only of the craft coming through, but also of their occupants. One feature I latched on to was the variety of tiller poses they adopted. Some stood on crates or on specially built platforms, the better to look over the roof; others were tucked away neatly inside the beginning of their cabins, only the top half of their torso visible. Still others sat casually, like I tended to do, their bodies slumped down like a bag of sand, their state of relaxation aiding the forces of gravity.

In time, I found myself becoming a conduit of information, a kind of policeman on the corner, letting people know what was causing the hold-up and what their position was in the queue. If I was exasperated by the hold-up, their situation was worse, assuming, of course, that they were in a hurry.

When we did finally get going again it was clear that all my calculations had been ripped apart. There is an immutable law of canal travel which states that time lost can never be made up. The speed you need to attain, and sustain, to regain even five lost minutes is (a) simply not possible and, even if you had a fuel-injected answer, (b) not permissible. I picked up the Nerdy and, in between glances up at the oncoming traffic and water conditions, began a rethink.

In the end we agreed to try for Lichfield, fully six miles nearer, an eternity in canal terms. The book said that there was a cinema there, even though by then we were old enough and wise enough to know that this meant precisely diddly-squat. Thus reconciled, we finally got going again once the last boat in the procession came through.

At last we seemed to have lost the railway and the scene had a Sunday afternoon quietness about it so we decided to get back to enjoying ourselves, the slight aberration into self-induced stress now behind us. Once again, the sun was behaving itself and a welcoming, if slight, wind had built up. This was plucking seeds from the bankside rosebay willowherb and throwing them randomly about in the air. As they floated, they took on the appearance of the first flecks of snow of winter, catching the light as they finally fell, glistening like diamonds before they hit the water.

This section of the canal seemed unloved, in places overgrown and certainly in need of dredging near the edges, as I knew to my cost. These facts made it especially important to maintain centre channel. The neglect did have some positive aspects, with occasional patches of bulrushes and outcrops of flag irises lining the banks. The state of the canal here may have had something to do with the chequered history of the Coventry Canal and the wheeling and dealing which had gone on behind its eventual completion. The stretch immediately after Fradley was in fact cut by the Trent and Mersey Company after an attempt by the Coventry Canal to get one over on its rivals in Birmingham had failed.

The history of the Coventry is in part a history of the at times bitter feuding between these two towns to gain primacy in the West Midlands. Both were granted parliamentary approval to cut a new canal in the same year, 1768, and both, with depressing predictability, promptly hired James Brindley as their engineer. The prize they were both chasing was access to the local coalfields and a means of getting their output into the centre of each respective town.

The Coventry also had half an eye on a wider vision and had thought it had the upper hand in its alliance with the Oxford Canal. By linking with the Trent and Mersey to the north and the Oxford in the south the Coventry would become the final and vital last piece in the jigsaw which would make up Brindley's Grand Cross. They reckoned without the tenacity and financial backing of the good burghers of Birmingham, and it was the Birmingham Canal which opened first, to pretty much instant success. The battle lost, the Coventry first ran out of enthusiasm and then of money. The canal got stuck at Atherstone and James Brindley, incredibly, got the sack. Getting as far as Atherstone wasn't bad though. Although the canal stood in splendid isolation for seven years, it was long enough to provide access to the coalfields north of Coventry and it served its purpose in supplying the industry in that town with its required fuel.

The canal's proponents didn't let go of their grander visions and continued to see their strategic position to the east of Birmingham and close to the Trent and Mersey as an advantage capable of exploitation. In 1782, at a meeting in Coleshill, in a rare example of inter-company co-operation, a deal was struck to cut a new canal from Wednesbury to Fazeley. This was to provide access to the Black Country coalfields, with the new company formed to carry out this task earmarked to work together with the Trent and Mersey to build the missing link from Fradley.

This deal was also potentially good news for the Oxford Canal which, likewise, had been sitting all on its own, looking for somewhere to go, like a wallflower at someone else's party. Once again, however, Birmingham was having none of it and did everything possible to block the plans. Eventually parliament had to mediate and awarded the project to Birmingham. Although the Coventry Canal Company was allocated the work to complete the final parts of the canal, it did so rather petulantly and had to be persuaded to complete the final section between Atherstone and Fazeley, the stretch we were on now.

Thereafter the Coventry Canal endured both good and bad times. For a while it was a vital link in the first route into London via Oxford and the Thames, but equally it suffered badly when the new Grand Junction Canal shortened this journey by sixty miles. There was room for two routes, due both to the high number of locks on the shorter route and the high tolls charged by the Oxford Canal on the short stretch of the canal it owned between Braunston and Napton. The Coventry also continued to do well out of the coal trade and also from its links with other canals, notably the Ashby. Indeed, the Coventry Canal Company continued to pay dividends until its nationalisation in 1947.

Although the stretch we were on had been built by the Trent and Mersey Company, it shared none of that canal's particularly endearing characteristics. Its narrowness made it seem mean and its bridges were nothing like as neat and well preserved as those further north. I was in two minds about how I felt about the absence of the regular milestones. During our passage south these had become a source of both comfort and frustration, depending upon one's mood at the time. Sometimes the thought of having travelled fifty miles since Preston Brook generated a sense of pride – fifty miles, long way – at other times it felt puny and insignificant. Fifty miles? I could have walked it in less time! A thought which was invariably true. While these ideas filled my head, as if to prove a point an orange tip butterfly overtook us and settled on a bush just ahead.

Before too long, Streethay Wharf boatyard came into view and we throttled back for a landing. Once safely moored up we connected our water hose and bought some more gas. The yard had a happy haphazardness about it, which somehow seemed to work. We were served by one of the mechanics, still wearing his oil-smeared overalls. However, while he was very probably a wonder when it came to tinkering with engines, he was completely dumbfounded by the workings of a credit card authorising machine.

For this he called on Ray, the owner, and after a couple of minutes we made our first acquaintance with this individual's eccentric charm. We learnt later that he used to be a farmer and had given up the land to set up this boatyard. A twinge of envy shivered down my spine when I learnt this. Not only did he offer a full range of services, but there was clearly a thriving marina side to the business as well. He was one of those people for whom the epithet 'larger than life' could have been invented and he bounded around his boatyard with all the enthusiasm of a gambolling lamb. We liked him.

A complete sense of lassitude had by now completely replaced our earlier manic state (what had we been thinking?), and as the tank slowly filled up with water we took the opportunity to quiz Ray over our options for a winter painting job on *Florrie*. His immediate recognition of her as one of Randall's Rammers was impressive, as was the fact that he'd just finished painting another in its class, which unfortunately had just left the yard. He ran his fingers along her surface and under the sills, brushing off the rust which remained on his fingers as if it was a mere bagatelle.

'You've got two options with boats this age,' he recommended, 'the cat's whiskers or the dog's bollocks.'

Annette and I stole a glance at each other, uncertain how to grade these choices.

'You either strip her right down, prime her and put gloss on top, or you get one of those machines over there' – he nodded towards a collection of assorted industrial hardware which seemed to include everything from sanders through to crushers – 'and attack the worst rust spots' – and with this point he rubbed vigorously with the flat of his hand along one of *Florrie*'s flanks – 'and give her a good seeing to.' This seemed reasonable enough we agreed, giving him a chance to pause for breath. 'Let's face it,' he added, 'she's what, twenty-five years old. The rust'll always come back, the only issue is how long will it take?'

'Can you give us any ballpark idea of cost?' I asked, innocently.

He sucked his teeth in best builder asked for an estimate mode and pulled a face. 'Oh, around forty pound a foot.'

We nodded sagely; this was in line with other estimates we'd been given, if anything slightly better, and we told him we'd think about it. As time was getting on, we asked if there was any chance of an overnight mooring and, thinking there probably was, Ray disappeared in a whirlwind to check his records to see who was away.

'Was that forty quid a foot for the cat's whiskers or the dog's bollocks?' Annette asked.

'Search me,' I replied. 'Do you want to ask when he gets back?' I suggested and went to the front to check the hose. While she contemplated this the mechanic came over, rubbing something indistinguishable and shiny in a cloth as he walked.

'Lister, is it?' he asked. Annette nodded. 'Thought so.' His curiosity satisfied, he turned and walked back into his shed.

Best of all, Streethay Wharf even had its own on-site cab driver, Paul, who was living temporarily on a converted butty with his wife and two boys aged eight and ten while they were selling their house. This alignment of ages with our own children made us feel slightly homesick, but we managed to conquer it. The worry lines on his forehead weren't too obvious, but he seemed unnaturally keen to take the job of taking us into Lichfield, which no doubt offered the prospect of at least a few minutes' peace at the end of the weekend.

'So, where's it to be then?' he asked once we'd got in.

'The cinema in Lichfield,' we replied in unison, at which point he burst out laughing. From this we deduced that Nerdy was once again out of date, as we'd probably always known all along. He went on to describe what Lichfield had to offer, a description sufficiently graphic for me to remember that I'd been there before, and although it sounded a charming place, it offered little to the entertainment starved other than a cathedral and some tea rooms. According to Paul there was a local by-law that nothing was allowed to be open after eleven at night; whether or not this was true, the fact that it had passed into local mythology said enough. Although we were not necessarily in the market for a late night, his commentary had the effect of diverting any investment of expectations back towards Tamworth. So we'd been right all along in our instincts.

In practice, when it came to entertainment, there was little that Tamworth didn't have to offer, as we were to find out. A Snow-drome, a bowling alley, one of those laser shoot-out 'bang bang you're dead' sort of places, a nightclub and, joy of joys, a multiplex cinema; all tacked on the edge of this ancient town like a strap-on beard on a middle-aged woman. We were not bothered about aesthetics, however, and were simply pleased that our quest was finally about to be fulfilled. There were even places to eat, although once we'd bought our tickets and were safe in the knowledge that we were actually going to see a film we eschewed the worst of the excesses of the leisure park and wandered into the centre of town.

This was clean and ordered but, it being a Sunday afternoon, was predictably pretty dead. Occasional packs of bored teenagers cruised the streets, but other than that it was the usual mixture of chain stores and charity shops. We wandered the pedestrianised main street and fell into some kind of café bar which suited our requirements and followed this with the film. In the end it took just over three hours to satiate our appetite for the big city, and we summoned Paul to take us back to *Florrie* with a sense of almost guilty relief that it was all over. As we pulled out of the car park I reflected that the local youths were either extremely law-abiding or lacking in imagination as I noticed that the sign for the local Ankerside Shopping Centre had remained gloriously ungraffitied.

After our somewhat leisurely progress of the previous four days we agreed that it was time to swallow some serious water. Although by now we had practical experience of the danger of setting ourselves deadlines, we did have a commitment to reach Coventry by the end of the following day. This was so we could travel back to Stoke to pick up the children somewhere in the northern reaches of the motorway system the day after that. Furthermore, I had to reach somewhere with a sufficient level of civilisation to pick up a fax and conduct some business before then. The commitments were piling up, and taken together they meant that we would have to pace ourselves and plan rather more than we had done to date.

So it was that once the magic hour of eight arrived we were ready to proceed and set off without further delay. The passage into Tamworth that followed confirmed the impossibility of the target we'd set ourselves the day before and we completed the stretch through to the historic junction at Fazeley without incident, despite passing through a high-risk military firing zone.

Fazeley itself was marked by a lot of recent building develop-ment, including some rather bijou mini-marinas for those who lived in the new flats we saw, which no doubt had been converted from old warehouses. The whole thing had been achieved with a modicum of taste, even if the junction was, like most of the historic or important junctions we'd encountered on the canals, understated and easy to miss.

We chugged straight through the heart of Tamworth and confirmed our earlier impression from the taxi window the day before that it had clearly become some kind of designated area for population growth, the housing having seemed to have sprawled like a spilt coffee over the map. We stopped for lunch on the edge of the town at a pub called the Anchor, having worked our way through the only two locks on this stretch. New management at the Anchor was making a respectable effort to cultivate the passing canal trade and we agreed that they would probably succeed if it maintained its admirable prices, which were especially reasonable. It was also the only pub I know of to have produced its own newspaper, *Well Anchored*, which also acted as the menu.

It was from this that I learnt that Thomas Guy, founder of Guy's Hospital in London, had been the MP for Tamworth at the end of the seventeenth century, as, more famously, had Sir Robert Peel. It was in Tamworth, quite reasonably, that the founder of the Metropolitan Police and some time prime minister had read his Tamworth Manifesto from the steps of the town hall, the document which redefined Toryism at the time. The paper also included a short history of the town which I can recommend as wholesome reading, especially when absorbed over a pint of M&B mild.

Suitably fortified and back in the countryside, we noticed that there seemed to be a switch to more of a market garden economy, with massively long polythene tunnels stretching out over the fields, lined vein-like with complicated irrigation systems. Elsewhere, undressed skeletons made up of what looked like curved scaffolding poles suggested that there were plans to extend operations. Once again, the variety of uses to which the land is put outside of towns surprised me.

The canal began to open out after Tamworth, as if it was beginning to take itself seriously, although this may have been more to do with the fact that we were now approaching the one-time terminus at Atherstone. As it became wider, at times becoming reminiscent of the Leeds and Liverpool, it also became better maintained. The robustness of the canal at this point could have been a reflection of the initial enthusiasm of the navigators to get the damned thing finished, although this was an enthusiasm which, as we'd experienced, had obviously soon waned.

Evidence of the coalfields which lay at the heart of the canal's success began to litter the landscape. Now closed and long gone, their fecundity was evidenced by the huge spoil heaps, now greened over, which lay all around. It remained difficult to comprehend that once this land would have been the scene of tremendous activity, the canal laden with boats carrying the fruits of the labour of thousands of unseen miners to the cities, literally fuelling the beginnings of the industrial age, both for England and, in time, for the world. Great times for the country, but probably less wonderful for those whose muscle power they were built on.

Now all that was left was an artificial horizon, not yet fully bedded in, despite the efforts of local authorities to designate the area a nature reserve and thus give it some kind of status. Passing through I did manage to spot the occasional rabbit and even a kingfisher, my eye taken by its golden headband. Its needle-like beak looked set fair for a day's fishing – a true canalside dweller. Signs erected on the towpath proclaimed the area's purpose and gave an indication of things to look out for, but the place was singularly unpopulated by people taking advantage of it. It was as if man had run out of uses for the land, having taken it, wrung what he could out of it and thrown it back, rumpled and dry.

Neither had the death of mining meant a return to Rolt's agrarian idyll, even if that had ever existed. Instead there was, well, nothing really, not a wasteland, but not exactly anything useful, or yet beautiful, either. It was as if the land hereabouts existed as some kind of neutral territory, a stand-off between man and nature, a stand-off from which nature was steadily, and inevitably, destined to emerge the victor. Don't get me wrong, this fact was in no way depressing. On the contrary, the area was a perfectly pleasant one to chug through on a sunny summer's afternoon after a pint of the local brew, and we appreciated the local wildlife that had become attracted to it. It just didn't seem natural somehow, whatever natural is.

Time for reflection evaporated suddenly as we began to approach Atherstone and the first of eleven locks. These started slowly in three batches of two and then culminated in a run of five into the centre of the town. As usual, we'd been looking forward to the chance for some social intercourse at the lockside, but our meetings confirmed what had become a growing suspicion, namely that people had grown less friendly as we'd entered the Midlands proper, probably since after Rugeley. The accents were noticeably more Brum, more nasal and drawn out, as if speech was an effort, communication a chore. Although people were not actually rude, they seemed to be more in their shells, reluctant to expose their thoughts or share reflections. What had once been detailed conversations were now courtesies, an exchange of pleasantries rather than a discussion.

A typical exchange on this stretch would start with a statement of the obvious, like 'Sunny today' or 'Two locks to go then,' rather than questions or a conversational opener. The statements were closed, not open, inviting confirmation, not progression. It hadn't seemed that long ago that meeting someone lockside had meant a sometimes protracted exchange of destinations and thoughts on good places to stop, advice – not always wanted or indeed heeded – or even an invitation to come aboard and share a cup of something. Not any more.

Feeling charitable, we put this down to the high proportion of hire boats on this stretch, hirers being the convenient boat owners' scapegoats for anything that might be wrong on the waterways – when it wasn't British Waterways' fault. Perhaps, we reasoned, they were concentrating harder on the task in hand, being unfamiliar with lock technique or more anxious not to make fools of themselves. Or perhaps they had yet to tune into the otherwise highly open culture of the canals?

We knew in our heart of hearts, however, that this was an inadequate explanation. Many of the owners were just as guilty, seeming to be happier in their immaculate cocoons, trying hard not to share the state secrets of any part of their lives or, God forbid, their feelings.

Ascending the Atherstone flight of looks took longer than we'd expected, but we were safely tied up by six, in time to make a rendezvous with an old friend and a couple of pints in a local hostelry. The town's status as a key canal location was barely noticeable, although we did spot an old Rothens boat and butty at an old coal yard at the top of the flight. More attention was devoted to the town's position as the one-time centre of the wool felt hatting industry. Well, somewhere had to be. Although at the turn of the century there had been seven hat factories in the town, only one remained, Wilson and Stafford. Another proud local industry to have gone the way of mass production.

Atherstone is also famous for its annual Shrove Tuesday ball game, which as far as I could make out was an excuse for the local youths of the town to get together and settle a few old scores. Nominal goals are erected either end of the town and after that, well, after that there didn't seem to be much in the way of rules.

More a case of shut up and get on with it. Still, it was nice to see that some local traditions had survived.

Don't Mention the War

The first bridge we saw the following day was number forty. We knew we had to reach number one at Coventry Basin by the end of the day, preferably by mid-afternoon. Conscious, once again, of the dangers of setting ourselves a deadline, we were prepared to take the implied pressure in order to buy enough time to visit Coventry Cathedral, somewhere we'd both last been to independently over twenty years before.

By mid-morning things were going well, with nearly half the bridges passed and steady progress amongst light traffic. As such, we decided to moor up in Nuneaton to receive my fax and clear the decks work-wise. The approach to Nuneaton had been marked by more spoil heaps, reinforcing the impressions of the day before. The largest of these was known locally as Mount Judd, after the Judkins Quarry just outside the town, but the one I enjoyed most came before that. This was erect and pert, having all the perfection of a recumbent virgin's breast. One side was slightly steeper than the other, which sloped away gently to merge in with the otherwise flat surroundings. The hill itself had the odd tree dotted on its side however, something a young virgin would probably have regarded as unflattering.

In the few places where there were fields, the farmers had been taking advantage of the warm weather to get the harvest in, the sheer pace of their frantic activity transmitting a hint of panic which in turn reflected the forecast of thunderstorms. The more efficient of them had parked their tractors rather self-righteously under hay barns, the golden fruits of their efforts stacked neatly alongside. Elsewhere, combine harvesters would creep up on us from nowhere and blast us not only with noise but with a fine dust, which would settle on the surface of the water like flour, and through which *Florrie* subsequently described an inelegant path. The smell they left in their wake was one of the distinctive scents of summer, all fresh and musky, baker's shops and *Cider with*

Rosie.

These fields were rare however, although the sheen the mid-morning sun bestowed upon them gave them a distinctiveness undeserved by their number. They were patches of gold in an otherwise dull green-grey landscape, the spoil from the quarries resisting the efforts of the quick-growing grass and weeds to colonise it. Occasional oak apples stood out on the sides of the trees lining the bank, while rose hips lent a splash of vivid colour to the hedgerows.

As if they were aware of the nature reserve status of this stretch, a number of highly territorial herons had colonised the banks. These would launch themselves into the air on our approach, their bills stretched out before them like the chin of a sprinter making for the tape. Swooping majestically, they would describe a semi circle, their light charcoal and white plumage at once merging into the sky. Once satisfied all was well, these would invariably return to the exact same spot where they'd started, tucking in their wings and becoming perfectly static in an instant.

A number of new marinas were also being developed along the route, many of which were far from full, although where all the boats might be was a mystery as we had had the canal more or less to ourselves for some time. One possibility was that they'd taken the Birmingham and Fazeley or Ashby Canals, both favourites for the regular cruiser. Another was that these new developments were speculative, built in the anticipation of a growth in canal traffic, an entirely feasible possibility.

One thing was for sure, they hadn't moored up around Nuneaton. To approach the town by canal meant a long game of 'tease' as the banks either side were lined with a curtain of tall trees. Sticking up irregularly from amongst these were disused telegraph poles of the old-fashioned type, with a myriad of small bell-shaped porcelain junction boxes jutting out from their sides, waiting patiently like birds preparing to migrate.

Judkins Quarry itself was unmistakable, a huge red hole gouged out of the side of a hill, a feat of digging almost as awe-inspiring as the cutting of the canal itself. Luckily, this too was mostly hidden by trees from our view. What seemed like the centre of the town was reached quickly enough, and we moored up beside a couple of other boats, following the theory that there is safety in numbers. A wide day tripper boat was using the winding hole nearby to turn round, and it warmed my heart to observe that even professionals can make a complete hash of reverse.

We wandered into the town with a single-minded air. We simply wanted to get our respective jobs done (Annette had felt the urge to buy a mop) and get out. This feeling was reinforced when we actually came to sample the place. On the basis of this experience we quickly concluded that Nuneaton was not the sort of place you'd take your granny for a day out. To judge by the shops, the local residents seemed to have an unhealthy obsession with personal appearance, with tattoo parlours, body piercers and second-hand clothes shops proliferating. Practically every single one of the people we passed seemed to sport the products of at least one of these emporiums. At the same time, the people each seemed to wear that 'got to get through the day' look which suggested a deep unhappiness with their lot.

We found a charity shop of our own and had a cup of coffee with a toasted teacake while I read through my fax and made the necessary corrections. Job done, we dropped Annette back at the boat and I got the bike down in order to find a quiet telephone booth for what was inevitably going to be a long conversation discussing my suggested revisions.

Finding quiet proved to be impossible, and in the end I spent forty-five minutes trying to make myself heard against the rumble of a busy main road whilst holding paper down with one hand and a pen in the other. At the same time, the telephone's receiver was cradled against the top of my shoulder, while I tried to keep at least one eye on my bike. At last I finished and prepared to sign off to my colleague on the other end, no doubt warm and comfortable at his desk.

'Let me give you some advice, should chance ever deal you an opportunity to come to Nuneaton,' I offered.

'Don't,' we yelled in unison.

There was no doubt about it, Nuneaton had not been a comfortable experience. It was as if we'd been fooled by Stoke into thinking that we'd left the threat of urban decay behind. In fact, Nuneaton was the worst case of it we'd come across so far, with one notable exception. We had felt like tourists there, observers of a culture we hadn't been invited to join and certainly hadn't been born into.

It was only as we were leaving the place that Annette informed me that, incredibly, Nuneaton had been the birthplace of George Eliot, one of her heroines. What was more, we had been but yards away from a museum housing personal George Eliot memorabilia. She'd clearly been perusing Nerdy in my absence. I think my observation that if Nerdy said that then it was almost certainly wrong came as little comfort. More importantly, however, we wouldn't have had time for a visit if we were to make Coventry in time. The news came as both a sort of redemption – if the town had produced Ms Eliot it couldn't be all bad – and condemnation. What had happened in the interim, we wondered, between the time when her imagination had been seeded and now? The answer was a lot, most of it probably not worth speculating upon.

On exiting the town we were struck once again by the absolute perfection of so many of the gardens we passed. The lawns were neatly manicured and had an almost golf course-like smoothness and verdancy. Allotments too were well kept and tended, with a recurring motif of runaway runner beans, their orange flowers almost all gone and the first fruits ready for the picking.

South of Nuneaton lay Bedworth, the heart of the coal industry that had fed the Coventry furnaces. A series of long straits made for easy, if dull, motoring before the approach of Hawkesbury Junction and we managed to make up some time. I had been looking forward to this landmark with special interest, as it would mark the first time I had revisited somewhere I'd cruised before, if you excluded the return up the Runcorn arm, which I had by now blotted out of my memory. It was here that I'd carried out my Inland Helmsman's training with Keith, what seemed like an age before.

Hawkesbury was important also for its significance in latter-day canal history. Ten years after the canals were nationalised the local council in Coventry had announced plans to fill in the canal from Hawkesbury to the city centre, a distance of five and a half miles. This would have effectively killed the canal by decapitation, and the fact that the proposition could have been taken seriously says a lot about the negative mood towards canals at the time.

Thankfully, the announcement couldn't have been timed worse, or better, depending upon your point of view, as it acted as a rallying call for the boat troops, who were just beginning to get themselves properly organised, thanks in no small measure to the efforts of LTC Rolt and his comrades. In time, they were successful in reversing the council's plans, a result that proved to be a turning point for the canals in general, causing those in authority with similar plans elsewhere to pause and consider before going forward. This victory has not prevented further crazy ideas from rearing their head from time to time of course, as my last visit to Hawkesbury had shown, with the historic wharf there apparently the latest target.

By the time we reached Hawkesbury the dreadful feeling that we were chasing the clock once again materialised. The Nerdy suggested that the visitors' centre at the cathedral was open until six, but we didn't want to rush ourselves and besides, what did that mean anyway? In theory we were only two hours away, but in practice would also have to moor up and find our way in. All this was assuming that we would be okay to moor in the basin, our preference by some distance given the fact that we were planning to leave *Florrie* by herself for almost all of the following day.

By the time we had debated these issues we found ourselves committed to pressing on. The canal bank, not to say the surrounding environment, was distinctly unpromising, with the former lined with freshly laid red gravel and defiantly resistant to a secure mooring. Furthermore, there were no mooring rings. On the far bank I thought I saw a rat emerging from the water, its skin chamois smooth and glistening, although later reading suggested there was a chance, just a chance, it might have been a water vole. The signals the canal was sending were clear: no one in their right minds moored this side of bridge number one.

The only alternative, one we considered seriously for a while, was to find a winding hole, retrace our steps and moor up at Hawkesbury, but by the time we'd agreed this might be sensible we'd travelled more than half the distance, making this option self-defeating. Besides, there was a distinct absence of winding holes. We were effectively trapped.

Eventually we decided to risk it and chose a spot outside a boatyard, which we reasoned would be regularly patrolled. Mooring was accomplished without difficulty, but *Florrie* looked terribly lonely and vulnerable left on her own with no boat in view for miles around. We clambered up the bank and found ourselves on a main road. As chance would have it, a bus was leaving just as we realised it was exactly the one we needed. It was at this point that luck finally favoured us and a taxi went past, its orange light aglow. In an instinctive reaction I hailed it and we were whisked into the centre of Coventry in less than five minutes. For the price of three pounds our conundrum had been solved. Delivered to a spot right outside the cathedral itself. Fortune, it seemed, was favouring the brave, and brave was what we felt we'd been in leaving *Florrie* where we had.

The outside of the cathedral was as we'd both remembered it, although more accurately this should be expressed in the plural, for the new building lies adjacent to the previous cathedral, which was bombed to smithereens by the *Luftwaffe* in 1940. Visitors were channelled through a narrow entrance designed to ensure that the non-obligatory contribution to the cathedral's upkeep was made all the same, an approach that took away some of the initial impact of the inside. Standing back, however, it was possible to appreciate very quickly what Sir Basil Spence had intended when designing the place, with one's eyes drawn insistently to the altar and the famous tapestry by Sir Graham Sutherland.

The angular lines and use of concrete shouted late 1950s, early 1960s, but the cathedral was none the worse for that; every cathedral is a product of its time – just ask anyone who's been to Barcelona. It was something other than that which made me uneasy as I wandered around, and I eventually put it down to two things. Firstly, the sheer overpowering nature of the set pieces. At times I felt I was visiting an art gallery as much as a place of worship. Again, this can be said of many churches, but the trick surely is to achieve a synthesis between the art and the purpose of the building, such as I'd seen earlier on the trip at Blackburn. I did not really get the impression that I was visiting a centre of worship for the local community. In a way, Coventry seemed to have sold its soul, if not to the devil then to the tourist. It seemed to belong not to the local people but to the world, acting as a sort of keeper of the global conscience when it came to matters of conflict.

This leads to the second reason I found myself becoming uncomfortable as we walked around, namely the constant harking on about the war, in a Basil Fawltyesque-type way. Okay, so the cathedral represents a triumph of hope over experience, or peace over war, and only exists because its predecessor was cruelly bombed out of existence, but there is a limit. Every conceivable anniversary of the war – its beginning, its ending, thirty, forty, fifty years on – seems to have been marked by the dedication of some new work of art. I couldn't help feeling that if the place was to become self-sufficient and last for hundreds of years, as surely was the intention, at some point it needed to move on.

That point might be now, and an appeal was in force when we were there to raise money for a commemoration of the millennium. However, unless I read it wrong, funds raised from this were going to be spent on the building of a new chapel, whereas a more pragmatic purpose might be a less visible but ultimately more useful endowment of money directed towards the upkeep of the cathedral. All the church's available long-term capital had been used up building the place, hence its currently being in hock to the Deutschmarks, yen and dollars of tourists. Until this dependence was broken, I felt the church was unlikely to really develop a personality of its own.

All this said, the place is impressive, and worth a visit. My favourite place was the Baptistery, with its use of a rock from Bethlehem as the font, with a scallop carved out of it, the whole overlooked by a Piper window. I also liked the etchings on the glass looking out towards the old cathedral, which were simple but effective. I doubt I am the first to remain untouched by the Sutherland. Call me a philistine if you like, and this is a purely personal view, but if I'd been told that the tapestry had been the result of a competition amongst final year art school graduates I'd probably have believed you. Big it may be, the biggest single tapestry in the world in fact, but inspiring, I think not.

Having gained a map from the tourist information office, we made our way to the Canal Basin to check out the form. Although easily found, this necessitated going through the centre of the city in the peak of rush hour. This came as something of a culture shock after so long away, and we found ourselves keen to get it over with. We had lost the habit of dodging buses and cars. Things soon quietened down when we entered the side street taking us to the basin. On the way we passed a funeral director's which also advertised the provision of wedding cars. With a little bit of thought this seemed a perfectly reasonable business proposition (presumably they just added a few ribbons), although trying to persuade the happy couple to lie down together quite so soon after the ceremony, and quite so publicly, might, we thought, be tricky.

The final hurdle in what was becoming something of a stee-plechase across Coventry was a bridge. This was built, it seemed, in the Chinese style, all zigzags to confuse evil spirits, a series of acute angles which made the crossing twice as long as it might otherwise have been. The basin itself was announced in bold letters eight feet high, forged in steel, the place having clearly been the subject of recent investment.

The basin was an unusual Y shape, with each arm long enough to fit eight or nine boats maximum. Originally opened in 1769, it was extended in 1788 at the time when hopes were high for the future of the canal, the Oxford then having recently been completed and the new link into Birmingham, it seemed, soon to become a reality. More recently money had been spent on creating a collection of rather esoteric retail units (only a news-agent seemed to be doing any business) as well as office buildings converted from old warehouses. These were occupied mainly by advertising companies, consultants and PR people, the sort of companies which would see a canalside location as distinctly right-on. The place was a curious mixture of the clean and newly painted and the more ancient, the site itself.

There was even a statue of an engineer at the junction of the Y, looking out pensively over the canal, a quill pen in one hand and a folio of papers spread out before him. I looked, but was unable to find anything to say who it was. Presumably it was meant to be our old friend Mr Brindley, the main office building being named after him. If so, this would have been something of a cheek, the Coventry Canal having had the distinction of having sacked him less than a year into his service.

At last we were the right side of bridge number one, albeit without *Florrie*, and we were relieved to see that there seemed to be spaces. We made for the boats moored on the far side, near the bridge, for a chat. The first good news was that the moorings were forty-eight-hour visitors' moorings, so we would be okay, although further interrogation revealed that the boat owner we were talking to had been there for five weeks and no one had bothered him. The story was that British Waterways was simply keen to see the place used and busy. We asked how safe we'd be there and were told not to worry: 'It's like Blackpool Illuminations here at night.' Suitably convinced, there was nothing for it but to go back and fetch *Florrie*.

An hour later we were moored precisely at the spot where we'd been so reassured. In doing so, the final run-in had confirmed the wisdom of pressing on. The scenery had become decidedly industrial, with uninspiring, mainly disused factories. One, a mass of pipework seemingly put together by an avant-garde artist, was belching steam (at least I hope it was steam) in a number of unlikely places, including over the canal.

The water was dirty and carrying more flotsam and jetsam than I'd seen since the worst of the mill country in Lancashire, and to make matters worse a steady drizzle of rain had settled in. Some attempts had been made to please the eye, including a series of sculptures along the towpath, mainly designed to provide seating areas, although why anyone would want to stop unless they were facing an imminent heart attack I didn't know. Our favourite was a stone sofa on a stone bamboo raft. Someone had also installed some railing painted to give a wave effect along its top, but these were oases in an otherwise unrelenting desert of awfulness. Certainly not stopping places for the night.

For the second time I was at the dead end of a canal, the first occasion being the Bridgewater in a place beginning with an 'R', the name of which now fails me. The circumstances this time round were more propitious. We had intended all along to come to this spot and we had a purpose in being there. To have made it,

on schedule and without serious mishap, represented an achievement.

In completing the whole of the Coventry we had also effectively reached the end of another leg of the journey. After a day's
shenanigans on other parts of the transport system, the next time
we stepped on board *Florrie* we would do so as a complete family
unit. In many ways what happened next was the ultimate test, for
we knew now what we could do with *Florrie*, both her limitations
and her strengths. We also knew that we liked being on her
immensely. My initial concerns over whether Annette would
enjoy herself sufficiently had evaporated soon after we'd left
Stoke, although it was clear that she was significantly less comfortable in an urban environment. This was possibly as much because
of the implications for dust and filth on her curtains and furniture
as any personal discomfort.

As we cooked our dinner together, we speculated on how
things might be different with the boys on board. I for one was
looking forward to sharing some of the experience and knowledge
I'd accumulated as well as some of the wildlife that normally
passed us by. Annette on the other hand was simply looking
forward to us being a family again.

We had also accumulated an undercurrent of confidence.
Surely we had experienced most of the things that could possibly
go wrong, and as such we could afford to sit back and relax a bit,
certainly a lot more than in the early days. In a short space of time
we seemed to have become old canal hands. From that point of
view our timing, which owed as much to circumstances as
planning, seemed, on the surface at least, to be propitious. Most
important of all was the question of how we would perform as a
family on board. This, after all, had been the general idea of
buying *Florrie*. Were we going to have fun?

We settled down to sleep early. This was despite a growing
gathering of boat owners outside, who were swapping stories and
experiences in between cracking open bottles of beer. Neither of
us knew where they'd materialised from, but there was no
denying their existence. As they settled in the temptation to join
them was almost overwhelming, and no doubt if I'd been on the
previous leg of the journey we would have. We knew, however,

that we had to cross town early in the morning to get to the railway station and subsequently onwards to Stoke and the car.

As we settled down we reflected that our earlier informant hadn't been joking when he'd compared the basin to Blackpool Illuminations. It felt odd to be trying to get to sleep under the glare of cream-coloured security lighting on one side and the more orange tones of sodium lights on the other. We were both shattered however, and dropped off more despite them rather than because of the comfort provided by the security they offered. Outside, the hubbub of conversation became a *sotto voce* murmur, punctuated occasionally by drink-inspired laughter.

Escaping the Slime

'...but more, much more than this, I did it myyyyyyy way!'

The sound made by a boatful of fifty-something women competing (and unfortunately winning) against Frank Sinatra was enough to wake the dead, and dead we had been, dead beat anyway. We had been warned the night before against going into the centre of Coventry because of the Premiership clash against the local side and Manchester United (was I never to escape them?), but no one had warned us against the matrons of Coventry. As we waited for the torture to end we couldn't help but think that Lady Godiva had a lot to answer for.

I groped for my watch. Midnight. It took all of twenty minutes for the disco boat to disembark fully, a period during which intense drunken giggles competed with sharp shrieks. These were both issued with delight, although at times I suspected that there was an element of fear as people stopped themselves from falling in – an uninviting prospect sober or drunk. All these were accompanied by the sort of sexist verbal abuse directed towards the (male) skipper of the boat which would have been enough to constitute a court case had the sexes been reversed. Eventually they dispersed, and we silently thanked the instinct which had led us to moor on the far side, so they didn't have to walk past us. We drifted back to sleep, literally.

At six o'clock, half an hour before our alarm, the boat in front of us started his engine, but left it in neutral. It turned out he'd fallen asleep in front of his television (television!) after the booze-up the night before and had run his battery flat. To give him his due, he thought we'd already left as we'd made clear our plans for an early start the previous day, but there's early and there's *early*.

Our detailed planning turned out to be immaculate and the pick-up of the boys went according to schedule. Even the weather had performed, being utterly dreadful, wet, thundery and ugly. This was the day the weather forecasters had been predicting for a while and we'd avoided being on the water for it. The good news was the same forecasters were unanimous in their view that the storm clouds would pass straight through and the high pressure we had been enjoying would resume.

The railway accomplished in ninety minutes what it had taken us the best part of a week to achieve by canal, and for once we had reason to be grateful to Richard Branson and his trains. It was clear to see why steel had held the advantage over water from the start. The F-in-L and M-in-L arrived more or less on time and the boys were scrubbed and ready to go. The first was keen to know how we'd got on, and seemed particularly concerned to know how we'd been coping with the locks. I was happy to reassure him.

We motored back to Coventry and I dropped off the rest of the family before resuming the journey to Banbury. From there it was one last trip back to Coventry before we were fully together again. Once reunited, I became aware of feeling absolutely shattered; I'd lost the habit of modern transport. My mood of irritability born of tiredness contrasted poorly with the boys' boisterousness, but any potential conflict was leavened by the comfort of us all being together again. Before long we were settling down once more, having taken the precaution of rigging up a boom across the bridge capable of being activated by the opening notes of 'New York, New York'. Well, it was a thought anyway.

After the growing sense of confidence I'd so recently felt, both in *Florrie* and my own abilities as a helmsman, it probably shouldn't have come as a tremendous shock when the engine refused to start the next day. A little voice of reason had niggled away in the back of my mind all the previous day, and the subject of its niggling had been our old friend Mr Fridge. With reason. Once again the battery was flat, and although this time there was a modicum of life still left in her it was still not enough to turn the engine.

After Adlington, however, I was less ready to rush for help, convinced there was at least a chance that I could sort it out for myself. Not a tremendous chance, but a chance all the same. At least I now knew what a valve lifter was. So it was that we found ourselves with the engine hatch lifted and me in the well of the boat ready to flick the lifters over as soon as Annette turned the ignition. The sounds that followed were encouraging, but in the final analysis represented only teasing. The noise we all wanted to hear, the womb-like comfort of the Lister chugging away, was only hinted at, and it refused to materialise.

As I sought inspiration, my gaze landed on the starting handle. Desperate times required desperate measures. I lifted the valves and gave Annette instructions to flick them back on the command 'Now!' She didn't look happy. By this point we were both standing in the engine well, to the outsider up to our knees in the water. I made sure the clutch was in neutral and that there were some revs and stood up to flex my shoulders, ready to devote my all to the effort ahead. Employing my best double-handed backhand, I spun the handle and was surprised to find the ease with which it turned. The shock of this prevented me from issuing the command, so we tried again.

'Now!' I yelled, and Annette flicked the lifters over exactly on cue.

Almost immediately something clicked, followed straight afterwards by the reassuring, the beautiful, the musical sound of the engine spluttering, starting up and, finally, chugging. That perfect one-two, one-two rhythm, with an occasional emphasis on the two, as if it was trying to sing, once again rent the air. A miracle! Black smoke plumed out of the exhaust in a parody of the papal selection process and the scent of burning diesel filled our nostrils. Perfume! The only disappointment of the whole episode had been that there had been no one around to witness our triumph.

A combination of exultation and pure, unrefined relief washed through me like a wave as I executed a perfect three-point turn at the apex of the Y and directed us out of the basin. Bridge number one beckoned and we passed through it without so much as kissing the sides before turning sharp right. The final leg of the journey had begun.

Our feelings were mixed on leaving Coventry. Whereas I would have liked longer to get under the skin of the place, Annette had once again begun to feel uncomfortable, exposed perhaps, in the big city – a rootless stranger living in an alien environment. The truth was, however, that neither of us had been totally comfortable in the place. This was probably partly because of the environment, of the signals the city sent out, and partly because we had only gone there to leave, not to savour. Like much of the Midlands, Coventry seemed highly self-contained, unwilling to give of itself. And yet, I was left with a sneaking suspicion that, like an introvert friend, the effort of getting to know the place would, in time, have been rewarded. I left feeling that one day I'd like to come back and give it a second chance.

The culture shock of moving from canalside to big city had been part of our experience. By now, nothing could beat the experience of slow movement on water for us, the sensation of moving on – not quickly, it's true, but moving all the same. To be static was almost to betray our purpose. In this frame of mind we reasoned that two hours' solid chugging down the Coventry arm would recharge both *Florrie*'s batteries and our own and, as luck would have it, this was exactly what we knew would be required to get us to Hawkesbury.

Almost straight away I let each of the boys have a go at the tiller, allowing them to experience the weight of the water behind it and the effort required to move it. They'd had their lecture-ettes on canal safety and had watched the British Waterways safety video, but I was keen to instil some kind of appreciation of the numerous things that had to be taken into account if we were to maintain a safe passage. The realist in me knew that creating a sense of responsibility in them would not come instantly, but equally we had to start somewhere.

We were on old ground once again, although this time without the stress of a deadline. In fact, I was taking things deliberately slowly, reasoning that this would be good both for the batteries and in order to break in our new crew. Using a pamphlet I'd picked up somewhere the boys began to play 'spot the towpath art' and I promised them that the scenery would pick up soon, although they both still seemed to be in thrall to the novelty of it all and perfectly happy with their lot. Out of place apple trees draped their branches over the water and I reached up to pluck some fruit from them, but the apples were small and mottled, unripe and inedible anyway, given the air pollution hereabouts. Their desiccation seemed somehow to be symbolic.

We soon approached the short, floodlit Stoke Heath Tunnel, and its orange and pink light threw exaggerated caricatures of us all on the opposite wall. The boys' profiles were made grotesque by the bulk of their life jackets, while *Florrie*'s high brow pointed forward proudly, like a Roman nose. The boys looked up and emitted a series of 'Boop!' sounds at the ceiling in an effort to get an echo. This was to become a habit adopted from that moment on. Even if busy in the cabin, the encroaching shadow of a passing bridge would always be enough to make at least one of them run out and yell 'Boop!' even if their cause was usually hopeless.

One of the original motives for pausing at Hawkesbury had been to look up Keith, as I'd promised during my Inland Helmsman's training, but without warning I suddenly spotted *Narroway* coming towards us, Keith's familiar insouciant figure perched at the back, possibly communing with his God. I immediately stood up, as if meeting my ex-headmaster, anxious to prove I had taken all his lessons on board. We had only moments to exchange greetings, and I had the advantage on him in that he'd been on my mind.

'Hi! Keith, remember me, Nick, you trained me.'

He looked up and waved, with just the hint of a bemused smile. I remembered the F-in-L once telling me how, as a teacher, you become practised in the art of feigning recognition, most ex-pupils tending to merge into one. I hoped he did remember me, but there was no way of knowing for sure. Then, as quickly as it had arrived, the moment had gone. We decided to stick to our plans anyway, and after another hour or so moored up at the first convenient spot we found.

On this, my second visit to this historical spot, there was time to stop and read the noticeboards, and I was surprised to find that the real reason for the stop lock (beyond the collection of tolls) was because of a miscalculation. A cock-up in other words. Also, the drop was a full six and seven-eighth inches, not the six inches I'd reckoned it was on my last visit. Finally, I learnt that the cast-iron bridge I'd admired three months before was apparently known as a roving bridge and had cost a total of £630. What was more it had been brought there by canal. If so, it must have come in stages, I reasoned, either that or it predated the stone bridges that now dotted the route.

We'd also planned to visit the chandlery shop that Nerdy claimed was there but – you've guessed it – it was shut. I made do with a visit to the British Waterways facilities, taking great pleasure as I entered in proving that the key did work, as Keith had shown the couple we'd met at the end of my training day. I felt less pleased when I wanted to leave, however, as I found myself thoroughly locked in. An extended period of thumping on the door and yelling for help duly followed, in the hope of attracting either Annette or one of the boys. In the end I was rescued by a fellow traveller, my family unaccountably clearly of the opinion that twenty minutes was a perfectly normal length of time for Dad to spend in the loo.

As we walked back to the boat my eye was taken by the activity of a pair of men working on the Hawkesbury Wharf building. Their power tools were loud and potentially threatening, and the building was now fenced in, and at first I feared the worst. The demolition squad. On closer inspection I noticed that they were working from the bottom up and seemed to be replacing bricks rather than removing them. Could it be that they were renovating the place? It would be interesting to monitor progress over the years I now knew stretched before me travelling on the canals. This realisation, that this journey was only a beginning, not an end in itself, slammed into my consciousness from nowhere. As it settled and permeated its way through my brain I found it was something to welcome. Yes, I would be here again, and again, and again. Why not?

Although the stop lock may only have dropped by a distance the boys would have recognised as seventeen centimetres, it was, as Keith had appreciated, an ideal training vehicle. I was able to get out of the boat and work with Annette in showing the boys both the theory and practice of working a lock. They'd seen locks before, of course, but this was different. This time we were on our own boat and getting through was something we had to achieve, not simply something nice to watch.

Getting through was also symbolic for marking our departure from the Coventry Canal. The significance of this was not so much in the departure of a canal itself, but in the underlying implications of the canal we had now joined. The Oxford Canal was to be our last. Somewhere towards the end of the line we would be home. As always at the prospect of a journey's end, the thought carried mixed emotions, of satisfaction but also, ultimately, of disappointment. I shunted these to the back of my mind. There was a long way to go yet.

Almost immediately after the junction the canal entered a series of the wide sweeps and curves of the sort for which it is justly famous. These, combined with the plethora of craft lining each bank, meant that the only possible progress was slow. Normally this wouldn't have mattered, but on this occasion the surface of the water had taken on a layer of disgusting lime-green algae, of unknown origin. Varying in thickness between a sheen and a carpet, this stretched from bank to bank without a break, as if the canal had misunderstood that just because it is coloured green in the Nicholson doesn't mean it has to be green in real life. We felt as if we were wading our way through the discharge of an unfortunate industrial accident, hoping as we approached each corner that clear water lay beyond, but it didn't.

As we charted a way through it, we carved open a path that the slime then closed in on again in seconds. If we were to stop we would have been surrounded by it. Thick custard skin-like folds gathered on the brim of our wake and left a deposit on the bankside, which would then slowly drip back into the water. Its only saving grace was that it was odourless, and after a while it seemed to take on a fascination, like a science experiment at school.

The curves immediately after Hawkesbury turned out to be a tease. Soon great long green straits appeared, often raised up on embankments, a result of the 'straightenings' carried out on the canal in the 1820s, which eventually chopped fourteen miles off the original thirty-six to the junction with the Grand Union at Braunston. The fact that this fairly drastic action had been necessary at all was a reflection of the Oxford Canal's early origins. It gained its Act of Parliament in 1769, at the same time as the Coventry and, surprise surprise, our old friend JB was appointed engineer. He did devote considerable individual attention to the Oxford, and the winding route it eventually followed in its first form has come to be seen as his personal hallmark on the canal.

The idea of a canal along this stretch had been alluring to the pioneers for two reasons. Firstly, the idea of linking the coalfields of Warwickshire with the industry of Banbury and Oxford seemed like a good one at the time; secondly, the Holy Grail of cutting into the Thames at Oxford, and thence to London, also seemed to make sense. The first of these goals was achieved in 1778, not by JB but by his successor Samuel Simcock, although the second took a bit longer, another twelve years in fact.

As we have seen, the informal alliance between the Coventry and the Oxford was never an easy one and it fell to the Grand Junction Canal to gain the prize of a route to London first, in 1780. The Oxford had a trick up its sleeve, however, in that it owned the short five-mile stretch from Braunston and Napton which constitutes the dog-leg between what are known as the North Oxford and South Oxford canals. This was a minor but critical part of the Grand Junction route, something the owners of the Oxford exploited to the full, demanding extortionate tolls, perhaps offering a lesson to those who now propose tolled motorways.

The rest of the canal prospered too, with traffic being decidedly two-way. Boats brought in pig iron, coal, slate and salt and took away grain, hay and straw from the rural hinterlands of Northamptonshire and Oxfordshire, as well as malt and beer. A number of industries were also stimulated by the presence of the canal, especially on the southern stretch, not least the manufacture of bricks.

The 'straightenings' were also a symptom of the canal's success, as well as a response to constant threats to cut newer and more efficient alternatives. The works involved were prodigious, requiring the building of embankments, aqueducts and deep cuttings. They also left a legacy in the form of a number of lonely cast-iron bridges along the bankside, which mark where the canal used to flow, usually visible at the beginning and end of a long stretch. The course of the old canal is rarely visible now, although the occasional dead end leads to a set of private moorings or a marina. The scene a hundred plus years ago must have been an odd one, with great curves of water going nowhere and slowly stagnating.

Much more visible was the railway, which after a short break now rejoined us as we made our way towards Rugby. Gradually, and only gradually, the green slime began to fade. Only when we managed to reach Rugby did it go altogether, although throughout the following day we were never really sure if it would reappear round the next corner like an unwelcome relative. The one thing that could be said for the slime was that it certainly kept the anglers away, and it was only when they started to pop up again, in ones and twos like the birds in Hitchcock's film, that we were able to feel confident that we were finally rid of it.

The 'straightenings' had a disruptive effect on the bridge numbering in this section of the canal, with the opportunity to carry out a renumbering exercise clearly having been botched. As a consequence, huge gaps appeared in the system, and the problem of identifying where we were was compounded by the fact that roughly half the bridges were completely numberless. On some the plates had clearly been removed deliberately, on others I suspected the bridges themselves had shrugged them off in frustration and confusion.

The landscape through this stretch was dominated by dense woodland, making it difficult to gauge what was going on in the real world. Keeping the trees manageable was the task of the British Waterways staff, whose distinctive jade green uniforms and dredging boats made them instantly recognisable along this stretch. Not once throughout our journey did we see one of these men working without their uniform on. This was a tribute both to their discipline and, no doubt, to their sense of safety, as with that colour on their back the excuse 'I just didn't see them, Your Honour' simply wouldn't have stood up in court.

Ploughing on, quite literally, through the slime, we stopped at Ansty, a village that seemed to be comprised of some delightful houses and a pub, the appropriately named Rose and Castle. When we asked if there was a village shop we were greeted with a

laughter, which we took to be a negative. The menu they offered
was varied and tempting, so we stopped and supped, enjoying one
of the privileges of canal travel which says you can do what you
damned well like on these occasions. Back at the boat we lazily
picked blackberries and fed the ducks some bread so that their diet
got some variety. After all, green slime might be okay for starters,
but main course and dessert as well?

Having let our lunch digest we got going again and it immediately became apparent that the oncoming traffic was definitely
picking up, with a particular feature being the higher proportion
of river cruisers. Up until now these had been something of a
curiosity on the system, but there were now occasions when they
formed the majority along a towpath. Their enviable manoeuvrability, and yet obvious fragility, with wooden hulls protected by
whole necklaces of fenders, added to the variety of the canal. At
the same time they provided a reminder of the fact that we were
moving out of the Midlands-based heart of the canal system and
closer to the Thames, although that remained some way off yet.

River cruisers also added a further dimension to the water-
based community, their obvious minority status perhaps
encouraging them to stick together. Although we found ourselves
striking up conversations with them when waiting at locks, the
people on board them tended to keep more of their own company
on the overnight moorings. Given that these conversations tended
to be very canal-centric this was perhaps not surprising, the river
cruisers perhaps still feeling that they were to some degree
interlopers in someone else's backyards. If so, this was something
to be regretted.

They were, to a boat, also crewed by the people who owned
them. None of the marinas we passed seemed to be offering
cruisers as an alternative along this stretch, although some did hire
out a curious hybrid of narrowboat with a sliding roof in the
middle, a sort of cabriolet boat. I wasn't sure these worked for me.

'Ordinary' hirers were also more in evidence along this stretch,
adding to the general sense of a build-up of traffic, a fact which
was probably not unconnected to the oncoming bank holiday
weekend. With the addition of these, the whole range of different
craft and communities became visible on this stretch, highlighting

the differences between them. We were now experienced enough to spot the telltale signs that made it possible to place a boat in its rightful place in the spectrum from a hundred paces and it became fun to compare and contrast.

The cruisers apart, which represented a class unto themselves with their own subcategories, three main classes of narrowboat seemed to exist. The first of these belonged to the residents, or live-aboards. These tended to be long, sixty- or seventy-foot boats, usually with a mini-garden of pots posited delicately on the roof, as if to say the owner was experienced enough to steer without upsetting them. They also sent out oblique messages about having put down roots. Amongst these there would normally be at least one pot growing a range of herbs, located strategically towards the galley end of the boat. Otherwise, geraniums proved to be a favourite. Owners who only lived aboard at the weekends tended to go in more for flowers.

Permanent residents also tended to carry sacks of coal or timber on their roof. The more the timber resembled driftwood the better, as it gave the impression that they were living from the water, in union with it. Their boats were also by and large less highly decorated, as if there wasn't really time for that sort of thing when you lived aboard. There were exceptions to this rule, usually those who made a living from offering canal art for sale, whose boats tended, if anything, to be over-decorated. Residents tended to paint their boats themselves, recognisable from telltale brush marks, whilst owners and part-timers more often went for a professional job.

Residents had also usually succumbed to television, sometimes with impressive collapsible aerials which they placed either on the roof or even, sometimes, in the slot where the tiller went, a location which could also be convenient for a rotary washing line. Another ad hoc arrangement was the collapsible windmill, a contraption I was keen to know more about after our experience in Coventry. If the fridge could drain the battery in under forty-eight hours, we needed to come up with a solution if we were to spend any length of time on the boat once she was home. No way was I going to drink warm beer.

While residents' boats tended to be scruffier, albeit more 'lived in,' owners tended to go in more for the immaculate look. Some, as we had already witnessed personally, took this to an extreme, worried lest a single scratch occur on their highly varnished paintwork. Hire craft were also instantly recognisable. Boats in the distinctive liveries of individual companies would swarm around their bases, their plumage invariably dull and functional, usually two primary colours only, with maybe a splash of a third.

Observations complete, our next destination was Rugby, where we intended to pause for a while and maybe take in the museum dedicated to the famous school. Nerdy also suggested that there was a Tesco superstore just off the towpath, and we reasoned that surely even the book couldn't have got this wrong. As the need for supplies was becoming pressing this was a clincher.

Later, our shopping done, while Edward and Annette were busy preparing dinner, Peter and I went for a walk along the towpath. He was quiet and I could tell there was something on his mind, but I decided to let it brew for a while until he had found a way of expressing it to his satisfaction. Eventually it came out.

'Dad?'

'Yes,' I replied, unconcerned.

'Can I ask you something?'

'Of course, what is it?'

'Well…' and at this point he paused a second, as if to remind himself of what he was going to say before starting again, perhaps checking himself to make sure he was on solid ground. 'Well, I was just wondering.'

'Yes?'

'Who will get *Florrie* when you kick the bucket?' I felt pleased rather than perplexed. Clearly he was beginning to fall in love with her too.

Gits in Peaked Caps

Complacency is a perfidious emotion. It enters you slowly and gradually takes hold in an unassuming but ultimately dangerous way, choosing the moment and manner in which it erupts and makes a fool of you. In our case, an explosion from the taps, followed by what can only be described as an oozing of dirty orange water, vaguely reminiscent of the canal at Worsley, was how it selected to make itself known. This time we really had run out of water.

Thankfully we only had to get through the night, and as there was a plentiful supply of alternative liquid refreshment available the hardships involved were not too great, even if it meant our already deteriorating standards of personal cleanliness fell further, albeit temporarily. Thankfully, there was a water point a hundred yards further on, so as stealthily as we could, which wasn't in truth very stealthily at all, we set off at seven thirty the next morning and hooked up to the bankside hose.

Florrie's manual said we had a six-hundred-gallon tank on board, which even on the most optimistic of reckonings I calculated equated into a two-hour wait, so two separate shopping trips were executed. Mine resulted in doughnuts, Annette's in doormats, both useful in their different ways. During the wait we decided to cancel the trip into Rugby. The canal ran to the north of the town and we were too entrenched into the boat's rhythm to want to start getting involved in taxis or buses. In the event, it took only forty-minutes to replenish ourselves, and whilst this made little logical sense, we accepted it without question and moved on.

This was to be a significant day, with some proper locks for the first time on this leg as well as our exit from the North Oxford Canal looming. We were also looking forward to Braunston, which has an iconic status in the canal pantheon. The locks came at Hillmorton, under the proud but fragile gaze of the Rugby radio masts, a landmark that up until then I had associated more with the motorway. Both the boys were insistent that they wanted to help, and help they did, under Annette's watchful eye, contributing to the group effort which was taking us forward.

After this burst of excitement the countryside became open and sparse. Cows stood in the fields completely static, as if they were playing at statues, and sheep grazed nonchalantly, untroubled by our passing. The fields along this stretch were small and less suited to arable cultivation. Small ridges gave the land a corrugated feel, with the Nicholson suggesting that this was due to the medieval ridge and furrow system. Each ridge apparently represented where an individual farmer's own strip had been, often for hundreds of years, with linear ploughing having had the effect of throwing soil towards the centre, creating the mounds between them. It seemed a plausible theory, although why evidence of this system had survived here and nowhere else wasn't explained. The boys and I agreed that the ridges looked like they would be good fun on a bike, or perhaps for creeping up on people, or even cows, to see if it was possible to shake them out of their somnolence.

As it was, it was Braunston which crept up on us, even though we'd known it was coming. Approached from the north the place seemed to be almost self-effacing. Indeed, we almost missed our turning, and if it hadn't been for the by now familiar black and white iron bridges of the Oxford Canal we would have carried on down the Grand Union towards London. The signpost which told us where to go was placed rather unintelligently on top of the bridges (there were two), completely beyond the eyeline of whoever might be at the tiller.

Braunston has been called the Brussels of the canal system, and it seemed to share many characteristics with that famous city. One of these was that you would be unlikely to visit it unless you had a reason; for us it had a slightly dowdy air about it, something enhanced by its having more than its fair share of hangers-on. In Braunston's case the latter included some rather second-rate souvenir sellers, although to its credit it also had one of the last surviving on-water tradesmen selling coal.

We eventually moored at the end of the visitors' moorings, just as we were close to giving up finding a spot and even contemplating going on without stopping. Braunston, however, had become an enigma, and we felt we must have been missing its point. As such, we were keen to investigate. One possible explanation for the lack of presence about the place, we speculated, might have been because we had approached from the north rather than the east. We had literally dropped in via the Oxford Canal, rather than made the more traditional entrance via the Grand Union. Whatever, we decided to give it a second chance.

An hour later, although we had given it our best shot, the attraction of the place continued to elude us. We had initially aimed for the British Waterways centre at the Stop House, keen to take in an exhibition we'd been promised through posters along the towpath for the past few days, but when we got there it proved to be a disappointment, over in less than five minutes. This just about summed up the place for us – a massive anticlimax. Long on promise, short on delivery.

Retracing our steps, we visited the marina to see what intelligence we could gain for the future, and although this was impressive in both its size and the number of craftsmen working there, neither of us was in the mood for detailed discussions. In fact, at one point Edward staged a full-blown rebellion, refusing to go any further. To be honest, we all shared some sympathy with him. We felt like disappointed tourists and were overwhelmed by a wish, unarticulated but no less shared or real, to get going again.

We made our way back to the boat and, just as we got there, Edward, by now, as if by magic, thoroughly rejuvenated, skipped on ahead, promptly slipping on the unstable bankside and falling into the muddy water right up to his shoulders. Although we were never to find out for sure, we think he was leaping to get onto the boat, but it was moored a little way out from the bank due to inadequate dredging.

A wail went up, born more of surprise than genuine fear, but before we got to him he'd managed to scramble his own way out, although he was clearly less than pleased by the whole affair. A rapid towpath strip followed, accompanied by a scurrying around for dry towels inside. We consoled ourselves with the thought that this had been bound to happen somewhere and that it could have been a lot worse. At least it provided us with something to remember Braunston by, even if, like the place, it resulted in a washout.

All cleaned up, we made our way along the short but signifi-cant stretch to Napton, the lode seam which had allowed the canal company to continue to pay dividends to its shareholders right into the twentieth century. As we got going the countryside around us underwent an immediate transformation, with rolling hills and intensive cultivation. The fields here were huge, well organised and symmetrical. As far as the eye could see cylindrical hay bales were scattered seemingly at random on a closely cropped carpet. These Northamptonshire prairies had a sanded down kind of quality about them, with just a sprinkle of dust. It was as if all the gold paint had spilled off God's palette when He'd stretched for His cup of tea. Sunglasses were a necessity to avoid glare.

It was as we moved along this stretch that I was finally able to formulate a theory, the fundamentals of which had been gurgling away inside me for some time. The essence of this was the advisability of always avoiding gits in peaked caps. Through experience I had discovered a linkage between those who felt that the normal rules of courtesy and forbearance on the water were for other people, not them, and peaked caps. The absolute understanding of this breed seemed to be that they always came first and that the water existed for their convenience, a fact that was surely obvious to everyone. Their hats marked them out, a sort of aquatic Masonic handshake. They were the canal equiva-lent of Volvo drivers and probably had one of those at home.

It was gits in peaked caps that invariably decided to run you to bridges which normal protocol would dictate were yours by dint of your position. It was gits in peaked caps who would chug towards you as if you were invisible, assuming that you would move aside and leave the centre channel to them, playing a sort of 'canal chicken'. Inside every perfectly varnished static showpiece boat there was invariably a git in a peaked cap.

My theory had yet to determine whether the behaviour of gits in peaked caps was intentional or simply inbred, although I suspected the latter. Their behaviour was what they had in common, their caps their badge of membership. They had become noticeably more numerous the closer we had moved south and I made a mental note to keep a special eye open for them as we approached the turning for the South Oxford Canal. From here on the canal was due to become noticeably narrower, with more hidden corners. I was going to need to keep my wits about me.

Napton Junction itself was especially well signalled, although mainly by traders who were keen to ensure you paid their pub or shop a visit. In deference to the origins of this stretch of the canal, it was the Grand Union boats that had to make a right turn; we Oxford chaps simply kept straight on. Sensibly though, the pool around the Junction was wide and deep, as mistakes must have occurred on a daily, if not hourly, basis.

Instantly we were plunged into a world of mystery, the bridges having gone thoroughly ex-directory. Up in the front, the boys had taken to performing some kind of cabaret to passers-by, which thankfully I could neither see nor hear, other than the regular 'Boop!' every time we went under a bridge. We consulted Nerdy and agreed that although it would be possible to go through the eight locks of the flight before evening, what was the point? The late afternoon radiated tranquillity and was urging us to stop, relax and enjoy some peace and quiet. We therefore moored up at the base of Napton Hill, along with a couple of dozen other craft. In fact the only spot we could find was a space between two boats, but by the time we'd realised this was our only option it was almost too late. As a result, we were forced to reverse into the space like a car, rather than go in front first, by far the preferred method.

One set of our soon-to-be neighbours seemed untroubled by the fact that we were about to invade their space and rushed out to help us. Without bidding they took our ropes and pulled us into the space, returning to their deckchairs as soon as it was clear we were safely in, leaving us alone in a very English sort of way. It's possible that they were more concerned about the damage we might do to their boat, but this would be uncharitable thinking; their boat looked loved but lived in, not a single peaked cap in sight.

As soon as we choked the Lister off we were struck immediately by total quiet all around us, interrupted only occasionally by the flick of a page being turned or, in the far distance, a radio playing music discreetly. Quite reasonably, the canal at this point passes by the village of Napton, which is perched on top of a hill, a windmill on its brow. Everything was as it should be. Cows were lowing in the field behind us, anxious to attend the afternoon milking, the water was still and the sun was generous in its warmth. Annette extracted one of our own deckchairs and established herself with her book and a bottle of lager. By her actions she was making it clear that even the cleaning could wait.

I went up front and rigged up a fishing rod, pulling hard on long repressed memories of the correct procedure. The last time I'd fished I'd probably been as old as Peter was now, and it had been my dad putting the rod together. My plan was simple: get the boys established watching a float, open up the second deckchair and get my own extremely neglected book out. I had no expectation at all of them catching anything, a suspicion which was only reinforced by the total lack of fellow fishermen, and the fact that the only bait we had to hand was bread and cheese. I had no intention of starting to dig for worms.

The opportunity to go fishing with my sons was something that definitely wouldn't have occurred if it hadn't have been for *Florrie*. There had been a rod on board and it seemed a shame not to use it. My own dad had been a keen angler, and had taken Chris and me out many a time, although I never remembered catching much. It was a father and son kind of a thing, and I was grateful for the opportunity to follow the tradition.

This mix of memories and emotions swirled around my head as I baited the hook and explained the fundamentals to the boys. Edward was particularly interested in the bait, which he enjoyed rolling up into what he called cheese sandwiches, whilst Peter, ever the 'doer', was keener to get it in the water. The most basic of the fundamentals, I explained, was the need to maintain absolute stillness and quiet. If they needed to talk then they should do so only in whispers. That way, I reasoned, I'd be able to concentrate on my book.

I performed the first cast and we watched as the float plopped into the water, about a third of the way out. Its slight orange tip floated gently and independently, drifting back and forth depending on whether the lock round the corner was being filled or emptied. As we waited, I casually whispered how much better this was than being stuck inside watching TV.

'How many times on this trip have you said that?' asked Edward.

'Seventeen,' I replied, *sotto voce*, 'I've been counting.'

Perhaps inevitably, given the overall perfection of the moment, and the fact that I was about to reach for my book, Peter caught something. It was a perch, no more than four or five inches long. The float had gone down with a rush and Peter had obviously felt the weight on the end of the line. He lifted the rod and there was the poor fish, squirming for dear life.

At that point all hell broke loose. Annette was called from the front to witness the great event and take a photograph. Edward also wanted a photo with his camera, but he couldn't find it. Meanwhile, I was frantically trying to remember how to extract a hook, wetting my hands before grabbing the fish and holding its gills so it opened its mouth. There was some blood in there, but it seemed all right. I prayed it wouldn't die, as that would definitely have taken the gloss off the occasion. Eventually we were ready and I released the fish back into the water. For a dreadful second it hesitated, the silver of its underside seeming to float on the water, but then it shot back into the murk, never to be seen again, no doubt as relieved as I was that the whole episode was over.

Of course, after that we had to go on, Edward quite reasonably thinking it was his turn now, despite the comment of a lady walking past that it was the first time she'd ever seen anyone catch something on this stretch in twenty years. Clearly anglers thereabouts didn't know about the attractiveness of Tesco extra strong cheddar to the average perch. As he stood patiently leaning over the edge of the boat I could swear I could see freckles coming out on Edward's nose, little pinholes on previously unblemished peach-smooth skin.

While we gave the fish a chance to impale themselves, we were joined by a family of swans, two parents and two adolescents, not much smaller than their mum and dad, but a dirty grey rather than a magnificent white. They were distinguishable also by the sounds they made, and they made a lot as they pecked the last bits of green slime off the side of *Florrie*'s hull. The parents gave pig-like grunts, issuing instructions – 'come this way' – 'don't do that' and so on, while their children could only manage a squeaking like dry machinery. All of them seemed to plead for food we were disinclined to provide, their presence distracting us from our fishing. They were not easily put off, however, and would return if we made even the slightest ambiguous gesture.

If the fishing had stirred mixed emotions, this stretch of the journey was doing likewise. We were now only a hard day's chugging away from our destination, although we were going to spread it out over a day and two nights. It now looked as if I was going to succeed in my goal, something which had never been certain. What it had been possible to regard as merely hypothetical up until that point now looked like becoming a reality. All the finality of an ending was creeping up on me, with the normal uncertainty of what lies beyond. Events that had taken place only weeks before were already taking on the status of memories.

In running the last two legs of the journey together like we had, living on the boat had become a way of life. I'd even stopped swaying when shoreside. The noise, the constantly changing scenery, the need to make up the bed every night and the cramped position I had to adopt every morning to shave – all these had become normal, life outside abnormal.

There were still a few miles and twenty-five locks to go through before the long-awaited moment, so we fortified ourselves that night with a meal in the Folly Pie pub. The food offered in the pub was unusual, as were the ingredients which made up the atmosphere within it. The first of these was the barmaid's absolute refusal to change the CD of Abba's *Greatest Hits* which kept on getting stuck. This jarred insistently on the ears, especially when it came to the chorus of 'Money Money Money'. The urge to get up and kick it, or more constructively, to eject the disc and clean it, was almost irresistible. When I made a joke about it when ordering our meals the best I could get out of her was, 'Yes, it keeps on doing it.'

Light relief was provided by a couple behind us. This was clearly an agency date, with the male side of the equation completely oblivious of the fact that endless stories about amusing incidents that had happened at work do not constitute effective chat-up. Especially if you work in engineering. He was, in short, a total prolonged yawn, a motorway pile-up of a crashing bore. Before long, the woman's contributions were limited to nasal grunts that may or may not have been meant to be encouraging. Either way it didn't matter, as no matter what she said or did the stories kept on coming, as if he'd been rehearsing them, which he probably had. Being a practised engineer, he was operating to a checklist. Amusing tale about a cock-up in the supplies department. Check. Side-splitting anecdote about the day the lathes went haywire. Check. Sensibly, the woman stuck to a single glass of wine. They didn't stay for coffee. 'Waterloo' played as they left.

To the right of us were a couple with two boys, both about five years older than ours. Here the dad and eldest boy insisted on playing out an entire game of rugby, including demonstrations of particular tackles, to the complete and utter bemusement of the mum and younger child, who seemed used to the scene. We ate our pies and left.

The next morning, Edward and I went for a walk up the hill into Napton proper for some milk. This was to be our last full day's chugging and the sky was the sort of brilliant blue which promised to repel even a suggestion of clouds. It was already warm, although not enough to bring out a sweat as we climbed towards the summit. Against this backdrop, the village was rural England personified, although the chapel of the Christadelphians, which stood on its own near the centre, hinted at another side to the village. Apparently this sect believes that only the righteous will achieve eternal life, with the wicked and sinners being utterly destroyed, basing its teachings on an absolute literal interpretation of the Bible. I hoped they only came out at night.

Walking back, we came across a farmer herding a flock of geese away from the grassy verge back into their pen. They formed a neat crocodile two by two as they did so, but complained vociferously immediately the gate was shut behind them. The din rent the Sunday calm asunder and he barked at them to shut up. They obeyed immediately, as if controlled by a switch. I envied him his control and told him. He replied it was simply a knack and went about his business as if it was nothing out of the ordinary. Napton was wonderful, but I felt like we'd wandered onto the set of an Ealing comedy. I kept expecting Alistair Sim or Peter Sellers to pop their head over a hedge and beckon us towards them to share a secret.

Inevitably, although not in a frustrating way, once we got going there was a queue for the locks, and the bad news was that the boat in front of us was flying the red ensign. This was an absolute giveaway sign of a git in a peaked cap. Worse than that, it was flying from a river cruiser, the git in question moving his boat around with tiny movements of his pinkie on the tiny steering wheel in his cabin, his face hidden behind the high windscreen such boats tended to have. The shield they provided giving them a convenient window behind which they could cower.

The boat was festooned with fenders, but despite this its skipper had the cheek to give me a lecture on the need to watch out for fenders in locks as it was easy to get stuck. He'd seen it happen so many times, he told me, taking such a pleasure in it that I almost expected him to utter a few chuckles.

We managed to lose him at the next lock, having to wait for a boat to come down, which had presumably, in turn, left him the next lock primed and ready, speeding him on his way. Such was the way of locking. Left to our own devices, I wallowed in the acknowledgement that this was probably going to be a special day, one which would be burnt into our family psyche for ever. All of us working together as a team, the glorious backdrop, the satisfaction of hard work resulting in progress. I wished there was a way in which it could be preserved in ice, so that it could be looked at whenever we wanted, slightly distorted for sure, but its essence remaining untouched. I contemplated taking some photographs, but decided against it. Our memories would be a richer record, the perfect filter to produce a purer recollection.

As we went through each lock, my head would slowly sink below the parapet, and the angle at which I viewed my helpers would become more acute. The fall was never sudden, however, rather a gentle and gradual descent, as if I'd stumbled into some quicksand. As we left each lock, the boys would reach down and we'd execute a high five, sharing a mantra of 'Good lock!' as we did so. I was immensely proud of them, of their concentration and willingness to get involved. Peter was just strong enough to operate a gate paddle under supervision, whilst Edward preferred to sunbathe until the time came to help push the gate open.

Just as the locks seemed to have lost their capacity to worry us, they sprang a surprise. We entered one as normal, but suddenly found our forward progress impeded. Visions of the stranded boat at Middlewich loomed, but I kept my calm, put the engine into neutral and walked forward on the roof. After a couple of seconds I diagnosed the problem; we were wedged in – by a fender. Further inspection showed that it was a fender on both sides: double trouble. My first reaction was to make sure the git in a peaked cap hadn't come back, my second to attack it with a pole, which I didn't really expect to shift it, but it made me feel better.

Eventually I lay on top of the roof, gripped the handrail behind my back and braced my feet against the lock wall like someone preparing to leg through a tunnel. I then pushed with all my strength, which was just enough to move the boat up and for Annette to drag one of the fenders free. This then gave us enough leeway to tug at the offending article on the other side. It had taken ten minutes, but we were free.

'I always knew you'd sort it out, Daddy,' said one of the boys as I wandered back down to the business end, showing the sort of faith and belief in me that probably only had a few more years left before it reached its sell-by date.

Beyond the Napton locks the landscape became extremely flat, and it was as if the canal was a groove cut into the soil, like a linocut master. Here there was no 'wasted' or fallow land; every square inch seemed to be cultivated. Despite this flatness, the canal insisted on going through a series of omega-shaped bends, a pattern which seemed almost perverse, as if Brindley had been drunk when drawing up his plans or was simply bored, hoping no one would notice. Either way, it made steering a challenge, and I was grateful for my two young self-styled navigators up front who jumped up and down gleefully, waving their arms every time they spotted something coming in the opposite direction. A further perversity of this stretch was a number of stone bridges which led from nowhere to roughly nowhere, solid structures whose only beneficiaries seemed to be livestock. As we passed beneath them, lava lamp reflections of the sunlight on the water danced on their undersides, something that was both surreal as well as deeply relaxing.

Working our way through this stretch was actually quite physically demanding, pushing the tiller in a direction it didn't want to go. I came to the conclusion that although a boating holiday was a great way to blow the cobwebs away, to leave physically relaxed you really needed at least one other person on board who knew what they were doing. By the end of the day my shoulder ached quite badly.

As lunchtime faded into mid-afternoon some clouds did manage to escape over the horizon and started to race each other over the fields, causing waves of shadows to pass over the prairies of deepest Warwickshire in a competition none of them could win. Their appearance failed to spoil the perfection of the day.

Conscious that the next morning would be our last of the trip, we girded ourselves for a final pump-out, and were dismayed to find that the boatyard we'd earmarked for the job operated a DIY system, using tokens like a service station car wash. In a way this seemed perfectly reasonable, a version of getting your own back, so there was nothing for it but to knuckle down to the task in hand. First, however, we had to buy a pump-out key, having relied on boatyards to provide their own in the past. This was hexagonal and unexceptional, betraying nothing in its shape of its ultimate purpose, although I didn't know what to expect otherwise.

The instructions by the machine were perfectly clear and we lined everything up where we'd need it, like a surgeon's tray.

'Pipe?'

'Pipe.'

'Hose?'

'Hose.'

A pause. 'Bottle of blue?'

'Bottle of blue.'

The key to the whole thing seemed to be to ensure you had the shit sucker firmly in place before turning it on. The consequences of failure on this point were too awful to contemplate. I had foolishly put a clean shirt on that morning. The boys were confined to barracks and we dropped the token in the machine, shutting our eyes instinctively as it clunked into the mechanism. Nothing happened. I twisted the lever on the pipe ninety degrees and placed all my weight on top of it, turning away as I did so.

It sucked. Cleanly.

We in turn breathed out, a collective sigh of relief.

Ride a Cock Horse

Is there any more humiliating way to start the day than to be soundly beaten in a game of Pest by a nine-year-old? So much for the triumph of experience over youth. It was clearly time to let slip the ropes, a feeling confirmed by someone chugging past. The big hand had passed the unofficial curfew of eight in the morning, before which nothing moves on the water unless it's got feathers.

We passed through the Claydon Locks without mishap, likewise a further pair a mile further on. After that Cropredy beckoned, the village where LTC Rolt had spent his first night on his journey aboard *Cressy*, so seeing as we were so close to finishing our own odyssey, I decided to moor up and take a look around. It struck me in doing so that since Napton we'd passed by so many villages without stopping it had become difficult to take the temperature of the area. Besides, I wasn't sure how representative Napton had been. I still had my suspicions that it was a sort of rural English version of Amityville.

Besides, Cropredy clearly had something to recommend it, as the gongoozlers had returned, lining up like ducks to watch us as we locked through. The village is famous in some circles for being the site of a Civil War battle in 1644, in which the Roundheads, led by a General Walker, were put to flight by the Royalists, led by King Charles himself, thus relieving Oxford itself from attack. In other circles its fame comes more from it being the site of an annual folk festival, which has a claim to being Europe's largest. It was possible that the battlefield scenes after each might bear comparison.

This latter tradition started twenty years ago when Fairport Convention played their last ever gig there, and have continued to do so every year since during the second weekend in August. We had therefore missed it by a fortnight. The festival is now known locally and beyond simply as Fairport, a word which is also used as a unit of time as in, 'Oh, that must have been a couple of Fairports ago.'

The village was a mixture of building styles, with stone being the predominant theme. Brick was rare enough to be noticeable, and had been used mainly for important buildings such as the church rooms, the bakehouse or the building which was now the post office (and may always have been). At some point there had been the near obligatory addition of some municipal housing, which just about managed to keep in character with the rest of the village. More recent houses, which seemed to be owned by the BMW and four-wheel drive set, had clearly had to pass some pretty stringent planning guidelines and merged in more easily.

Given its history, the village did not owe its existence to the canal, neither now nor in the past. Indeed it was mentioned in the Domesday Book and records show that in 1524 the local manor house had been owned by Brasenose College in Oxford, with one of the local pubs still called the Brasenose Arms. It was not backward in coming forward in exploiting its position on the canal though, being the site of both a toll house, which still stands today, as well as a brickworks and a corn granary, which do not. There is a shop on the wharfside which does teas though.

Rolt hadn't wandered into the Brasenose, being tempted instead by the Red Lion, so we decided to follow suit. This he had described as having 'escaped both stuffy Victorianism and the olde-worlde reconstruction of our own age. The bar parlour was as simple and unpretentious as it always had been: a stone-flagged floor, benches and tables of wood whitened by constant scouring, a great open fireplace with its crane and ratchet hooks, sunken ash-pit and snug seats beneath the yawning chimney breast'.

I have to say we found it much the same, even if I had to stop Annette from getting to work on the scourer as the tables looked distinctly stained and varnished to me. The Red Lion was an archetypal English inn, with an 'e' on the end, thatch roofed on the outside and lined with ancient beams on the inside. The walls and ceiling were a reassuring cigarette-stained yellow, speaking of many a contemplative conversation over a pint of the local brew. Tube train straps hung from the ceiling, no doubt useful after a few pints.

The place was surprisingly empty, save for the landlady and a regular who were themselves engaged in a discussion. The former was clearly not happy, openly voicing her complaints about the village that she'd moved to four years before but had found it hard to settle in. She volunteered, in a voice loud enough for anyone who wanted to hear, that it was an open secret that she was seeking a buyer, perhaps seeing us as a possibility.

The regular, supping out of his own mug and sitting in his own corner of the bar, nodded his understanding. The place was ruled by cliques, he opined, later refining this to a single clique, in a 'they know who they are' kind of a voice. Thus, together, this pair epitomised modern-day village life, with the fresh blood coming in but rarely staying and the old families pulling up their drawbridges and fighting desperately to maintain the status quo. In the meantime, individual identities disappeared. It was a shame, but perhaps inevitable. Having seen, and perhaps heard, what we'd come for, we drank up and left.

Chugging out of the village, we passed what looked like a community of live-aboards, who had colonised a part of the bank. An alternative theory was that they were remnants from the folk festival, still to go home, but none of them seemed to be wandering about with a finger in their ear and neither did they appear to be wailing unfathomable laments. What they were doing was having a barbecue in a cutting in the woods, an area which was surrounded with the detritus of everyday living, not organic matter, just sheets of steel, old bikes and plastic bottles. A sign stapled to a British Waterways post gave an official warning to the residents to clean up or be cleaned up, its existence made worse by the fact that it was a year out of date, so this situation had clearly been going on some time.

Feeling charitable, I wondered if perhaps these might be the modern-day inheritors of the Romany traditions of the old 'number ones', the canalfolk who had owned and operated their own boats. Further reflection left me with the feeling that these people hadn't been members of any distinct group worthy of respect because of their ancient traditions. This group had had their own cars and mobile phones and had simply adopted this way of life, not that this lessened their right to do so.

After Cropredy the countryside opened out again, with an occasional smattering of single locks and a bridge crossing under the M40. We were now dangerously close to the finishing line. The crimson colour of the Oxfordshire Redlands tinged the edge of the fields like an early sunset as the rural landscape began to fade into the almost definitely urban surround of Banbury. The first thing to hit us as we approached the town was the sweet smell of baking from the Krafts-Suchard factory hidden behind the hedge, part of a dense concentration of works. The second was the sheer scale of redevelopment taking place in the town, with a whole new quarter being developed, taking advantage of the previously underexploited canalside.

With the possible exception of Stoke, nowhere gets a worse press in canal literature than Banbury. Part of the cause of this resentment can be traced back to plans to build a bus station next to the canal, filling it in, back in the days when the waterways were seen more as a nuisance than an asset. These plans would have effectively killed off the canal in the town and decapitated the canal. Although from a modern perspective this can be seen as a proposed act of vandalism, these plans need to be seen in the context of their times. According to Rolt, who started his journey from Banbury, the canal was a well-kept secret, with many of the locals he spoke to ignorant of its existence at all.

That said, Banbury was also the spot where, in 1955, over fifty boats gathered to lobby in favour of the retention of the Oxford Canal. At the time, the canal was under threat from the official British Waterways' view that the narrow canals, of which the Oxford was one, had a limited future. This rally effectively saved the canal. The town clearly had a schizophrenic relationship with its waterway, and I had put aside a few hours from our journey to help me make up my own mind.

Banbury was our first real town for a long time and I was keen to form my own impressions of the area. I knew a little about the place already from previous acquaintance, notably the concept of 'Banburyshire'. This idea was one in which the locals took some pride, but was the subject of behind the hand giggles by compatriots in Oxfordshire, Banbury's true home county.

On paper at least, the idea of Banburyshire is a sensible one, in that the town's position at the junction between three counties, Northamptonshire, Warwickshire and Oxfordshire, means that it acts as a focal point for a disparate group of populations which go beyond normal classification. This jigsaw puzzle of boundaries had been something I'd noticed going past on the canal, and it seemed reasonable to invent something new if this reflected the reality. The trick was to avoid falling between the two stools of practicality and reality. By the time I left I wasn't totally convinced that this was a trick Banbury had succeeded in mastering.

In recent years Banbury has also sought to reinvent its economy, this time more successfully, and as such was not that dissimilar to some of the towns I'd visited earlier in my journey such as Burnley and Blackburn. From being a market town dependent upon trading in produce from the land, along with a few value-added activities such as brewing and brick-making, the town has twice reinvented itself.

This had been achieved the first time through the encouragement of manufacturing plants, of which Krafts-Suchard had been one example. At one point so many people working at the local Bird's Custard factory lived on the same estate that it had become known locally as The Aviary. The second occasion was more recent and was born of the town's strategic location on the M40, which had opened in 1991. Halfway between Birmingham and London, the town has developed as a significant distribution centre, along the way becoming something of a centre for the highly successful UK motor racing industry.

This acute specialism is totally in tune with the town's past, when it was for a whole century from the mid-1700s the country's leading manufacturer of plush. This velvet-like material, although with a more open pile, was produced in all colours and used to embellish the often ridiculous uniforms of servants in landed homes across all of Europe.

My first port of call was St Mary's Church, which Rolt had visited, witnessing at first hand the clarion performed by its bells. I was keen to see if the clarion still rang. Even from the outside, St Mary's was remarkable. Built in 1822 to replace its predecessor, which fell down one night, the church says much about the confidence, and indeed wealth, of early Victorians. The outer

286

fabric has a 'pepper pot' tower and two levels of turquoise roofing. On the top is a dome, supported by twelve classical columns. The real surprise hits you when you go inside, for nothing can prepare you for the fact that the church is in fact square in shape. One is so used to rectangular churches, with a nave pulling the eye towards the altar, that the room and space created by a square comes as something of a shock. Should this idea have been seen to be to the diminishment of the glory of God, however, the architect had a solution, with some rich golden mosaics on the far wall pulling the eye to the centrepiece of the church. These were extraordinary, more suited to a hillside church in Tuscany than a Victorian edifice in a small market town in Middle England.

As I looked up, further surprises followed, not least the installation of a second tier and a balcony, which gave the place the feel more of a lecture hall or theatre, roles which it has no doubt also fulfilled during its time. Back at the front, the pulpit was also imposing, not because of its ornateness, nor by virtue of its height, which was tall, but not ridiculously so, more because of its no-nonsense angularity, with a straight flight of steps up – none of those fancy semicircular structures for this church.

Much to my surprise the clarion did still ring out, at nine, midday, three and six in the evening, and I was disappointed not to be around for any of these. It turned out it plays a selection of six Victorian tunes, in line with its origin as a commemoration of that queen's golden jubilee. I was surprised because Rolt had noted the poor state of repair of some of the keys and his tone had suggested that it didn't have long to go.

A final curiosity caught my eye on leaving. Apparently Jonathan Swift, in a 1726 preface to *Gulliver's Travels*, mentioned that he got the name Gulliver from a tombstone in St Mary's graveyard. Unfortunately there is no evidence of this today, presumably because it was a victim of the previous church's collapse, so the story remains wonderfully apocryphal.

A similar symbol of Victoriana is the Banbury Cross, possibly the one symbol most people associate with the town through childhood memories of the nursery rhyme 'Ride a Cock Horse'. The current incumbent is not the cross mentioned in the rhyme, indeed it is difficult to place which of the original three crosses the rhyme refers to, the High Cross, the Bread Cross or the Market Cross. These were all torn down during a period of Puritan zeal towards the end of the sixteenth century, a time which also saw the loss of the town's maypole.

In truth the current cross is an ugly affair; neo-Gothic and over-decorated, it was erected in 1859 to celebrate the queen's daughter's marriage to Prince Frederic of Russia. Sycophantic or what? It was further adorned, if that is the right description, in 1914 with statues in its nooks and crannies with likenesses of the late queen herself, Edward VII and George V, whose coronation was being somewhat belatedly celebrated. If the intent was to make the cross more pleasing to the eye then, in my opinion at least, they failed.

On the issue of the cross I must admit to being on the side of the dissenters, of whom there were quite a few at the time, who were against its construction in the first place, this being a time of general anti-monarchy sentiment. They may well have been right, for the townspeople had clearly forgotten what it was like to have a cross bang in the middle of the street and the local newspapers were full of tales of people bumping into it on foggy nights. As a result it was later lit by gas lamps. It has been a nuisance ever since, but it is hard to imagine it being torn down. Indeed, it now has its own traffic island, which in today's car-obsessed society is probably as close as you can get to permanence.

Having seen two of the three things we'd come to see, we made our way through the town towards the canal. On the way we picked up some Banbury cakes, our last local delicacy of the journey. These were flat and pitta bread shaped, a sort of Eccles cake which has been passed under a steamroller. They were slightly spicier though, with a hint of Christmas cake and quite sweet. We enjoyed them.

It was market day in the town, although these days a car park sufficed as the place where the stallholders gathered, the original market having been knocked down years before. As such, there were crowds milling about, heads down and in a hurry. Grandparents were pushing pre-school children around in prams and young boys still on holiday were terrorising old ladies by rushing towards them on their rollerblades.

In the town centre a number of reminders of the town's past remained, including a Victorian postbox and a one-time agricultural and seed merchants at a busy corner near the market. This still had painted on its side in letters eight feet tall the range of goods it offered, which included:

FORAGE, COKE, LIME, CORN, CAKE, COAL AND SEEDS

The building was now a combination of estate agent and insurance broker, which summed up neatly the town's shift of economic emphasis.

Our third port of call was perhaps the most poignant. Going through on the canal we'd seen a huge banner draped over a bridge which lauded the redevelopment of the local museum, along with the town's commitment to the canal, including the creation of a canalside craft centre and a working boatyard. This, I realised, was Tooley's Boatyard, where Rolt's *Cressy* had been repaired, repainted and refitted, and the spot from which he'd set out on his famous journey. This had to be a place of pilgrimage as we came to the end of our own tour of parts of the English canal system. It was something I wanted to do on my own, and Annette and the boys agreed to meet me back at the boat. I promised not to be long.

The yard could only be viewed from across the canal, and there was a certain sense of irony in the fact that the best way to reach it was by crossing the bus station that had been the cause of so much of the canalfolk's ill feeling towards Banbury. The water itself was busy with people passing through on their way to Oxford, boats queuing up to pass through the lock impeding their progress. Many seemed to be regular travellers, calling each other by their first names and swapping impressions of the scene before them, either marvelling or despairing at all the building work.

It turned out that the renovation scheme was part of a much bigger project. A car park was finished, and the retail units which it would service looked as if they weren't far behind. Amongst this hive of activity, and its associated cacophony of noise, Tooley's Yard stood sadly exposed and out of place, with not so much as some scaffolding or a protective roof to keep it from the certain danger presented by the ravages going on around it.

It looked decrepit and close to ruin. Frankly, if it hadn't been for its historical significance it would have been difficult to build a case for its retention at all. The roof and sides were comprised of corrugated metal, with what looked in the sun like red paint peeling from the sides, although it could just as easily have been rust. All the windows down the side closest to me were broken, and looked as if they had been for some time. All in all it resembled a stretched allotment shed which had been left out in a hurricane. The space around it had been pared down to the absolute minimum, a forgotten corner of an otherwise vibrant spot.

Unsurprisingly, the yard seemed to have been left at the bottom of the list when it came to setting priorities. Indeed, when I visited it seemed to be undergoing a trial of strength with a piledriver right next door to it, perhaps in the hope that it would collapse and thereby solve an inconvenient problem.

This was suspended from a honey-coloured crane, a thick metal sausage that was being repeatedly dropped into a hole, causing muddy water to splash out from its sides when it fell. Every now and then, the operator would pause and lower a giant corkscrew into the hole to churn up the mud some more. The whole process was mesmerising to witness, and I wasn't the only one standing on the towpath watching it. In fact, there was a whole set of OAPs sat on a bench, staring at the scene with vacant expressions on their faces. Although there were no ripples on the surface of the canal, the thuds travelled under the ground and up through my feet. I couldn't help but wonder what it was doing to the boatyard's undoubtedly fragile foundations. The publicity said it was due to be up and running by Easter 2001. I couldn't help but think that it was going to take an awful lot of investment and tender loving care to turn what I'd just seen into a working boatyard and a fitting testament to the glory days of the canals.

I turned and walked away, the thumps of the piledriver receding as I went. Maybe, I thought, just maybe they'd do it. This was Banbury's chance to redeem itself. At a time when the town's planners were trying to forge a new role for the town, to reinvent its role as a magnet for its sprawling hinterland, their focus had been on trade, on a huge retail development and parking for as many cars as could make it. As they looked to the past in their search for a role for the future, they had also picked up on the potential of the canal, but how real was their commitment? Was it genuine or mere artifice? Only time would tell. Perhaps this was a chance not only for the town to redeem its reputation, but to take a lead for all those other towns who still kept a hidden jewel in their backyard to take it out, burnish it and show it off to the world. I'd witnessed how others had tried, and how Manchester for one was succeeding, and hoped they were the pacesetters.

Now that our journey was at an end I knew that *Florrie* for one would never be far away. We'd be there to keep an eye on the place and chivvy it up if it started to show any signs of slacking. Although we still had a little way to go before we reached our permanent mooring, Tooley's Yard seems an appropriate place to conclude this account of our journey. Banbury had marked both the beginning and the end for Rolt. Equally, it marked the end of our journey and the beginning of what we hoped would be many more good times ahead on England's canals.

So finally, in conclusion and in a spirit of thanks, here's to *Florrie*, without whom it would never have been possible. Together we had both taken a risk, but it had paid off. Over the summer we had travelled a total of 270 miles, negotiated 165 locks and endured three pump-outs. What had started off as a casual affair had matured into a fully fledged relationship, one destined, we hoped, to last for years.

When we'd set out we hadn't known if we were going to make it or what lay in store. Together we'd lived and learnt, forming a bond that I knew now it was going to be awfully hard to break. Even as I write this I yearn to be back on board. To feel the swaying of the water and to experience the strange nomad-like existence that is life on the canals. I want to pick up my boat and chug and am comforted by the fact that I will again, and again.

Ladies and gentlemen, raise your glasses to *Florrie*. She might not have been the prettiest little thing on the water, but she was one of the most distinctive. Her high brow, pimpled skin, angular features and clear need for a makeover could, in many eyes, have counted against her. But for us they were simply part of her

charm. We had come to love her, our *Florrie*; warts and all.
    Cheers.

Postscript

Two weeks after securing *Florrie* at her permanent mooring, the withdrawal symptoms had become too painful and we were drawn back to at least sample the pleasures we'd felt during the summer once more, even if it was only for a weekend. Already we were hooked and were making plans for a tour of virgin territory the following summer. When I checked the weed hatch before setting off it was with some surprise that I registered a film of the green algae we'd first encountered an age ago, on joining the North Oxford Canal. It was a vivid reminder, in more ways than one, of the trip that was, as I'd predicted, already fading into a memory, kept alive to some extent by the writing of this book.

The act of writing also reminded me that at the beginning of the journey I had put forward three pretty high-minded questions which I had hoped the trip would go some way to helping me to answer, at least for my own sake. Although I had recognised at the time that these were to some extent a sort of personal justification for what, even then, looked like a huge act of personal self-indulgence, I believe that they still hold some validity and will attempt in this postscript to address them.

These three questions, I now realise, were connected and got steadily grander. The first wondered whether there was still a sense of regional diversity across the country, or whether differences had been steadily ironed out until they were invisible. The second considered the extent that we English still had what may best be described as some spirit left in us. Was the vibrancy, the quirkiness, if you like the creative greatness, what I had labelled the life force, still flowing in our veins? I had looked forward to the opportunity canal travel would provide to peek over the country's fences to take a look and at the same time take the nation's temperature. The third was the biggest and hardest of all and asked whether we, the English, could still regard ourselves as a cohesive nation at all, in the face of a confusion of competing identities.

In addressing these issues I recognised two things: that my sample was selective and that any perspective gained would be entirely personal and therefore irrational and certainly not academically robust. What I could offer was likely to be more observation than insight. This book represents but one version of a single trip. Other members of my crew, even though on the same journey, would probably have written a different book; the things that struck and tickled them would have ordered themselves in a different way. Different crews following the same route would have had their own experiences. It's entirely likely that Runcorn on a Wednesday afternoon is a completely different proposition from a Saturday night, but Saturday night was when we were there, so that's the experience I recorded. Braunston must have something going for it, it's just that we missed it. That, it seems to me, is the very essence of travel.

What was more, with the best will in the world I sampled only a small part of the country, although in my defence this included a fairly extensive swathe from the tip of North Yorkshire to the heart of the southern Home Counties. Furthermore, given the links between my questions, any conclusions would inevitably overlap. Still, recognising these limitations, it seems only fair to share some reflections, however flawed they might be and however biased.

Starting at the top with the question of the state of regionalism. At the outset of the journey I struggled with the difficulties of differentiating between what might be regarded as givens, such as geographical diversity and physical appearance, and the less tangible, more cultural differences between regions. There was little doubt, for example, that the wide rolling moors of Lancashire, where nowt grows but grass and people can exist for days without meeting a soul outside their immediate circle, represented a very different environment from the relative claustrophobia of the Midlands.

At the same time, during our journey I sensed very definite variations between how you might be received in different places as a stranger, as well as the vibrations picked up by wandering around unfamiliar streets. The messages transmitted by civic authorities in both their words and their deeds about an area's aspirations and sense of community often varied considerably. In other words, leaving aside physical differences, the less tangible cultural differences between regions seemed to be driven by a combination of interaction with individuals and with the municipal whole.

Over time, however, I realised that the physical and the intangible were not mutually exclusive, that environment has an inevitable impact upon what makes a place tick, as does history. In other words, any discussion on regionalism is subject to the age-old debate around nature versus nurture.

The comfort to be drawn from this is that, as a minimum, given the fact that environments will inevitably vary, there will also always be an element of regional diversity, whatever the efforts of the multinational homogenising brigade. If every day you look out on to moorland or cows grazing in the fields, your outlook on life is bound to be different from someone who stares out at an industrial wasteland that has remained unchanged for decades, and is unlikely to change for a while yet, if ever. Furthermore, the degree of this variation can be influenced by the actions of community representatives.

This is where history comes in, and how an area deals with it. A region's past can either become a millstone, constantly dragging it down, or a launching pad. The position adopted towards their history by the various towns and regions my different crews and I passed through on the trip varied enormously between these two extremes.

For example in the early stages, the disused mills represented a solid physical statement of what had made the area great. They also served as a living reminder that things would probably never be the same again. In such circumstances it is perhaps understandable if the natural reaction becomes one of trying to arrest an inevitable decline, and, even if this is successfully resisted, the effort involved in that resistance inevitably depletes the resources left for investing in the future.

Equally, we witnessed many examples of places which had tried to bounce off from their past into a new future. The problem is that no one can now visualise what the future might look like.

Municipal reactions to fundamental shifts in an area's economy have traditionally varied. One response has been to build advance factory units in order to encourage new industries and spread the economic base as wide as possible in order to avoid being caught out by the decline of a single industry again. Another has been to encourage a large single, usually foreign, investor – the car factory syndrome. The success of these measures has varied greatly, and we saw numerous examples of half-empty (half-full?) industrial estates on our travels. The problem these days is that the employers of the future are likely to be invisible, operating in cyberspace rather than factories. It seems inevitable that the work once done in factories will, wherever possible, be shunted out into the low wage cost economies, a process which if anything is almost complete.

Given this backdrop, the need to have a vibrant, fun, want-to-live-in feel about a place will become at least as important as physical infrastructure if a region is to attract and maintain the talent who will be the wealth creators of the future. Perhaps the model here is Ireland, a country with a population roughly equivalent to one of our major cities, which the young left in droves for years, regarding it as a basket case, both economically and psychologically. Now they are returning by the planeload and the place has one of the fastest growing economies in Europe.

However, despite this imperative, efforts to make areas more exciting and attractive were perhaps the greatest source of disappointment during the journey. It is in this field that imaginative responses seem to be at an absolute premium, with town upon town falling into the trap of granting permission to build the multinational's version of 'fun': an off-the-shelf leisure park. It was these mini-Americas, with their shopping malls and flat one-storey diners and entertainment complexes, which seemed to me to provide the most abrasive sandpaper wearing down regional differences. Dropped into one of these and you could be anywhere. Useful perhaps, but at what cost?

Although undeniably popular, I couldn't help but wonder if these places succeeded more because they were all that was on offer rather than because of what they offered. In a desert, a thirsty man will drink anything. Given the investment such places must represent, not least in the despoliation of a town's outskirts, couldn't the time and effort be better spent? It seems to me, perhaps naively, that the whole attitude that these places represent is off beam with the future.

Leisure facilities are only part of 'feel-good', of making a place worth staying in, and even moving to. Neither is leisure a commodity, to be bought and sold in units of time, consumed without any discernible worthwhile output. Finally, these places are aimed at a narrow market, a market furthermore which should probably not be the primary target of an area seeking to attract the people who will secure its future.

Why would a potential wealth creator, who could live and work practically anywhere, choose to move to somewhere offering exactly the same mix of sensations as the place they're currently in? The attraction is in diversity and uniqueness, not sameness. The best thing that can probably be said about these parks is that they might contain a potential problem, the young, who might otherwise trash the place. How true is this, and what does it say about trust? The whole idea seems so Orwellian, so *Nineteen Eighty-four*, a time, coincidentally, when many of these places began to be built. For music for the proles, read leisure for the proles.

Elements of the philosophy which seemed to underpin entertainment and leisure also seemed to be visible in housing. During the journey we saw some pretty dire, in some cases near criminal, examples of both architecture and housing estate design. Housing for the neo-proles, the ones with money and aspirations, but no apparent interest in building a wider community. I was left with the impression that many of the estates we saw being built were the middle classes' equivalent of the sixties' high-rise flats, mere storehouses for future social problems. And yet we also saw some excellent examples of new housing, as well as conversions. Buildings tend to be around for a long time, a highly visible and tangible representation of a location and how much the local population cares. I can't help but think that they're something worth getting right.

For places looking to the future and trying to find a way of making themselves attractive, possibly even distinctive, these two areas of housing and the broader issue of environment are probably crucial. Some of the places we went through seemed to be beginning to get the message. What we saw of the heart of Manchester shouted out the fact that it was a 'happening' place. If only the same could have been said about Runcorn, less than twenty miles away.

With all this said, it has to be recognised that a fundamental premise of future change is a stable society. Although pockets of what is now called social exclusion undoubtedly existed, throughout our journey we were rarely, if indeed ever, placed in a situation of real danger, whether real or simply felt, despite exposing ourselves to its potential and despite a number of warnings and stories. Perhaps we were lucky, but the closest we came was a young lad of nine or ten perched on a bridge pretending to throw stones at passing boats, and that was in the middle of the countryside!

To move on to the second of my questions then, there is still some get up and go, some vibrancy in the backyards of England, but, and there is a but, it is sporadic at best. We English perceive ourselves as a people who tend to stay down once we've received a devastating blow. All this pick yourself up, dust yourself down stuff is all very American; after all, it's embarrassing to show your face in public if everyone knows you're a failure. Well, this is probably only partially true, although we do seem to stay down a long time before we do eventually start to look for a clothes brush.

The prolonged recession of the early eighties was followed by another shorter one in the early nineties, just as a few places had got around to staggering to their feet again. This double whammy was cruel to many regions and if getting up after one blow is hard, getting up after two is perhaps nigh on impossible. And yet there is no choice if these places are to survive as communities rather than sinkholes. They know who they are and most are trying, but the answer may be to skip a generation of regeneration thinking and miss out the fancy roads, leisure complex phase and move into the opening years of the twenty-first century with a bit of lateral thinking.

Our experiences suggested that, geography, history and economy aside, a kernel of regional differences did exist in different places we visited. These were more to do with local pride, in Burnley and Stoke for example, as with more tangible differences. My expected variation in the types of foods on offer, for example, was a huge disappointment. Only very rarely was something on offer I'd never seen before in my local supermarket. Oatcakes were an example, as was the Banbury cake; after that I'm struggling. Some differences in emphasis could be seen, with bakeries and the cheese counter the best places to look if you're seeking variety, but efforts to detect regional differences via my palate were largely wasted, and I tried quite hard.

So, is there a sense of Englishness still? Much better writers than me, and indeed great statesmen, have struggled with defining what constitutes Englishness and most have failed to come up with a precise definition. It seems to include elements of pride, aloofness, almost arrogance and introversion; but also of eccentricity, an ability to make fun of ourselves (as well as others) along with creativity and inventiveness.

For us, the most distinctive and noticeable of these was the first, specifically the pride the English seem to invest in their home and garden. This seems to be the single unifying characteristic of us as a race; the statement that an Englishman's home is his castle has, like most old sayings, more than a modicum of truth. No matter where we chugged, the immaculate nature of the vast majority of gardens was a wonder to behold. Before this trip I regarded myself as a conscientious gardener; now I feel inadequate and a disappointment to my countrymen.

Lawns like carpets and flower beds straight off the front cover of a magazine were the norm. Patios and conservatories proliferated, planned and built with a lot more of an eye to line and design than most of the houses they surrounded. Whatever the time of day, people were clipping bushes, deadheading annuals or mixing concrete. Evidence of projects still being put together or recently completed were everywhere. Neighbours were helping in the sure and certain knowledge than a favour given is a favour owed, and children would look on admiringly, as the love of gardens was passed down the generations.

They too had a vested interest, as the mutual gathering place of the public park has now been replaced by an array of swings, slides and climbing frames in almost every garden where there are children or grandchildren to be seen. Few, sadly, ever seemed to be in action when we passed by. The latest fad during our trip seemed to be a mini-bouncy castle, offering often surreal images of yellow or orange ramparts peeping over hedges. This fetish of the home was replicated on the canals, with boats personalised to the nth degree, varying from the palatial and untouchable to the downright lived-in.

Working backwards, we detected no real sense amongst our sample of the English thinking of themselves as Europeans. Nowhere was the EU flag flown as it is with pride on municipal buildings throughout mainland Europe, with even the smallest Mediterranean village proud to proclaim its part in the wider European dream. This did not mean that the English had declared UDI from Europe. Local councils showed a keen alacrity to take the Euro-shilling, or should that be Euro schilling (or even Euro-Euro?), if it meant funds for the development of infrastructure or towpaths. One couldn't help but feel that the money was taken on a false promise, like a child taking a pound off his granny with a promise to be good and promptly pulling his sister's pigtails.

Although such schemes were well intentioned, I couldn't help but wonder about the efficiency with which these funds were spent. All too often a European Union-sponsored project was painfully obvious, being an oasis in a desert of decline. As such, the period in which it remained pristine was necessarily limited; in all too short a time these 'improvements' seemed to become dragged down to the level of their surroundings, either through physical vandalism or the action of a midnight spray painter. These schemes seemed to be the victim of big project mentality: if it didn't cost at least half a million it wasn't worthwhile applying. I wondered if there was a contrast to be had here with lottery money, the total of which must now compete with that received from Brussels, but tends by and large to be spent less visibly.

Another widely accepted feature of the English is their aloofness, their relative lack of friendliness, and our experiences would reject this, although I would acknowledge that most of our contacts were within the cocoon of the boating community and as such were certainly unrepresentative. That is not to say that we had an evenness of experience. Rather, we came across a phenomenon that we labelled the 'friendliness funnel', with people being generally extremely open and unselfconscious in the north, in line with popular perceptions, becoming steadily less so as we approached the Midlands.

Here people were much more introverted, communication between strangers limited at times to grunts and waves, before the friendliness factor picked up again the other side of Birmingham, albeit in a revised, partially filtered form. People became open again, happy to chat and swap experiences, but in a time-limited, on their own terms kind of way. During these conversations it often became very clear when your time was up or if you were straying beyond the bounds of acceptability in terms of topic. Further north, these boundaries were less apparent, and people seemingly had all the time in the world. This was, for us, much more attractive, if at times counterculture and hard to get used to.

As for the famed English sense of humour, this too was in ample evidence, even if at times it swayed more towards the tradition of the seaside postcard than that of Oscar Wilde. Perhaps the best example of this was the eccentric names some people felt obliged to give their boats, often the sorts of names which might seem hilarious after a few pints, but should perhaps be forgotten in the cold light of day. This is, I think, a peculiarly English tradition, one taken from house names, or possibly vice versa, and not something you could imagine the Germans or Danes pursuing. Many names reflected the boat's provenance, such as *Jake's Legacy* or *Kid's Inheritance*, others were more corny, such as the awful *Awayfromit Owl* or *Toad's Haul*, whilst some were downright crude, such as *Far Canal* (say it quickly). Humour was also expressed, inevitably, in garden design, although not always, I suspected, intentionally.

Going back to the outset of this adventure, I set myself some personal goals alongside the more lofty questions covered above. These included teaching myself how to slow down, to rediscover the pleasures of travel for its own sake and, most important of all, to have some fun.

As to the first of these I would say I was partially successful. The bald fact is you simply cannot hurry on a canal boat. That is a statement of velocity rather than momentum. In a sense it is too early to tell, for reversing the habits of an adult lifetime will take more than a single summer. Our trip was not exactly stress free, although when stress did arise it was because we were fighting a self-imposed deadline or target, an action which goes against the grain of canal travel.

Conversely, I surprised myself on a number of occasions by my ability to rise above conditions which might otherwise have been extremely stressful (no water, no power, no idea) and conquering them each in turn. Many of these were in areas where my natural inclination would have been to call out an expert. Sorting them out on my own allowed me to discover a new emotion, the obverse of stress, a sense of exultation and liberation, as well as smug self-satisfaction.

As for the pleasures of travel for its own sake, this certainly was a benefit. The freedom to moor up in places we would never normally have gone to, and the sheer serendipity that usually resulted, good or bad, was terrific fun. The cathedral in Blackburn, the pleasures of rural Staffordshire, the hope inherent in Banbury, the horror of Runcorn – all these made me feel by the end of the trip that I knew my own country so much better, and yet I was still hungry to know more.

I also enjoyed the companionship of fellow travellers immensely. One of the greatest surprises, and a refreshing one at that, was the lack of a generational divide. Boaters ranged from the young not quite weds through types like us with young children and on to the high number of retired couples. The last I had expected, less so the proportion of them who spent half their life on the system.

The trip also allowed me to recalibrate my sense of distance, something the car, train and plane have taken away from us. On the map, England appears to be a relatively small country, and a crowded one at that. After all, it is possible to drive from Dover to Carlisle in under a day. The impression I took away from my journey was that it was actually quite large and spacious. There were vast tracts of land which appeared to be largely idle, possibly as a result in part of the ridiculous set-aside policies of the European Union, or because no one knew what to do with the land after the natural resources had been extracted from them. Indeed, their inactivity was often because of the very fact that their foundations had been sucked out from underneath them.

Two recurring themes dominated the headlines during the summer of our journey. The first was the refuge of the lazy journalist of a widening north/south divide, an issue where I have already aired my thoughts. The second was the perceived crisis in farming, of how the rural economy was facing its worst spell in fifty years. The evidence of my eyes both confirmed and contradicted this assertion at the same time.

Confirmed because of the sheer lack of activity in so much of the country where there plainly had once been working farms. These had presumably been abandoned because they no longer made sense according to the economic laws they were being made to abide by. Contradicted because of the obvious success and self-evident efficiency of some of the larger farms further south. Although these were most definitely not of the single farmer with a couple of workers and a tractor variety, they seemed to be doing all right, although I'll happily admit there was no way of telling what kind of an income they were receiving. Appearances could easily have been deceptive. For all I knew they may have been on the edge of bankruptcy, as much a victim of global markets as the mills and manufacturers were.

Either way, it was clear that farming in this country is in a state of redefinition. The newspapers and the farmers themselves perhaps quite reasonably assess this in negative terms. An alternative might be to see it as an opportunity, not only to ask what we could and should be growing and how, but also to ask what role we are asking of the countryside and the part it can play in helping to shape and encourage regional diversity. But perhaps this is another characteristic of the English, the tendency to start by protecting what we have now, however past its sell-by date it may be, rather than opening ourselves to the challenges of the future.

Finally, the question of fun. If you have read the whole of this book, I hope you will have gathered through my words the answer to this question. Fun was an ever-present through the trip. Not often laugh out loud fun (although sometimes), but more of a redefinition of what we mean by the word. A sense of being at one with the world, of having your yin and yang in balance, of lowering the threshold at which simple everyday living becomes a pleasure – these were what I experienced.

In an age where it has become a cliché to say that change has become a constant, my journey generated a whole range of issues and challenges without, of course, producing any definitive answers. Although not even close to an academic study, my meanderings resulted in the usual conclusion of any research paper, namely that more research is required. It has been unrealistic to expect solutions, because, of course, there aren't any.

Perhaps ironically, one area where these challenges became explicit during my trip was the future of the canal system. At pretty much the same time that we were first setting out from Skipton, British Waterways was producing its consultation document 'Partnership with the People'. This in turn was a direct result from a policy paper put out by the government called 'Unlocking the potential... a new future for British Waterways' released the previous February.

Governments are rarely pushed into such action unless they perceive an interest. The fact that the inland waterways are taken seriously and are seen as something that are here to stay is a testament to the effort of LTC Rolt and his many collaborators and successors. These include the unsung thousands who stemmed the tide of destruction of the canal system in the late 1950s and early 1960s.

The issue currently on the table is how best to take the canals into the future, starting with the mountain of backlog maintenance, estimated at over £250 million. Some innovative ideas are being put forward. Many are worth supporting. Already the towpaths have been used to lay eight hundred miles of fibre-optic cable, a use which is allowing the transport system of the past to become a lane of the information superhighway of the future.

Whether we stand at the brink of a fresh start or a false dawn is unknown. As I vowed in Banbury, the role of those of us who are interested, and over ten million people visit the waterways a year, is to become active in our interest. To build upon the work of those pioneers and learn from their example that change, positive change, directed change, is not only possible, but also desirable.

References

Although this book is based on my own personal experiences, and those of my different crews, a number of external sources of information have also been of considerable value. These are listed below with my thanks to the various authors and publishers involved.

Paget-Tomlinson, Edward, 'The Big Lift', *Waterways World*, May 1999. This informative article on the Anderton boat lift itself draws heavily on David Tew's *Canal Inclines and Lifts*, Alan Sutton, 1984

History of English Canals (web site) – Mike Clarke, Milepost Research

Evans, Martin, and Reichenfeld, Robert, *Canals of England*, Weidenfield & Nicholson, 1994

Paxman, Jeremy, *The English, A Portrait of a People*, Michael Joseph, 1998

Theroux, Paul, *Fresh Air Fiend*, Hamish Hamilton, 2000

Liley, John, *Journeys of the Swan*, George Allen and Unwin, 1971

Rolt, LTC, *Narrow Boat*, Alan Sutton Publishing, 1994, First published 1944

Nicholson *Guide to the Waterways*, Harper Collins, 1997
1. *London, Grand Union, Oxford & Lee*
3. *Birmingham & the Heart of England*
4. *Four Counties & the Welsh Counties*
5. *North West & the Pennines*

Gagg, John, *Observers Book of Canals*, Claremont Books, 1996

'Partnership with the People' – Consultation document from British Waterways on the future of the canal system

www.banbury-index.co.uk/history – web site on Banbury
www.blackburn.gov.uk/ – Blackburn and Darwen Borough Council official web site

www.british-waterways.org/ – British Waterways web site

www.zen.co.uk/home/page/mike.clarke/EnglishCanals – a brief history of the canal system

www.canals.com – an introduction to the canals and the main signposting web site available

www.canals.org.uk/rootsandroutes/ – comprehensive series of pages by Peter Hardcastle covering the history and geography of the main UK inland waterways

www.lancs.ac.uk/users/history/lanchhistory/pendle – Lancaster University 'History in the Community' Internet Project 1997–98 web site page on the Pendle witches by Nicola Estelle Hargraves

www.Stoke.gov.uk – web site with an excellent overview of the history of the Potteries

www.waterways.org.uk – web site of the Inland Waterways Association